A Mind to Stay

A Mind to Stay

White Plantation, Black Homeland

Sydney Nathans

HARVARD UNIVERSITY PRESS

Cambridge, Massachusetts · London, England · 2017

LIBRARY OF CONGRESS CATALOGING-IN-PUBLICATION DATA

Names: Nathans, Sydney, author.
Title: A mind to stay : White plantation, Black homeland /
    Sydney Nathans.
Description: Cambridge, Massachusetts : Harvard University
    Press, 2017. | Includes bibliographical references and index.
Identifiers: LCCN 2016038913 | ISBN 9780674972148 (hardcover :
    alk. paper)
Subjects: LCSH: Freedmen—Alabama—Hale County. |
    Rural African Americans—Alabama—Hale County—History. |
    African Americans—Land tenure—Alabama—Hale County. |
    Land tenure—Alabama—Hale County. | Plantation
    owners—Alabama—Hale County.
Classification: LCC HT731 .N36 2017 |
    DDC 306.3/620976143—dc23
LC record available at https://lccn.loc.gov/2016038913

In memory of Alice Sledge Hargress,

guide and blessing to generations

Contents

Preface

A Mind to Stay is the story of a plantation that became a homeland to formerly enslaved people. Through the prism of a single place and of black families that dwelt on it, the book illuminates the changing meaning of land and landowning to successive generations of rural African Americans. Located in western Alabama, the land has gone from family member to family member—starting with the white planter who bought it in the 1840s with his father's funds as a proving ground, shifting to blacks who purchased the plantation in the 1870s as a foothold in freedom, and extending to descendants who held it throughout the twentieth century as a possession and refuge for "all the heirs." A dominant narrative of black life in the twentieth century is the Great Migration, the response to oppression and dispossession in the rural South that propelled millions of African Americans to leave the land. *A Mind to Stay* focuses on those who stayed and fought to hold on, not just for themselves but also for those who might someday return.

Oral testimony and archival research provide the mainstays of the book. I focus on a 1,600-acre plantation acquired by Paul Cameron—an absentee owner and wealthy planter from North Carolina who brought 114 enslaved workers to Alabama in 1844 and who owned the land into the 1870s. The Cameron Family Papers, housed at the Southern Historical Collection of the University of North Carolina, allowed me to draw on the prolific correspondence of Paul Cameron, decades of overseers' reports, and hundreds of lists of enslaved workers, frequently enumerated in family groups. Manuscripts were just the beginning. I sought and by good fortune found descendants who possessed an oral tradition about the 1840s migration experience—and much more. Formerly enslaved people bought the land from Paul Cameron in the 1870s; their descendants remain there now. I center especially on experiences of one black family whose members span the full two centuries of the story, from its beginnings in bondage in the 1820s to today. In extensive interviews, descendants shared their accounts of generations of landowners from past to present.

The modern quest to draw on oral testimony to fathom African American family history began with Alex Haley and *Roots* in 1976. In decades since, Edward Ball's *Slaves in the Family*, Henry Wiencek's *The Hairstons*, and Rachel Swarn's *American Tapestry* produced models of the genre, focusing extensively on those who moved and made the most of movement from the plantation South. Historian Dylan Penningroth and law professor Thomas Mitchell have concentrated on the practice and legal standing of rural black property-holding in the nineteenth and twentieth centuries, and especially on sources and vulnerabilities of "heir land." In *Breaking the Land* and *Dispossession*, Pete Daniel detailed the forces acting to push black farmers off the land. Isabel Wilkerson artfully humanized the Great Migration in *The Warmth of Other Suns*; anthropologist Carol Stack vivified late twentieth-century return migration in *Call to Home*.

A Mind to Stay seeks to cast light on the counterpoint to exodus and return—to humanize what it took for African Americans to get land and to illuminate how and why successive generations held on to it against all odds and, as one observer put it, "against all comers."

A Mind to Stay

Prologue

Unexpected

This time they would be prepared.

Two days before, they had gone to the march in the morning, expecting to be among those at the demonstrations who might see the barricades come down and the courthouse open its doors to the registration of voters. They had not expected the tear gas. They had not expected the baby to be scalded. They had not expected to have to flee toward the church. The one thing they had expected was the heat—after all, it was July in Hale County, Alabama, where they had lived all their lives. They knew there would be heat.

Today was to be different. They knew they'd be standing in the heat. They knew they might be there a long time. So they prepared their lunches and put the chicken sandwiches in the car. They brought folding chairs as well. They planned to retrieve the sandwiches and chairs when they broke for lunch. At least that's what they thought they'd do when they parked the car.

Alice Hargress was fifty-one years old, her hair still dark, mother of three daughters and five sons, grandmother of more, none of whom lived any longer in Alabama. She lived fifteen miles south of the town where the demonstrations had been going on for more than a week. Greensboro, Alabama, was the seat of Hale County. She lived on land owned by her family since Reconstruction, in a community of black landowners whose forebears had purchased their lands in the 1870s and 1880s. A number of them were descendants of those who had worked that same land in bondage; all of them were descendants of enslaved people who had worked plantations nearby. Alice Hargress had been fierce about holding on to the land and equally fierce about others doing the same. Blacks who let their land go, whether because of bad management, deception on the part of others, or indifference, she regarded almost as "goats"—men (and it was usually men) who didn't see what it took to get and hold the land, or, above all, what having land meant for generations to come. Those who willfully or drunkenly relinquished the land she regarded as Judases.

Her land was in no danger, not as long as she was on it, not as long as her children and grandchildren understood that it was their sacred duty to keep it, undivided, in the family. It was heir land—land for all the heirs, to be held in common for all, to be divided among none. In July 1965, as she packed her lunch and drove to Greensboro and yet another day of demonstration in the town, she had no fear for her land—not if her family held fast.

Nor did she believe that without her and her neighbor and friend Bertha Wallace—two adults from the settlement to join in the July marches—the demonstrations would fall short of the crowd they needed. There were dozens there, of all ages but mostly younger. To supplement the numbers, dozens more had driven in from neighboring counties, Greene County to the west and Perry County to the east, joined by a handful of young white folks from New York and California there to help out. No, they had the numbers they needed to fill the street, press right up to the barricade, sing songs, and chant, "Ain't nobody gonna turn me 'round." They had been watching the unfolding of the demonstrations and marches on the black-and-white televisions in their homes. She and her neighbor knew full well about the Montgomery bus boycott of ten years before that had put Alabama in the center of

the struggle. They knew also of the protests just months before at Selma, the first routed by troopers on Bloody Sunday
and the second victorious in gaining the right to march from
Selma to Montgomery. It was just a matter of time before
the movement would reach their county in the rural Black
Belt and, if the pattern held, prevail there. "We knew it was
coming."

The fifty-one-year-old mother and grandmother felt she
"had to go." She had to march for her mother, born in 1890,
seventy-five years old, who had never voted. She had to go for
her heirs. She had to go even for those who had left Alabama.
The land was theirs to return to, but if they lacked the vote,
would they ever want to come back? She couldn't leave change
to others.

If she thought the day of demonstrations would be more
peaceful and orderly than two days before—that they'd get a
break to have lunch in their chairs—she quickly realized that
something was up as they walked from their parked car to the
barricade. There were four busses, empty and waiting. There
were more than a dozen deputies, some in ordinary work
clothes, all with badges and weapons. This was far more than
the town police force or the sheriff's men. This was more
than the skeletal crew of the state highway patrol, who had
beefed up the locals. It's not clear whether she recognized the
armed men as people she'd seen before in town and who had
been newly deputized for this occasion. What she did recognize
was the set on the jaws of the deputies, uniformed or not. Like
the demonstrators, they were in Greensboro on a mission. Their
missions were on a collision course.

Soon she would learn why the busses and deputies were
there. There would be no lunch.

I'd come out many years later, in the summer of 1978, embarked on a very
different mission. What I wanted to know was whether I could find people
with an oral tradition about the great forced migration of the antebellum

era, which took a million enslaved people from east to west and birthed the phrase "sold down the river." I, too, thought I was prepared.

I had trained as a nineteenth-century political historian. I knew how to use archives, to quote from letters and newspapers, to test claims, to confirm or question "facts." I'd done a biography. However, I had no formal training in doing interviews; I didn't own a tape recorder. I was learning oral history by osmosis, excited and envious as colleagues used the approach to capture the story of underchronicled Americans. In the mid-1970s, oral history had found a great popularizer and exponent in Alex Haley, whose epic account of his family history from Africa to Tennessee to freedom and into the twentieth century had become a runaway best-seller and record-breaking television series. *Roots* inspired extraordinary possibilities for oral history and for the recovery of the African American past. Could an archival historian be part of that?

Coincidences opened the way. I got invited to be an advisor to the opening of a new historic site just outside of my hometown, Durham, North Carolina. The state had acquired a plantation founded in the eighteenth century. Called Stagville, the plantation's buildings had remained in use from the 1780s to the 1930s. The 1787 "big house" had survived—unusual, but hardly unique. The surviving 1850s slave quarters were definitely unusual, a startling row of two-story wooden dwellings, four of them. Truly exceptional was the presence in the area of people who had dwelt in those buildings as tenants in the early twentieth century, who could tell about their lives there and share tales of their forebears. A young historian was on the case, modeling the marriage of oral and archival investigation to map the genealogy and uncover the stories of black families in bondage and freedom.

A second coincidence furthered and focused my quest. The same year that Alex Haley published *Roots*, historian Herbert Gutman published a book that addressed the issue of the impact of bondage on the black family. In *The Black Family in Slavery and Freedom*, Gutman challenged the prevailing view that forced sale, forced migration, and forced sex had subverted the attachment to family on the part of enslaved men and women. Not oral history but the records of the planters themselves provided the sources for his study. Brilliantly he used the planters' annual lists of enslaved people—inventories made for tax purposes and internal censuses—

to discern that clusters of names persisted year in and year out. They were family groups. Not only that, but enslaved blacks named children after parents, siblings, aunts, and uncles. The naming patterns and the maintenance of family clusters over the years suggested that attachment to family endured despite bondage. Among the records he relied on most heavily were hundreds of lists of people belonging to the owners of Stagville—the Bennehan and Cameron families of North Carolina's Piedmont region.

Like many owners of large-scale plantations, the Bennehans and Camerons preferred the benefit of keeping families together to the disruptions that came—to white owners and enslaved blacks alike—in the wake of separation or sale. But on this eastern plantation as on others, there was a powerful disruptive force that had nothing to do with sale or sex or with a slave owner's death and the division of human property that came with inheritance. The force was the opening of rich lands to the west. Land in the Deep South—Georgia, Alabama, Mississippi—was richer, blacker, and more fertile than land in the eastern states. Far more than soil in the East, western lands supported the crop that was the white gold of the nineteenth century—cotton. The West beckoned the son who stood to inherit Stagville and the plantation lands around it, enlarged to thousands of acres over the course of a half century by the son's grandfather, uncle, and father.

In 1844, with his father's money, thirty-six-year-old Paul Cameron purchased a western plantation near Greensboro, Alabama, in the heart of what was called the Black Belt, and sent out 114 enslaved people to work it. He was to be an absentee owner. His overseer reported to him monthly or more; the young owner came out once a year to check up on his plantation and his people. Most important, following a long-standing white family tradition, he made a gesture toward transplanting workers in family groups when he put together the list of "Negroes to Go South" in November 1844. But could he send people off and yet sustain families and the implicit plantation "pact"? In almost all narratives about slavery, being "sold down the river" brought separation, severance of families forever, a more feared and brutal bondage, and, above all, loss. What was the outcome of the young heir's attempt to stave off the worst? Many a western plantation was, like the Cameron's, owned absentee. Was there any difference whatsoever between being *"sold* down the river" and being *"sent* down the river"?

I knew that archives could tell me what the planter and his overseers did and thought. The Cameron family papers, housed at the Southern Historical Collection at the University of North Carolina at Chapel Hill, were among its largest cache of letters and documents. Those papers would hold answers about why Paul Cameron wanted a western plantation, why he chose a place in Alabama, and what he observed on his visits west. As important were overseers' reports, which spanned more than twenty-five years. There was a rich archival record.

Could I find an oral tradition—despite the lapse of 134 years—to shed light on the black perception of separation from home, the forced migration, and removal to a distant plantation? To say the very least, it was a long shot. I knew where the plantation was located. Beyond that, what I had to start with was a list of people with the names of those 114 "Negroes to Go South." The names on that 1844 list, as with almost all slave inventories, were first names only—with one exception. One of the 114 people, Jim, was listed with a last name: Hargis. If I could find that name after emancipation—in overseers' reports, in census returns, in Alabama in 1978—I could hope for a lifeline from the past to the present and, potentially, a source to guide me from the present to the past.

As I drove out to Alabama in August 1978, there were many ifs. Could I find descendants? If so, would they have an oral tradition about the migration of 1844 and its consequences? If so, would they share what they knew with *me*, a white professor, an utter stranger? All the imponderables boiled down to one: I'd need to be lucky. If I got lucky, I had much to ask.

I checked into The Inn, which looked to be the only motel in Greensboro, Alabama, and settled myself down. I took out my 1844 list of names and my printouts of census pages from 1870, 1880, 1900, and 1910. On all I'd found variations of the name Hargis, with many of those people still living in the vicinity of the old Cameron plantation. Sometime in the late nineteenth century, *Hargis* had migrated to *Hargress*. If there was anyone still left in Greensboro by that name in August 1978, that might be my tie into the story. I found the current Greensboro telephone directory, no thicker than my pinkie, and opened it to the *H*'s. There was the name: *Alice Hargress.* I took a deep breath, reached for the phone, and dialed her number. When she answered, I introduced myself the way I'd rehearsed it many times in my mind: "I'm Syd Nathans, a historian from Duke University in North Carolina. I'm doing research on black people brought out from North Carolina to Alabama in 1844 by a man named Paul Cameron."

"That's right," she said.

My heart skipped a beat. I went on, "He went back to North Carolina, but left the people, and after freedom came, it looks like many of them stayed."

Again Alice Hargress said, "That's right."

Those two words, repeated twice, told me that there was an oral tradition about the story I was looking for. I asked if I could come out and talk with her the next morning. There was no hesitation in her voice: "Come on."

I made my way south from Greensboro, fifteen miles down state Highway 69, turned right off the asphalt highway onto a red-clay and gravel road, drove in a hundred feet, and turned right again at the mailbox, as Alice Hargress had instructed me to do. As I drove up the sloping hill, I noted a small cabin on my left, with a porch in front. I passed it, paying attention mainly to cows on either side of the rutted dirt road, making sure to steer clear as I drove a hundred yards up to the house where Alice Hargress lived. She was sitting on the porch with a young woman, who turned out to be her seventeen-year-old granddaughter. Both of them were in white slat-backed rocking chairs; both seemed at ease as this bald white historian pulled up in his professor's car, a slate-blue nondescript Chevrolet with books, maps, and Xeroxes strewn on the backseat. Mrs. Hargress had a greeting that would grow familiar to me in years to come, a deep-voiced melodious "Hellooooo." She had a scrapbook on her lap.

"This is my granddaughter Henrietta," she said. I realized that they were both checking me out as I repeated and elaborated what I'd told Alice Hargress on the phone. I'd come to see if I could find out what happened to black folks sent out in 1844 from North Carolina by a planter named

Paul Cameron. "That's right," she said again, as she'd confirmed the day before. Then she quickly went from my story to hers. "This is called Cameron Place," she said, stretching her hand from the porch to the hill I'd just driven up and toward the land in front of the house. Paul Cameron sold his land to black folks—"all black, no white," she stressed—and black people owned it now. This was the answer to what had happened in the 1870s, when the overseer's letters to Paul Cameron had ceased. From the archives I'd learned that Paul Cameron had long been eager to rid himself of the plantation in Alabama, but I didn't know who'd gotten it. Alice Hargress was telling me from the porch of her house on what she called Cameron Place. She was emphatic that he had sold it to "all black, no white." Was it to give credit where credit was due that her house seat, and the hill it was on, had the name of the former slaveholder? What she made clear was that Cameron Place had been in black family hands ever since Paul Cameron sold it, from the 1870s to when I arrived a century later.

I knew I'd want to come back to how and why Paul Cameron sold his land to "all black, no white." That seemed almost as surprising to me as the desire of his former bondsmen to buy the plantation on which they'd been enslaved for two decades. Naive, I had a lot to learn about motivation on both sides. Nonetheless, I wanted to shift back to what I'd come out to learn. Had any stories been passed down about the 1844 migration and what happened to people in slavery times? I was getting ready to ask when she opened the scrapbook she had on her lap and said, "I suppose you've come out here to find out about Forrest." Baffled can hardly begin to describe my response. I had no idea what she was talking about.

She pointed to a newspaper article in the scrapbook. It had a photograph of two elderly sisters. A reporter had come to the community a few years back to talk with them about their father, who in June 1965 had died at the age of ninety-nine and a half. His full name was Ned Forrest Hargress. The story was that he was the son of one of the most brilliant officers of the South, Confederate general Nathan Bedford Forrest, and that their father was conceived in early April 1865. General Forrest and his troops had come through the area in the waning days of the Civil War and camped overnight near the Cameron plantation. Supposedly an enslaved woman named Dorothy was sent from the Cameron place to cook for the troops. Afterward, she was summoned to the tent of the general, who had his way with her. She returned to the plantation with his seed in her womb. When Dorothy had a son nine months later, on January 1, 1866, she believed that General Nathan Bedford Forrest was his father. She gave her son Forrest's name to affirm the link. Many thought "Ned" was an abbreviation—a contraction—of Nathan Bedford. Ned Forrest Hargress got his last name from his stepfather, the freedman whom Dorothy married later. Forrest Hargress believed the general to be his father. So did his wife and his daughters. So did many—but by no means all—blacks and whites in the county.

The reporter took down the story as the sisters told it. He judged it plausible but not provable, and noted facts that didn't match their version of what happened. Nonetheless, images held open the possibility that the story might be true. The reporter had viewed photographs of Forrest Hargress as a young man and again as a man in his seventies. He gazed carefully at the facial features of the sisters and invited the article readers to do the same at their picture in the newspaper. He examined photos and a portrait of the General, the most feared and celebrated raider of the Confederacy. He couldn't rule out the possibility. There were resemblances. Was it possible that Ned Forrest Hargress—who I would later learn had become the spiritual leader of this black community—truly was the general's son?

Startling new questions were eclipsing the one I arrived with. How had a man so conceived become a leader of the community? How had black folks gotten their former owner's plantation and kept it for a hundred years? I tried once more to get back on track, to steer my way back to 1844, to the migration and slavery times. Alice Hargress began to shake her head, as if to tell me that she didn't know. Or so I feared.

But that wasn't what she meant. "For that," she said, "you'll have to talk to Louie." She pointed down the hill, to the small cabin with the porch. It was the dwelling that I'd driven by on the way up. "Louie knows it all."

Louie Rainey, I came to find out, was the oral historian of the community. Born in 1906 in the settlement, he had lived there into his twenties.

He'd grown up in a place just across Highway 69, on land purchased from Paul Cameron by his grandfather Wilson Rainey, and had spent his youth in the household of his mother, Louisa, and his widowed grandmother Elizabeth Rainey. Elizabeth Rainey, like most in the community, was known by an informal name; hers was "Ma Vet." Born in slavery times on a plantation ten miles to the north, Ma Vet shared stories of those days and of freedom times with her inquisitive grandson Louie, who it turned out had an extraordinary memory that absorbed not just her stories but those of other elders in the settlement. He displayed early on a disposition to ponder things he was told, to fill in gaps where pieces of the puzzle were missing, and to recount others' stories or his own speculations with gusto. He'd left the community in the Depression, found day labor in Mobile, and relocated in the mid-1930s to nearby Uniontown, Alabama. In 1937, drink and a quarrel at a midnight dice game led to a fight. A knife flashed, and the next thing Louie knew, he was cut in the back—paralyzed from the waist down. Louie was brought back to the community, nursed by Alice Hargress's mother, and eventually set up in that small cabin where, nimbly working from his wheelchair, he rewove cane-bottom chairs for a living. For decades, Louie Rainey's porch became the place everyone came to visit, the old to share stories of the past, the young to hear Louie retell the tales, white customers to get their chairs redone.

It was no wonder that Alice Hargress pointed to the bottom of the hill and told me, "Louie knows it all." She told me she'd give him a call and let him know I'd be coming by. It was the first of many gates that Alice Hargress would open for me.

"Come!"

I had barely stepped onto Louie Rainey's porch and knocked on the door when his voice boomed out from within the dwelling that hot day. In his wheelchair, he was working inside, a big floor fan whirring and a black-and-white TV on, its picture splotchy and its sound blaring.

"Sit!"

I found a seat. Louie, I would later learn, was in his early seventies, but looked to be in his fifties. A broad-shouldered, muscular, strapping man, he wore a white T-shirt that contrasted with his dark mahogany skin. Both of us were bald and clean-shaven. We shook hands, and I noticed that he'd lost two fingers on his right hand. I began to explain myself, as I had to Alice Hargress, but she'd already tipped him off. He started right in. "So I hear you want to know about Old Man Paul Cameron—and Old Man Paul Hargress." He was off and running.

Paul Hargress had always said he came out on the coach from North Carolina with Paul Cameron, crossing over the Blue Ridge Mountains. "Me and old Paul C. Cameron came all the way together on a stagecoach. I didn't walk nary a step," Paul Hargress would say. As Louie Rainey told the story, the planter came out with a bushel of gold, and before he left, he gave a peck of it to Paul Hargress. Supposedly Paul Hargress had buried that bag of gold before he died, buried it by the cherry tree right in front of his house—and Louie Rainey pointed across the red-clay road to a place just opposite his dwelling. After Paul Hargress died, Louie Rainey told me, folks dug for that gold, night after night. Louie Rainey himself saw dirt piled up six feet high. The hole dug around the cherry tree was so big that the tree finally collapsed into it. But nobody ever did find that gold. Louie's guess? Paul Hargress used that gold to buy his part of Paul Cameron's land. "They say that Old Man Paul Cameron wanted black people to have his land—sold it to all black, not a foot of it to white," Louie Rainey concluded.

What in the world to make of such a story?

In the tale Paul Hargress had told over the years, Paul Cameron had taken him on as a kind of partner, privileging him with a place on a coach rather than consigning him to the coffle of slaves forced to walk out from North Carolina. Paul Hargress's special status and the gift of gold, Louie Rainey speculated, had enabled him to buy his part of the Cameron plantation, Alabama land that Louie Rainey and Alice Hargress believed the planter had sold purposely and exclusively to black people.

It all beggared belief. This was not the story of forced migration that I had expected, any more than I had expected Cameron Place to be named for the former master, or the onetime slave owner to provide a refuge for his former bondsmen, or one man in the community to believe he was Nathan Bedford Forrest's son. One thing was clear: nothing was going to keep this story confined to where it had started for me, to the twenty-one years between the forced migration of 1844 and the end of slavery in 1865.

As if all this weren't enough to explode the boundaries of the inquiry I'd begun with, a single word bridged the gap between past and present. From reading letters written by the Alabama overseer, I knew that people on the Cameron place after 1865 had been exposed to Reconstruction politics. Freedmen had repeatedly gone to meetings and had always come back with an elevated sense of rights and diminished willingness to work. So I asked both Louie Rainey and Alice Hargress if they'd ever heard stories about people going to meetings.

At first Louie Rainey said he'd never heard about meetings. Then, after a pause, he said, "You mean a speakin'?" And immediately he recalled hearing his grandmother Ma Vet talk about a "speakin'" that she'd gone up to in the town of Greensboro, fifteen miles away. There, Louie said she'd told him, she'd heard a man named Cryden White tell folks in June 1865, "You're free, you're free, you can go where you want to go and do what you want to do!" I'd come across the name before I came out to Alabama. The speaker was Henry Crydenwise, a New Yorker who'd moved to Alabama briefly to work in the newly established Freedmen's Bureau. In the town of Greensboro, where whites as well as blacks assembled, he'd told people of color that they were free, but that they had to work and must not become idle. They needed to make and abide by contracts. Whites approved. But those in the densely black crowd heard, and Ma Vet recollected, a different message: "You can do what you want to do!" Astoundingly, more than a century later, Louie Rainey was repeating to me what Crydenwise had said at the speakin' in 1865.

When I asked Alice Hargress about meetings, what came to the fore was *her* involvement in politics. It turned out that she'd marched in demonstrations in Greensboro, Alabama, in July 1965. She'd been arrested and taken to jail in Selma that month. In a small space with dozens of women and one toilet, she'd spent three days and nights in jail.

Oral history had opened up the freedom struggle as part of the story of this plantation's long history. It bridged a full century, from the freedom

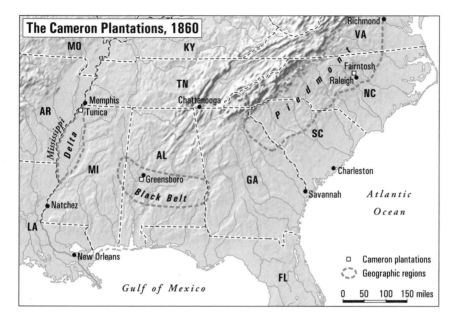

The Cameron Plantations, 1860.

pronouncement of Henry Crydenwise in June 1865 to the arrest of Alice Hargress in July 1965.

I left Alabama in July 1978 with dozens more questions than I had come with about this onetime plantation and the people on it—starting with those taken out in 1844, extending to those living there in 1978, and spanning generations in between.

Back home, I reverted to my archival roots. I decided to trace out the intertwined stories of Paul Cameron and Paul Hargis and see where the trail would lead me. In hundreds of lists and thousands of letters, I found a tale of two men—one heir to a birthright of wealth and land, the other to a legacy of bondage—and a plantation experience that defined them both. And I found more.

Paul Cameron, it turned out, opened not one western plantation but two—the first, in his view, a failure; the second, in his hopes, a bonanza. In the course of that changeover, he became a different kind of planter, and subjected his workers—both in the Deep South and back in North

Carolina—to a different kind of bondage. Though he never changed his place of residence from North Carolina, he made his own inward migration, one that mirrored and illustrated pervasive changes throughout the plantation South.

Paul Hargis, for his part, became a party and a witness to the western migration. Before exile, back in North Carolina, he and his family had escaped the worst that bondage brought others. The small but real leeway built into the Camerons' eastern version of enslavement shaped young Paul Hargis's experience and outlook. In the West, dramatic changes occurred, especially at midcentury, when the planter's ambitions took an imperial turn. Again Paul Hargis escaped the worst. But the changeover had lasting consequences for him as well as for the planter—consequences that spanned the next quarter century, until Paul Cameron permanently separated from Alabama and Paul Hargis (now Paul Hargress) permanently rooted there.

What happened after blacks got the land? Over the course of many years, I went back to Alabama a dozen times—with a tape recorder—to seek the answer.

What unfolded was a story of 1,600 acres of land in western Alabama and of the black people who dwelt on it for 170 years. It was an account of the meaning of land to those who lived on it, and of how the land's role and meaning changed over time. From emancipation onward, these were people who chose to stay rather than to leave. They purchased the plantation they'd worked in bondage. They held on to their land rather than sell it. They fought for it rather than be pushed off it. They marched in 1965 to fully free the land for those who remained and to remake it for those who might return.

Despite the massive departure of rural black people and their own children to the North and West as part of the Great Migration of the twentieth century, they held on to land for their heirs. Why they safeguarded their land with such tenacity, what they were up against, and what those who stayed achieved—this is the story that *A Mind to Stay* seeks to tell.

Part One ❧ Proving Ground

One ⟳ Spared

IN THE BLACK COMMUNITY of the former Cameron plantation in Hale County, Alabama, as in other black settlements throughout the rural South, many of those who'd lived through bondage passed on little of their experience to the next generation. Better that their children and grandchildren, nieces and nephews, shouldn't know all that had happened, lest they be embittered by anger or hatred or shame. So it was that Carrie Davis, born in 1906, heard almost nothing about slavery from her great-uncle—"Unc' Paul"—when she sat on his porch and heard him talk about days gone by.

Carrie Davis knew her uncle by the altered last name that he and other family members had adopted by the turn of the twentieth century. The family changed the last name from Hargis—the surname of the man who once owned their forebears—to the recomposed name Hargress.

The Paul Hargress that she recalled was "a huge of a man, with a high fine voice," who wore his hair plaited in a single braid that ran partway down his back. Eighty-seven in 1914, Unc' Paul was still imposing. Unable any longer to farm, he turned his cabin into a sometime store that sold candy and a few canned goods. His wares brought a token income, and his store and storytelling kept a stream of visitors coming to his dwelling. Of the many stories that Paul Hargress told in Carrie Davis's hearing, there was only one about bondage, but that story he told over and over: namely, the tale of how he and he alone had come out on the coach with slave owner Paul Cameron, how together they had crossed the

Blue Ridge Mountains on the way to Alabama, and how before Paul Cameron left, the planter gave him a bag of gold.

Paul Hargress left it to Carrie Davis and other hearers to guess the meanings of that tale. Was it an account that proclaimed the partiality of the white slave owner toward his black worker—that Paul Hargress was a favorite of the planter, able to ride to Alabama while other enslaved companions had to walk? Did the story of the long coach ride, the bondsman and the planter sitting across from each other or side by side, hint at a full human relationship and a leveling trust between them? Did the ride and the claim of a parting gift of gold suggest something even more improbable, a bond between men more partners than master and servant?

Paul Hargress's account kaleidoscopically reconfigured the facts of his experience, just as he reconfigured his name after emancipation. Yet his story contained two essential truths. For more than a half century, Paul Hargress's life was bound with that of Paul Cameron—and his experience in bondage was one of repeated escapes from slavery's worst fates. Those realities would ultimately route and root him to the plantation in Alabama, and when freedom finally came, they would shape his account of the planter and how they both got there.

When twentieth-century descendants referred to the two Pauls—Paul Cameron and Paul Hargis—it didn't seem remarkable that master and bondsman both had the same first name. In actuality, it was. On the Cameron plantation in North Carolina's Piedmont, for owner and slave to have the same first name was rare, unless the name was common, such as John or Mary. Names given to enslaved people tended to be pet names, classical names, place names—Joe, Virgil, London—so as to keep distinct and subordinate the names of the owned from those of owners. In the case of Paul Hargis, however, the explanation was simple: he'd not been born on the Cameron place but rather acquired and brought into it. So no taboo was violated, no pretension asserted, in his having the same name as the heir to one of the largest plantations in North Carolina.

Other than a shared first name, the two Pauls were utterly different. Paul Cameron was born as heir to a fortune in land and enslaved workers begun by his grandfather Richard Bennehan on May 25, 1776, when Bennehan bought 893 acres of land from a former sheriff of Orange County, six weeks before the American declaration of independence from Great Britain. That same year, he wed Mary Amis, who came to the marriage with a dowry of five enslaved people bequeathed to her by her late father. Their daughter Rebecca Bennehan in turn married the most ambitious and successful lawyer in the county in 1803. Four years later, at the urging of his wife and father-in-law, Duncan Cameron reluctantly became a planter as well, when he moved to Richard Bennehan's home—called Stagville—and subsequently began to build his own dwelling two miles up the road. It was at Stagville that the Cameron's second son, Paul, was born on September 25, 1808.[1]

Carrie Davis would have thought it strange, even perverse, to describe Paul Hargis also as an heir. For his first thirty-eight years, until 1865, he remained enslaved—the property of others. Yet beneficiary he was, though of neither fortune nor freedom. He was an heir, for a time, to a version of slavery that was designed to be more benign than most. It grates against modern sensibilities—and those of many nineteenth-century contemporaries as well—to think of bondage as coming with benefits. Yet just as there were gradations of freedom, so there were variations of enslavement. Nothing was more important in Paul Hargis's life than the reality of those variations.

Paul Hargis was born in North Carolina's Piedmont region in 1827, almost two decades after the birth of Paul Cameron. The enslaved Paul was the youngest son of his parents, George and Agga, who had been brought from Virginia early in the nineteenth century.[2] Their three sons, Squire, Jim, and Paul, and their two daughters, Sally and Nancy, all were owned by a small farmer and neighbor of the Camerons, Lawrence Hargis.[3] Hargis lived in Person County, a dozen miles north of the Cameron plantation. By 1808, Lawrence Hargis had become a storekeeper and the partner of Duncan Cameron. Partnership was a way that Duncan Cameron, a large landowner, diversified his holdings and income. He provided a $2,000 bankroll for the nearby merchant, who in turn traded with neighbors—and paid Duncan Cameron a third of the store's profits.[4] George and Agga and their youngsters provided the labor for their owner's small farm, and Paul Hargis's father, George, was likely also a helper at the busy country store.[5]

Only later would Paul Hargis learn from his parents that ill health began to plague their owner in the 1820s.[6] The storekeeper got behind on his payments to Duncan Cameron. Hard times diminished his income and deepened his debts.[7] Near the end of the decade, Lawrence Hargis's physical decline was evident and his store was failing. Like many slave owners, small and large, he looked to his human property to settle his accounts. He needed only to turn to his brother, a small-time slave trader. Thomas V. Hargis periodically gathered enslaved persons from owners in the Piedmont and marched them further south, to be sold along the way or, if not, taken to the slave mart of Charleston, where buyers eager for labor in the low-country rice fields or cotton uplands of South Carolina could bid for their bodies.[8] There can be little doubt that the enslaved George Hargis and his wife, Agga, knew of their owner's dire condition. In early 1829, they were a step away from becoming part of the South's human cattle call.

Instead of turning the enslaved family over to his brother for sale, Lawrence Hargis chose a different way to settle his debt. He deeded the black Hargis family to Duncan Cameron, valuing the two adults and five children at $1,555.[9] By the 1820s, Duncan Cameron had acquired the reputation among fellow slave owners as a man "of good feelings." What this meant was that, as a buyer of enslaved persons, he had the wherewithal and disposition to purchase entire families, and a further reputation for keeping them intact. Other slaveholders who found themselves, like Lawrence Hargis, mired in debt and compelled to sell their human property turned to Duncan Cameron to ease their consciences. Because Cameron could and often did buy families entire, the sellers would not have to resort to "unfeeling speculators" who bought and sold without regard to family ties.[10]

Only two years old on the day of transfer—February 15, 1829—Paul Hargis would have had no understanding at the time of what it meant to be acquired by Duncan Cameron rather than dispatched to the slave-trading brother of their owner. His parents knew. They'd been spared.

The world that Paul Hargis and his family entered was the largest plantation in the North Carolina Piedmont. Begun in May 1776, it had grown rapidly over the course of two generations. Richard Bennehan, his daughter, Rebecca, and his son, Thomas Amis, sought to achieve the fidelity and forced labor of their "black family," as they referred to them, with attentive medical care, with good garb, and above all by keeping families together. When they added to their labor force, they often—though not always—purchased new people in small family groups. As a twentieth-century descendant of enslaved people put it, "They stole your labor but they kept you together."[11] After lawyer Duncan Cameron moved from Hillsborough to the countryside and commenced his career as a planter, he found benefit in the Bennehans' approach to their enslaved workers. Never a man to shy from compulsion, Cameron nonetheless adopted the Bennehan model of slavery—the trade-off of family cohesion for faithful work—as his own.

To the Bennehan principle, Duncan Cameron added a complementary strategy for extracting labor from the people he owned: incentives. Between 1810 and 1812, when he needed to clear land for his plantation house, he rewarded those who did work over and above time in the field with credit at his father-in-law's store. With their credits they bought calico cloth, ribbons, whiskey, Dutch ovens, and locks. In the course of clearing the land, Cameron learned who worked the hardest and who had the skills to do the specialized tasks of the place. He searched for the most able among his enslaved workers, and designated those few to be plantation wagon masters, shoemakers, carpenters, blacksmiths, couriers, manservants to accompany him on his travels, and in one case, a black overseer. These were the "first men" of the plantation. Though specific roles were not always designated, annual inventories of enslaved workers usually gave the names of adults in order of their value to the planter. Those who came first on the lists were those Duncan Cameron valued most highly, and with that ranking came duties and rewards.[12]

Slave inventories of the early 1830s indicate that Paul Hargis's father moved quickly to the top of Duncan Cameron's plantation hierarchy.

Cameron would have come to know George Hargis through his work for Cameron's Person County merchant partner. By 1834, the annual slave inventory listed the Hargis family as located at the "Home" quarter of the plantation and placed forty-six-year-old George Hargis immediately between the first man named, Anderson the foreman, and the third man listed, Joe the carter.[13] The "Home" quarter—one of five quarters on the vast plantation—was where Duncan Cameron lived with his wife, two sons, and six daughters. The astonishingly tall and thickly forested trees had prompted Cameron's wife, Rebecca, to call the home place Woodville. But the title Duncan Cameron chose was Fairntosh, after the ancestral home of his Scottish grandfather.[14] George Hargis's role as the number two man at Fairntosh was not identified on the 1834 slave inventory, but Cameron's correspondence suggests that he may have become a courier.[15] As a courier, he was entrusted to take mail, messages, and sometimes goods between plantation quarters—a distance of several miles or more—and on occasion to carry correspondence to Hillsborough, fifteen miles away, or even to Raleigh, thirty-some miles distant.

Though new to the Cameron plantation in 1829, George Hargis had joined a small group of trusted men and women, some descendants of the first enslaved generation of the eighteenth century, all valued by white owners for their skills and roles. George and Agga Hargis would also have found that there were enslaved people at the Home plantation who had overstepped their bounds and who lived there on probation. They were placed at Fairntosh to learn and illustrate the lesson that their owner—reputed among whites as a "man of feelings"—was not to be crossed. There was Sandy, a young man who took the day off from his role as a courier to visit a paramour in Raleigh. Found out, he was dispatched to Fairntosh and there made to receive "exemplary punishment"—a severe whipping. After his flogging, he was allowed to work his way back into the role of plantation carpenter, but he was kept under surveillance until he proved himself redeemed.[16] There was Pompey the wagoner, who twice was reported as illicitly trading goods during his trips to and from Petersburg, and finally was removed from that post. Never specified was the transgression of Joe the carter, who remained at Fairntosh through the 1830s but with a new designation: "Rascal Joe."[17]

Paul Hargis and his parents were present at Fairntosh as the promotions, demotions, and more fundamental dramas of the plantation's history played out in the 1830s. Even though he chose later not to talk about his childhood, Paul Hargis had much to witness and absorb about the black community and the Cameron system.

It was not only enslaved Paul Hargis who had lessons to take in. The other Paul—white heir Paul Cameron—had much to learn as well. Paul Cameron was off at college in the North at the time that indebted merchant Lawrence Hargis turned over the black Hargis family to Duncan Cameron in February 1829. The need to tame his son's turbulent temper and to discipline him for the role of heir had compelled Duncan Cameron to send Paul away from home in the early 1820s.

It was Paul's older brother, Thomas Cameron, who had first been sent north to school. Born in 1806, Thomas Cameron found reading difficult, writing laborious, arithmetic impossible, and frustration quick to come when he was asked to attempt script or sums. Duncan Cameron had to make the painful acknowledgment that his firstborn son would never be capable of self-sufficiency. The father sent eighteen-year-old Thomas to Middletown, Connecticut, to a military academy run there (and subsequently at Norwich, Vermont). Duncan Cameron conveyed to the academy head, Captain Alden Partridge—West Point graduate, instructor, and briefly West Point superintendent—that the son had a good heart and good intentions but that his impaired abilities required patience, nurturance, and above all, limited expectations.[18]

Younger than his brother by two years, redheaded Paul Cameron was by contrast a quick study, and was as impulsive as his brother was sluggish. Long before Paul Cameron understood that the role of male heir was to fall on him, that in a family of two boys and six girls he would eventually become the head of the family, he was aware of the wealth and prominence of his father. From an early age, he seemed to expect that privilege and deference were due him. Sent to Raleigh in 1821 to be prepared for college at a private school for boys of his social class, he balked at the teacher's demands.[19] The twelve-and-a-half-year-old Paul wished nothing more than to return home, where he could be in the midst of servants and the farm life he loved. A Raleigh friend of his father's had to be diplomatic in extracting him from the school; it would not do, even for one of the most powerful planters and lawyers in the state, to insult the school-master and openly indulge a spoiled son.[20] Private tutoring and schooling elsewhere got young Cameron enough of a foundation in English to enter the University of North Carolina at Chapel Hill in 1823, where his grand-father and uncle had been members of the board of trustees. Mastery of Greek was another matter, a laborious effort that again required demanding discipline.[21]

Though humbled by the need to receive extra help from his teachers to remedy his shortcomings, the young man expected proper esteem from classmates. At the start of his second year at the university, he believed that his due included preference in the front pew of the morning chapel service required of all students. When a first-year student from Tennessee sat in what the fifteen-year-old Cameron regarded as his place, the North Carolina youth demanded the seat, and was told that no places were owned or reserved. Promptly, in the front row of the chapel, Duncan Cameron's son cuffed the Tennessean. The fighting got him suspended from the school. Soon Paul Cameron found himself at the Connecticut military academy attended by his brother.[22]

Paul Cameron was sent to Partridge Academy to learn discipline.[23] Two years followed of what he regarded as a rigid schedule, total control, poor food, standardized clothing, and a deaf ear to all his complaints or requests for release, home visits, and extra cash. As he viewed it, he was treated much like enslaved workers back home, with no opportunity for appeal and no options beyond what the schoolmaster would grant.[24] But by the end of his time there, he got the message: he needed to control his temper and, like it or not, he must please the captain. "I do my best to gain his good will," Cameron wrote his sister. "I think I go very straight now and will try to continue so." Obedience won the captain's praise: "Paul appears to have become the Master of himself."[25]

Young Cameron stayed in the North to complete his schooling at Washington College in Hartford, Connecticut—later renamed Trinity College.[26] At college he came to understand the fundamental reason for self-mastery. He was being groomed to be an heir—to be *the* heir. With his brother impaired and his sisters unmarried, responsibilities for looking after the family would ultimately fall on him and him alone. He promised his parents that he had "left behind his wild youth," that he now saw clearly the duties that would fall on him in his manhood, the obligation he had to sustain the family.[27] For the next quarter century, dozens of letters to his father repeated the same refrain—expressions of obligation, gratitude, and debt.[28] Labor and duty were the keys to life.

Paul Cameron was a college senior in February 1829 when two-year-old Paul Hargis and his siblings came to Fairntosh. While away from North Carolina for the better part of five years, the son had to rely on reports from his sisters and his uncle and on brief bulletins from his father about what was going on in his absence. What he learned energized and amused him. The plantation was a hub of enterprise and improvements. As his father sought to get more out of the place, he bought iron for mills and a new thresher for wheat, and he had his enslaved workers dig new mill ponds. In the spring before his son's return, he ordered the construction of a tanyard. Writing his sister, Paul Cameron joshed: "What will he not have next"? . . . I am often amused to think of some of his plans. He has made Fairntosh a little city and you don't know what you have around you until you think an hour." Young Cameron was aware that even as his father added improvements, he increasingly retreated from direct supervision, delegating authority to overseers and to trusted black workers. The most valued worker was Luke, who on Paul Cameron's last visit had apparently regaled the planter's son with an account of all that "we" were doing to improve Fairntosh. The "young master"—as he was called by the enslaved people—picked up on the irony. When Paul Cameron wrote his sister in February 1829, two days after Paul Hargis and his family became Cameron property, he proposed that Fairntosh should be renamed "Hodgepodgiana." "Yes I expect to see his man Luke declare it a regular incorporated city and himself mayor and sole sovereign," Paul Cameron wrote, only half in jest.[29] It's clear in retrospect that the role of mayor and sovereign of Fairntosh was one that he foresaw for himself someday.

The career of planter was the last calling that Duncan Cameron wanted for his son. A quarter century had soured the onetime lawyer on plantation management as a lifelong vocation. As much as anything, Duncan Cameron valued control. The volatility of farm prices, the unpredictability of weather and harvests, the periodic epidemics that ravaged the health of his workers, and above all the need to discipline workers whose labor fell short persuaded the father that the plantation was a world of vexations.

When a young nephew asked Duncan Cameron's opinion about starting a plantation in the west, Cameron's answer was firm: *Don't do it.* There was nothing as exasperating as plantation management.

His own disappointments had in fact plunged Duncan Cameron into deep depression three times after he moved to the country to undertake the life of a planter. Each time Cameron made a comeback, threw himself more intensely into the work, acquired more land and people, and sought machinery to supplement human and animal power.[30] It was on one of his upswings that he added the Hargis family to his labor force in early 1829. Duncan Cameron was in a more positive frame of mind when young Paul Cameron returned from the north in June. Nonetheless, in December 1829, Duncan Cameron found an outlet that promised relief from the volatility of plantation life: he was invited to take the reins of the Bank of North Carolina, located in Raleigh, and to serve as its interim president. During the next year, he found the true calling and reward for his restless energy, decisive temperament, and desire to preside over an endeavor he could control.[31]

What Duncan Cameron found for himself in the year 1830 was he wanted for his son: escape from the trials of plantation life.

Law was the profession that Duncan Cameron had in mind for his son, and after a time of indecision, the son settled down to prepare for the bar at the Fairntosh plantation dwelling, while his father remained in Raleigh to extract the Bank of North Carolina from near-bankruptcy and to restore its standing with legislators and depositors in the state. At Fairntosh, once again the student, the son dutifully slogged through the classic tomes of legal principles and precedents. Mercifully, he reported, the tedium was relieved by the singing of workers in nearby fields. Those were the sounds Paul Cameron truly loved to hear, music that he imagined reflected not just harmony of voices but contentment of the singers.[32]

Paul Hargis's father and mother would have learned otherwise. Behind the blended voices at Fairntosh was hidden discontent, conveyed by different songs sung at secret sites. The Hargis parents would have come to know about the clandestine prayer meetings held in forested areas well away from plantation fields and the planter's dwelling. A household servant at Fairntosh recounted what went on at the midnight meetings. Those assembled for prayer stationed guards to make sure that no one discovered them; the guards took special care to watch for whites who patrolled at night on the lookout for black assemblies, so as to break them up and capture those involved. Blacks at the meetings believed that if a pot was turned over, it would capture the sound of songs and prayers to the Lord. If patrollers or owners heard one song in particular, worshippers expected, punishment would be heavy: "Our bondage it shall end / With our threescore years & ten / And to Canaan we'll return / By & Bye, by & bye."[33]

There is no way to know whether George and Agga Hargis were invited to the secret prayer meetings or, if invited, chose to join them. There were risks. Mary Walker, a seamstress and the personal servant of the Cameron daughters, declined to attend. She was afraid of being caught and punished with stripes.[34] She may have harbored the further fear that her young children would suffer reprisals as well. Paul Hargis's parents would have faced the same decision—to attend or not to attend. If discovered, they were at greater hazard than families who had served the plantation since its founding in 1776. The Hargises were newcomers, and gratitude, not defiance, was expected.

Paul Hargis's parents would have had another choice to make. They would certainly have known that the wagoners who took the plantation crops of wheat, tobacco, and cotton to Petersburg for sale traded on the side for coffee and supplies they brought back to the home plantation. Some of the booty they kept for themselves; other goods they bartered to fellow workers. The wagoners put themselves in line for demotion if discovered.[35] It's not clear whether those who bartered with them were at risk as well. Again, individuals with more longevity on the plantation had a cushion if caught. Far less would that have held for the Hargises, recently rescued. They needed to demonstrate compliance with plantation rules.

Despite his superior attraction to the life of a planter, Paul Cameron bowed to the wish of his father and persisted at the law. After the twenty-three-year-old Paul Cameron began to court seventeen-year-old Anne Ruffin, the daughter of state supreme court justice and planter-lawyer Thomas Ruffin, he received the same counsel from the jurist—stay with the law.[36] At the conclusion of Paul Cameron's legal apprenticeship, and on the occasion of his marriage in December 1832, Thomas Ruffin sold his new son-in-law land and a small cottage in Hillsborough. It was to be the base from which the young attorney would practice his profession, there and in nearby Granville and Person counties. After the cottage accidentally burned, the couple started again in the town and built a new home, Burnside, from scratch. Dutifully Paul Cameron began the practice of law. He was miserable, and the misery took physical form. His weight ballooned to well over 200 pounds. Kidney stones, a hereditary trait, plagued him. Traveling the circuit, riding to and from his Hillsborough home to courthouses in adjacent counties, put his great weight on the saddle for hours and induced hemorrhoids. He feared that all his father's physical ailments would befall him.[37]

Paul Cameron knew he was mediocre at law, scrambling to make a living and to win even petty cases. He was the student again, underprepared among the well prepared, upstaged by rivals, and, as he saw it, the object of imagined derision and mockery. His wife found him depressed, and was herself depressed by his low spirits.[38]

Then came a move that would alter the course of the lives of Paul Cameron and Paul Hargis both. The change would put Paul Cameron ultimately en route to the role of planter. For the Hargises and other enslaved workers, the young master's ascent would put to the test the principles of the plantation forged by generations before him. Would he keep families together? Would he still rely on first men and leaven compulsion with incentives?

In 1834, Duncan Cameron received the invitation to become permanent president of the Bank of North Carolina. He instantly accepted. He left Fairntosh for Raleigh, and in the months to come, he commissioned the construction of a city mansion befitting the president of the state bank. In the meantime, he managed the plantation in tandem with his wife and overseers, sending frequent letters to her or them, and on intermittent visits directing the sequence of harvests, the dispatches of crops to Petersburg, and the timing of sales of grains and tobacco. Rebecca Cameron prepared to leave for Raleigh when the mansion was finished and her banker-husband beckoned her and their six daughters to move.

Even at eight years old, Paul Hargis may have wondered, as surely did his parents and other enslaved workers, whether Paul Cameron would ultimately manage the plantation. Periodically, Duncan Cameron's twenty-seven-year-old son came to Fairntosh in 1835 to look in on his mother, to visit his uncle, and to report to his father. Then he would ride off to draw up legal documents for occasional clients. There was no signal from his father to take over Fairntosh.

It was in that limbo that young Paul Hargis and young master Paul Cameron found themselves at Fairntosh in April 1835, when a test came of what kind of ruler the Cameron heir might be. On the morning of April 25, Luke—Fairntosh's most trusted servant and one of the few allowed to come directly to the family residence—summoned Paul Cameron and his mother to report that a whipped worker stood at the outside gate. When the young master asked the man, Jim, what happened, he reported that he'd quarreled with his overseer and been beaten by him. Paul Cameron knew that Jim had been on the plantation for decades, indeed had arrived before any Cameron children were born. Jim had been a gift from Duncan Cameron's father. Paul Cameron also knew Jim's reputation—perhaps from longevity and his privileged status—as an "ungovernable slave." Jim's overseer, William Nichols, was new to that role on the Cameron place, and not disposed to keep his voice down or his temper contained, as other Cameron overseers had learned to do.[39] Standing in for his father, Paul Cameron instructed Jim to return to his quarter and his overseer—and to be obedient and submissive. The young master would go down the next day to get to the bottom of the episode.[40]

The next morning, however, Jim was again at the gate, this time with blood gushing from his head, barely able to stand. Paul Cameron immediately feared the wound would be mortal; he sent for a physician from Hillsborough. Dr. James Webb came and found a fractured skull and, with little hope of success, performed the most startling surgery Paul Cameron had ever seen. Cameron talked to Jim, then went to see the overseer, and learned what had happened. Jim had gone back the day before, as ordered, and had laid low, as told. But Nichols had accosted him early the next morning and demanded to know if he had gone to see his master the day before. Jim said he did. When Nichols asked what Jim had told him, Jim replied, "That is my business, Mr. Nichols." With that Jim turned his back and started away. Enraged, the overseer uttered "some harsh and angry words, got a hold of part of a [fence] rail as Jim was walking off from him, his back turned," and clubbed Jim to the ground. Somehow the wounded man, blood gushing from his mouth and nose, made it more than a mile back to the gate at Fairntosh.[41]

Both Paul Cameron and his mother realized that Duncan Cameron must be told. In cryptic language, perhaps cushioned so as not unduly to alarm her husband, Rebecca Cameron reported that Jim and Mr. Nichols had "had a difference" and that Jim was badly hurt. Paul Cameron wrote a far fuller account on the back of his mother's brief letter. Clearly the son was horrified at "the brutal transaction . . . I use the word brutal, because it is the only word that will express the conduct of Mr. Nichols toward Jim." The son felt "a *deep* solicitude that Jim should live." Even though he acknowledged that Jim was a bad and ungovernable slave, what had happened was something else again. He feared a murder on the plantation. It was the son who had sent Jim back to Nichols—"his thoughtless overseer!" If Jim died, it would be a death on Paul Cameron's watch. To be sure, the son had at once sent for the doctor, and both he and his mother hoped that Jim might live "for many reasons." That still left open the matter of what must be done with the overseer who had responded to Jim's impudence with a brutality that Paul Cameron—and perhaps the plantation in its long history—had never seen. The younger Cameron knew the stakes were high. What would his father think of him? How would the people of the plantation—"our black family"—judge the young master and how he managed the next step?

Duncan Cameron hastened back from Raleigh. Decisions that followed revealed what was to be done. William Nichols remained in place as overseer. Jim, who gradually recovered, was moved to a different quarter.[42] For the son, the lessons were clear. In a dispute between an overseer and an enslaved worker, owners must back the overseer. Moreover, when submission was at stake, force was a fact of life. Paul Cameron soon showed he understood. Two months after the beating of Jim, Paul Cameron reported that he was dissatisfied with the effort of some laborers and demanded a new spirit of industry. It wasn't long before he acquired the reputation among neighboring enslaved people as a young owner who whipped his workers just to show them who was master.[43]

The episode with Nichols and Jim forced Cameron to show his father and plantation workers that he was prepared to punish to gain compliance. More to his liking, however, was the model of his uncle, Thomas Bennehan, for whom medicine mediated the relationship with "his people." The unmarried uncle had invested himself in the medical treatment of his workers and had become the de facto physician of the Stagville plantation, adjacent to Fairntosh. Ailments that were endemic to his workers' demanding lives—malaria, fevers, colds, small injuries—he ministered to with intense care. Young Paul Cameron had witnessed his uncle's medical attention to his slaves, who referred to their owner as "Mas Tommy."[44] The nephew watched his uncle with admiration and witnessed displays of gratitude from those the uncle treated, despite their dislike of the purgatives and blistering he employed under the prevailing humoral theory of disease. Illnesses likewise provided the nephew with the need and opportunity to doctor the workers in their quarters. Paul Cameron threw himself into the role of lay physician. When measles broke out, the young master left behind his wife and law practice in Hillsborough so as to tend workers day and night. Whether or not his medical methods helped, his presence reassured the black families of his commitment and of his readiness—if life itself seemed at stake—to summon a doctor to the rescue.[45] Paul Cameron reported with relief and satisfaction that the epidemic subsided and that none had died.[46]

For another year and a half, Duncan Cameron sought to handle the affairs of his plantations by proxy. At the same time, there was little doubt that Paul Cameron, languishing at law, was depressed. Cameron's uncle

Thomas Bennehan, visiting Paul and Anne Cameron in May 1836, reported that they were both sunk in gloom. Duncan Cameron, who had left the plantation after epidemics and deaths and his awareness of lost control had made him a "melancholy hypochondriac," had to face the fact that the absence from the fray was putting his son in the same condition. At the end of 1837, Duncan Cameron conceded. If twenty-nine-year-old Paul Cameron wished to run the plantation and become its sole sovereign and mayor, his father would no longer stand in the way.[47]

What Paul Cameron's authority and ambition would mean for Paul Hargis and his family would emerge over the next half dozen years.

Two ❧ "Emigrants"

PAUL CAMERON'S FIRST YEAR was like no other, and signaled to his workers, and to his father, mother, and uncle, that this was the role he was meant for. Throughout 1838, good weather and good health favored the plantation, and by midyear Paul Cameron reported that an unprecedented wheat harvest was in the offing. He was in the field every day, riding his horse, urging on his overseers and first men. Though drenched in sweat by the effort, he reveled in the results. "I have . . . lived on buttermilk and lost some quarts of perspiration in the harvest fields. I would be willing to have my *shirt* wet every day in the year for *such* a harvest," he wrote his mother.[1] Depression free, he wrote in celebration rather than complaint.

For eleven-year-old Paul Hargis and his older brothers and sister, all now old enough to be workers in the field, as well as for their parents, the young master's drive meant that they, too, were sweating and straining to make good on Paul Cameron's brag. There was no need to see if he meant business. The episode with Jim in April 1835 had been a wake-up call. For three members of the Hargis family, however, there was more than the planter's push. After Paul Cameron took over the place, he moved George and Agga Hargis to one of the larger quarters of the Cameron place and made George the first man of the quarter run by overseer Arthur Bobbitt. George Hargis moved up to number one on the list of enslaved persons at Bobbitt's quarter.[2] From Paul Cameron's point of view, the role of slave foreman was one of trust and authority—a promotion within his hierarchy of enslaved people. No record indicates how George Hargis viewed the role, whether he felt ambivalence or even reluctance about the expectation that he would be the driver to push his fellow workers. Nor is there any record of how he and his wife, Agga, felt about their move away from other family members, most of whom remained at Fairntosh until 1842.[3] Perhaps less conflicted was the new role that Paul Cameron apparently assigned to the oldest Hargis son, Squire. There were several Squires on the plantation. By the time of the 1842 inventory of workers, Squire Hargis was twenty years old. It's plausible that the youthful son of George and Agga Hargis assumed the role of courier on Paul Cameron's watch. If so, he now acted as a frequent messenger and wagoner between quarters and to and from Cameron's father in Raleigh.[4]

Intensified work, intensified supervision, role shifts that suggested greater trust in the Hargises on the part of the planter—all these changes came with the ascent of the young master who sought to prove in 1838 that he was up to the job that his father had vacated. But unbeknownst to the Hargises and others, there was more, far more, in the offing. The new sovereign of Fairntosh, who just three years before had spoken modestly of wishing only to be self-dependent and to provide comfort for his wife and others, revealed an ambition that extended well beyond harvesting the best wheat crop in the Piedmont.[5] Like other young men of the 1830s, and especially young southern slave owners, Paul Cameron was looking to the West.

"I write to introduce one Paul Cameron, who is my son, and who is interested in acquiring land in the southwest." So wrote Duncan Cameron in January 1839.[6] For the elder Cameron, the endorsement of expansion outside the Piedmont had been slow in the making. Two decades earlier, on a trip to Knoxville, Tennessee, he had seen and heard of the rush of migrants to lands of the West, a zeal that was siphoning young men from Tennessee as well as from North Carolina. To the senior Cameron, who had managed to acquire thousands of acres incrementally in the Piedmont, the "pursuit of Happiness" by "changing from place to place" struck him as a delusion, as if "that unattainable quality was to be found in any *particular* place."[7] Later, of course, he himself found happiness in a new place as president of the state bank. In the early 1830s, his son had teased his sisters that he might join the western migration. When Paul settled in Hillsborough in 1834, he seemed to foreswear such a move.[8] By the late 1830s, however, the lure of western land, and above all the promise of cotton, was no longer a tease to either Paul Cameron or his father. For much of the decade, wheat in the Piedmont and elsewhere was overproduced and its selling price low and flat. During the same years, the demand for cotton seemed insatiable, and despite ever-increasing production, the price of cotton held. The Cameron and Bennehan lands did grow a modest amount of cotton, which sold immediately and well. But the real land for growing cotton, and for realizing its profits, was in the West.[9]

Flush with the triumph of his first year of planting at Fairntosh, Paul Cameron looked to do through cotton and expansion what he had done for wheat at home—to prove his mettle, to move from sufficiency to abundance, to go beyond simple custody of his inheritance. There was one key difference between his tease of heading west in 1834 and his genuine quest for western land in 1838: Paul Cameron had no intention of moving himself. He was looking for land to own in absentia. Once he found it, he would send workers from North Carolina to make the crop and bring in the profits. This time Duncan Cameron supported his son's undertaking. A distant place could enhance happiness—at least for the white family.

Starting out in November 1838, Paul Cameron scouted for a western plantation for two months. He went first to Greensboro, Alabama, a town in the western part of the state.[10] The land was called the "Black Belt" on account of its rich black soil and the black workers who grew cotton for their owners. He then made his way across the nearby state line to eastern Mississippi.[11] He turned back and returned home without making a purchase. He may have gotten cold feet in the midst of extravagant claims for riches waiting to be made. A close friend had described Mississippi as a land of swindlers and liars, a place where no one was to be trusted.[12] More likely, other forces had stymied Cameron's plan. A second wave of a severe economic panic had demoralized the country. Even for men of means, the winter of 1838–1839 seemed a risky time to invest. More overriding may have been tragedy in the Cameron family.

Consumption—the contemporary name for tuberculosis—had already taken the life of one of Paul's sisters, in July 1837, and now it imperiled the lives of others. Two others wasted away and perished in the summer of 1839; a fourth would die in 1840.[13] For Paul Cameron's distracted and distraught parents, the time was hardly right to buy another plantation and dispatch workers to it.

For those who might have been sent west if a buy had been made—including the once-spared Hargises—delay brought reprieve.

Our labor force "must turn a new leaf," Paul Cameron wrote his father at the end of 1842.[14]

Four years after the halcyon beginning of his ascent as the master of Fairntosh, Paul Cameron had discovered what his father had long since learned and tried without success to convey to him: "There is no permanent prosperity here."[15] "Mastery" dissipated against setbacks that befell the son after 1838. Illnesses induced by work in the wheat and aggravated by mill ponds and the earlier clearance of low-lying grounds that provided a breeding ground for malaria-infested mosquitoes kept Cameron busy treating sick workers. As had his uncle and his father, he threw himself into medical care. When one or two became mortally ill, he stayed with them till they died, performing the "melancholy duty of the master." As it had with his father, depression set in, aggravated by illness of his own—kidney stones, bladder infection, hemorrhoids, muscle spasms. He came to doubt that he or his workers would improve. Long past the point of reminding his son that he'd forecast what lay in store, the father could only encourage his son to meet stress with resignation, as did his mother. Outcomes were up to a higher power. As always, the father urged his son to battle against the blues, against depression of spirit, by concentrated effort at good cheer.[16]

No more was resignation an option for Paul Cameron than it had earlier been for his father. To the son, something beyond ill health was involved in what he regarded as diminished plantation productivity. Cameron seems to have concluded that despite his medical care and what he regarded as generous provisions, "his people" had settled into shared understandings about how hard they would push themselves or be pressed to do their work. Even with reliance on first men, even with a black overseer on one of the quarters, even with white overseers of long standing, it seemed as if nothing would move his workers beyond an un-spoken pact to cap their effort. Cameron acted to break up the understand-ings. At the end of 1842, he shuffled the makeup of the quarters.[17] For the first time in decades, he transferred people to new places and broke up family groups. Bygones would be bygones, old shortcomings forgotten, but now he expected results.

Paul Hargis was among those shifted about. He and his two sisters—Sally and Nancy, the first older, the second younger—were moved to a quarter in adjacent Person County. In Person, Paul Hargis and his sisters came under the supervision of either Jim Ray, the plantation's only black overseer, or William Nichols, the man who had almost killed Jim seven years before. The Hargises' father and mother remained at over-seer Arthur Bobbitt's quarter, where George Hargis continued as the first man and likely foreman. Son Jim Hargis had already moved to yet a dif-ferent quarter, where he'd started a family with an enslaved woman named Dilcy. The middle brother, Squire, stayed at Fairntosh, where he continued in his role as a courier among quarters and to destinations off the plantation.[18] Of course, members of the Hargis family were still not far from each other. One might view these moves as a vote of confidence for Paul Hargis's father, George, as an accommodation for his brothers Jim and Squire to be with their mates, and even a concession to Paul Hargis, who could look after his sisters. Paul Cameron may have seen it that way—not so much breaking up families as breaking up black labor arrangements.

It turned out to be a prelude to a far more sweeping shift.

Paul Cameron had for a time put a western plantation out of mind, looking instead to boost harvests in North Carolina by reshuffling his workers and expecting more of them. The plan failed, doomed not so much by foot-dragging as by worsening illness and weather. Physicians were called twenty-two times in the spring of 1843 to treat the sick at different plantation quarters, leading Duncan Cameron, in response to reports from Fairntosh, to lament the "pain and suffering" of black families and to fear for "the anxiety and fatigue" of his son. "God be with you in all your troubles," he said in a letter. Bad weather deepened the Camerons' sense of siege. "We have indeed had a desperate season," wrote the father from Raleigh. The small cotton crop of 1843 faced complete destruction; that of 1844 was little better, "the shortest crop ever made in this neighborhood." The wheat crop survived, only again to bring flat sales because of overproduction throughout the region and the country.[19] For Paul Cameron, there was only one way to break out of the cycle of failure and to relieve the despondency that once more was setting in. He persuaded his father to bankroll the purchase of a cotton plantation in the West, and to allow him to pick as many enslaved people as he needed to work it. In August 1844, preparations began for the move.

Paul Cameron concentrated his efforts on material provisions for the trek out. There must be leather for new shoes, 400 pounds of cloth and a thousand brass buttons for new shirts and frocks, new hats and fresh blankets, and medicines for the trip. They would need heavy cotton canvas sailcloth and stakes for two large tents to be hoisted thirty or forty feet high at overnight stops, so that women and children would have shelter. The son authorized the purchase of four heavy wagons and twenty-one mules to pull them. At the plantation, there was no secret about Cameron's purpose. On the contrary, in every quarter, people were put to work—women sewed garments, men dressed leather for shoes, wagoners gathered supplies for the trip.[20]

All also had plenty of time—five months from August to November 1844—to wonder and worry. Who would be on Cameron's final list of "Negroes to Go South"? Would Paul Hargis or his family members be among them?

Paul Cameron sought to reassure his father that all his expenses, including more and larger ones to come, would be rewarded: "I fear you will find yourself a good deal impoverished by this undertaking, but the land paid for, you will never regret the removal of your slaves."[21] Could he provide equal reassurance to the enslaved people he was about to remove? Could Paul Cameron hope to transfer not just people but the understandings that had been the hallmark of the Bennehan and Cameron plantations since before his birth? Could he take enslaved people west without breaking up families, thereby violating the unspoken pact of forced labor for family integrity? Could he expect to keep the allegiance of first men if he dispatched them to the Deep South, with its reputation among the enslaved as the hellhole of bondage?[22]

The black perception of bondage in the Southwest was stark, and if Paul Cameron had not known it before, he encountered it full force in December 1838 on his first reconnaissance for a western plantation, when he arrived in Greensboro, Alabama. Earlier that year, the first published narrative of an American slave's experience had gone to press. In *The Narrative of James Williams*, an enslaved man who had fled bondage and made it to New York and Boston told abolitionists his story of being sent from Virginia to Greene County, Alabama, in the 1830s.[23] His was a tale of separation from his family, betrayal by a planter he trusted, and brutality by an overseer determined to transform indulged eastern bondsmen into submissive western cotton pickers. The setting for his account was none other than an Alabama plantation located near Greensboro.

By the time Paul Cameron arrived in Greensboro at the end of 1838, the editor of the town newspaper, the *Alabama Beacon*, had challenged the authenticity of the *Narrative*, disputed the identity of the author, and refuted his claim to have been enslaved and maltreated in surrounding Greene County. Forced to withdraw the account, its abolitionist publishers claimed that there was still truth in this tale of a migration experience, even if names and places erred. Cameron came to Greensboro exactly at the time when the editor and the county's planters were still gloating that they had forced abolitionists to back down from a fraud—a slander on slaveholders who moved their workers to the West and an insult to slaveholders who dwelt there. A meticulous recent reexamination of the *Narrative* and the experience of its author has found that "James Williams" was a pseudonym for an enslaved man who indeed was taken from Virginia to Alabama—to a county fifty miles east of Greensboro—and concluded that his account was a composite of his own experience and the trials and fears of others.[24]

Paul Cameron's preparations for the move suggest that, whatever he thought of the furor over the *Narrative*, he sensed that his enslaved workers shared the fears it expressed. His choice of those to make the migration was designed to reassure "his people" that the move was not a betrayal. There was to be a parting, yes, but not a departure from the ethic of generations before him. Cameron drafted list after list of names, shifting names about, dropping some, adding others, and selecting individuals from all quarters. Each of the drafts included first men—Sandy the carpenter, Milton the courier, Charles the blacksmith, Edmund the foreman. Each draft sought to cluster family groups. Cameron was trying to hold together husbands and wives, parents and children, and sometimes adult sisters and brothers. From his vantage point, he was keeping the family pact, even as he moved people west.

Hargis family members were on every version of "Negroes to Go South," as Cameron titled his evolving list. Paul Hargis and his two sisters, transferred to the Person County quarter in 1842, were on the final register, along with the mates of the sisters. With his wife, their brother Jim was also on the final list—and indeed was the only enslaved person recorded with a first *and* last name, Jim Hargis. The Hargises' father and mother, George and Agga, were on all of the lists—save the last one.[25] Who decided they would *not* go to the Southwest, and why, can only be conjectured. As the first man on the Bobbitt quarters, was George Hargis too essential to send? At the age of fifty-six, was he deemed too old? Were the Hargis parents given the choice? Whatever the explanation, as the day arrived for gathering the group of 114 people from different quarters to the home plantation at Fairntosh, the parents knew that this was a final farewell. They knew because their son Squire—who was to stay behind at Fairntosh—received the assignment to go with overseer Arthur Bobbitt, the supervisor of the parents' quarter, to drive a wagon to Person County and collect Paul, Sally, and Nancy Hargis for the departure.[26] Whether Squire's assignment was a last consideration or an excruciating finale—or both—one can only guess.

As Paul Hargis and his siblings gathered at Fairntosh, wagons and mules at the ready, they could look around and see other families or fragments of families assembled with them. There was Sandy the carpenter and his beleaguered wife, Aggy, who'd lost every child she'd birthed and would lose more in years to come. There was Milton the courier, an enterprising man used to having the run of the region in North Carolina, an unconfined man moving to a confined place.[27] There was Rosezetta, bought with her daughters in 1818, one of the older women designated to go, who would accompany a daughter and granddaughter. A year later she would display how furious she was at the move. Rosezetta was paired with old Lewis, a onetime wagoner relieved of his role when young Paul Cameron had snitched that Lewis was bartering on the side. "Drops will empty an ocean," he had alerted his father.[28] There was Edmund, the foreman of the quarter at Eno, chosen to be the head man in Alabama, there to set the pace and be a model of loyalty, trusted to do his job and move others to do theirs.

All were in place on the day of departure, November 1, 1844—including the family patriarch himself, Duncan Cameron. His presence was the son's final effort at reassurance to the black "emigrants," as he called them, that this was not just the young master's undertaking but a full family venture. "Under all circumstances, I shall expect you *here*," Paul Cameron had written his father the week before. "I beg you will believe [me] that your presence will do much to make the *start easy*."[29]

Paul Cameron accompanied the people, their overseer for the trip, and the wagons and mules for the first two days and two nights of "the march and the encampment." He "reduced things to a good system & left them well organized" for the remainder of the journey. After he got "our people . . . just beyond Boon Station," at the edge of the Blue Ridge Mountains, he bade them farewell, returned home, and readied himself to travel west by train and coach. Confident that his preparations, his father's presence, and his personal escort had left "all well here," thirty-six-year-old Paul Cameron parted from the caravan in high spirits: "All things going on most prosperously."[30]

Whether all things would continue to go on "most prosperously," seventeen-year-old Paul Hargis—marching to Alabama along with 113 other "emigrants"—would soon learn.

Three ✐ "A Place Perfectly Detested"

DECADES AFTER HIS REMOVAL from North Carolina and resettlement in Alabama, eighty-year-old Paul Hargis provided only an idyllic account of the trip out—travel by coach along with the planter, followed by an amicable parting. His was a tale as different as could be from horrors chronicled in slave narratives such as *Twelve Years a Slave* and in the fictional bestseller *Uncle Tom's Cabin*. There was, however, a single literate person among those who traveled to Alabama in November 1844 who offered quite different testimony about the move. Writing to one he trusted, a year after the journey from North Carolina, his words were scathing:

> [The new plantation is a] place perfectly detested. . . . I have been wronged, grossly wronged; injustice, gross injustice has been done me. . . . If I ever felt willing to enter a room naked armed with a two edged sword to meet a foe from whom I could only escape by victory, it is now. . . . I know not how, when, or by whom the day of my emancipation shall come around, but I shall shout with a new born joy to know I am not again to see this spot of earth. . . . It is a long night upon which no light ever dawns.[1]

The person who wrote of "so hated a place," of his rage for revenge and yearning for emancipation, was not Paul Hargis nor one of the 113 other enslaved people who made the twenty-nine-day trek across North Carolina and Georgia to Alabama in 1844.

It was Paul Cameron, the planter who sent them there.

For the move to Alabama, Paul Cameron had taken every step in November 1844 to counter fears inevitably harbored in the hearts of those named to go west. Though Cameron made no note of words or actions that revealed the apprehensions of those listed as "Negroes to Go South," the anxieties of "emigrants" (as he called them) were no secret to him or his father or to other planters. By selecting persons to go in family groups, including Paul Hargis and his brother Jim and their sisters, Nancy and Sally, he had sought to cushion the irrevocable separation from friends and other relatives they would never see again. But what lay in store for them in the West? What kind of work, what kind of rule, what kind of treatment? On the plantation in North Carolina, there had always been some element of human relationships with Cameron slave owners and their wives and children, some knowledge of capacities and skills, health and limits. In the West, Paul Hargis and others would be blank slates to men who knew them not, and who saw them as needing to be toughened to meet the demands of a new overseer and a different crop. If harsh treatment came, their owner would be 400 miles away.

The possibility that he himself could be betrayed was the last thing on the mind of Paul Cameron as he prepared for the move of his enslaved laborers to their destination: Greensboro, Alabama, a village in the heart of Greene County and the Alabama Black Belt. Cameron had visited Greensboro six years earlier, on his initial scouting trip for a western plantation in December 1838. He made Greensboro his starting point that winter because it was near the plantation belonging to an uncle of his wife, Anne Ruffin Cameron. James Ruffin had moved to Alabama in 1834 and had settled on a place about twenty-five miles from Greensboro in Marengo County, just south of Greene County.[2] Cameron had then gone to eastern Mississippi, where a friend of his had written about land of inexhaustible fertility.[3] Cameron came back without making a buy. The friend guessed that his young compatriot found himself immobilized by all the claims and embellishments that he encountered among landowners eager to promote theirs as the best lands in the South. Who could be trusted?[4]

In the summer of 1844, Cameron decided to rely on James Ruffin, asking Ruffin for help locating a place and getting a promise of assistance. In September, with Cameron anxious as the time of departure neared, Ruffin told him of a place in Marengo County, not far from his own plantation, owned by the Gracie family of New York City. Ruffin expected the place soon to come on the market, pledged to write the owners, and even had Cameron's permission to make an offer on it. Paul Cameron assured his father that he felt at ease about following his relative's advice.[5] He would have inside information that he could rely on, and not have to cope with the hyperbole of self-interested strangers.

With his enslaved people still on their trek out, walking a dozen miles a day with most of the adults on foot, the group crossing rivers by ferry with their four heavy wagons and twenty-one mules, Cameron hastened ahead to Greensboro.[6] There James Ruffin explained to him that the Gracie sale hadn't worked out but that he'd found another place that he thought would suit. It belonged to Colonel William Armistead, who had owned and farmed the place since 1834. The amount of cotton produced had been good—between 400 and 500 bales annually—with the exception of one bad year. Ruffin stated that there were already built dwellings of good quality for all of Cameron's people. "As regards health, Armistead says he has lost but two grown negroes, from diseases of the climate, in ten years." Ruffin duly noted that the Armistead plantation was "not a first grade place." But there was not a first-grade place to be had.[7] Ruffin's conclusion was that the Armistead plantation was an excellent deal—it was worth its price in weighed gold—and he told young Cameron, "Had I your means and labor, I'd take it d——d quick!"[8] After several days of negotiations, Cameron did just that, agreeing to pay $29,305 for 1,674 acres, the amount to be paid out in annual installments over a three-year period. He was not totally persuaded by what he saw, but nonetheless was "governed either by the advice of friends or counsel and I trust all has been 'well done.'" Fervent was his hope, for every penny of the purchase was his father's: "I have never been more anxious to acquit myself faithfully to you."[9]

Cameron's workers, some weary and one gravely enfeebled by the monthlong journey west, waited in Greensboro under the supervision of their North Carolina overseer while Cameron concluded the agreement with William Armistead. Then Cameron accompanied them as they walked and caravanned the final fifteen miles down to the new plantation. By then, uncertainty had begun to gnaw at him. On close inspection, he had found the cabins less than desirable. The former owner's overseer was unhelpful, the supplies supposedly awaiting them smaller than promised. "The best that could be had" was James Ruffin's assurance and, for the moment, Cameron's consolation. Yet Cameron began to wonder. Perhaps it was more than a coincidence—which he was aware of before the signing—that William Armistead was indebted to James Ruffin, and indeed that the first payment to the seller was immediately transferred to Ruffin to pay off that obligation.[10] In the meantime, the trip-depleted worker named Edmund—the thirty-seven-year-old man that Cameron had counted on to be the black foreman of the Alabama place—grew weaker by the day and died a month after arrival in Alabama. Cameron had looked to Edmund, who had filled the foreman's role on the Eno quarter back in North Carolina, to be his first man in Alabama, a trusted leader to buffer the adjustment of fellow workers to their new overseer. For Cameron and the enslaved people alike, Edmund's death was a loss, and an omen. It threw the planter into depression.[11]

It's not known what happened during the month after Cameron made his purchase and moved his people and himself onto the plantation. Neighbors and nearby overseers may have come by to meet the new owner. One or more of them may have said, in so many knowing words, *Oh, so you're the one who bought the Colonel's place.* Did another, in a decidedly dubious tone of voice, wish him good luck with it, as if to intimate that he would need it? At some point Cameron seems to have asked, or been told, the neighbors' verdict about the Armistead place. The soils on that plantation varied wildly and couldn't be counted on; the seller had exhausted the topsoil for all it was worth; Colonel Armistead had been keen to get out; Cameron had wildly overpaid. The thirty-six-year-old buyer from North Carolina came to believe that he'd been taken.

Persuaded that he'd been misled—rendered "not just a dupe but a *victim*," as he later put it—Paul Cameron had a breakdown. He fell apart in front of the people he'd uprooted, those whose confidence—in him, in the move, in the transplantation of the Cameron plantation ethic—he had worked so carefully to build. Almost certainly fueled by drink, he raged that he was a deluded man, deceived by his wife's relative, derided by knowing neighbors. He lambasted his blindness; he confessed his folly; he uttered the wish to leave Alabama and never again to set eyes upon the place.[12]

Paul Hargis and the other enslaved people who witnessed their owner's collapse surely were flabbergasted. When Cameron recovered from his tirade—when he sobered up—he realized that his overseer, Charles Lewellyn, who had been recommended by James Ruffin, had witnessed the rant and would report it to Ruffin. Cameron knew he had to apologize to his wife's uncle. In response, Ruffin wrote back that he took no offense, that he knew that the stress of the trip and difficulty of adjustment, not to mention the death of the man he had counted on to be the foreman of the new place, had unsettled Cameron. Ruffin's main regret, as he put it obliquely, involved "the want of firmness and energy which you exhibited" and the fact that Cameron had temporarily lost "control of his mental and bodily powers." Ruffin thought "and still think that it was a gratuitous infliction of pain upon the members of your family"—that Cameron's outburst had wreaked needless harm on the people he'd brought to Alabama.[13] Ruffin and Cameron both knew that his workers inevitably came with apprehensions about what lay in store. The last thing they needed was for their owner to talk about his folly—and his wish to escape.

Shortly after the episode, James Ruffin wrote home to his brother Thomas Ruffin, Cameron's father-in-law. That letter is the only one in the family archive of thousands of letters with a paragraph carefully cut out and discarded.[14]

⌒◦

No more than Paul Cameron had seventeen-year-old Paul Hargis expected that the enslaved man Edmund, picked to be the foreman of the new plantation in Alabama, would die soon after their arrival in Greensboro. The record kept by the overseer who brought out the 114 people from North Carolina noted only the stops made on the way, along with entries of payments for feeding mules and for ferrying wagons, animals, and people across the half dozen rivers they encountered. There was no mention of weather—wet or cold or both—or of the health of the people. In retrospect, it's clear that the trip and then the change to the climate of Alabama took a toll, fatally for Edmund, chronically for Sandy, the plantation carpenter weakened by the trip and sick for much of 1845, and indeed for all the older men in the caravan.

The older men on the Alabama place proved to be the most vulnerable to the change in climate and perhaps to a different strain of malaria found in the Alabama Black Belt. Over the course of the next two years, a total of six men, three women, and one child died. Among the men, four were fifty or older—Old Simon, Old York, Old Peter, and sixty-year-old Abraham. Before the deaths, Cameron noted when he returned to Alabama in November 1845 that all the elders looked "thin and pale," "bleached and enfeebled." As one after another of the older men died, others came close to death, most with "congestive fever." Paul Hargis and his brother Jim and their sisters, Sally and Nancy—none of them over twenty-five—had to be grateful that their father, George, who turned fifty-six in 1844, had at the last moment been struck from the list of those chosen to go to Alabama.[15]

Of course, as the Hargis family members learned over the course of that first year, and as Cameron realized on his return to Alabama in November 1845, far more had changed than the climate. Cotton was a crop that made continuous and intense demands on field hands, far more than had grains and tobacco in North Carolina. In the dead of winter, plows had to furrow up the land. By early spring, seeds were to go in, and as the young plants came up, the weeds that rampantly flourished alongside the cotton had to be chopped out, hoed again and again so they didn't stunt or overwhelm the money crop. In the grueling heat of late summer, with blood-sucking mosquitoes at their worst, harvest time came. Picking cotton was a skill utterly different from harvesting corn or wheat. Once the bolls opened, there was a premium on picking cotton with speed and clean of trash. Summer's weather could change at any moment. Drought could wither, or rain could drench, the open cotton bolls, diminishing or destroying the crop's worth. It took skilled hands to pick each boll from the plant, separating it entirely from the hard but crumbly leaf at its base. Pressure fell on Cameron's workers, few of whom had come from North Carolina with experience in picking cotton.[16]

Given that Paul Cameron left Alabama with the belief that he'd bought a poor plantation, the overseer's 1845 reports of low returns were hardly surprising. Still, the news stung. The Alabama crop was small; his workers picked on average only 140 pounds a day. From his cotton broker in Mobile came complaints that the cotton arriving for sale was trashy and would go at a low price. When Cameron expressed disappointment, the overseer faulted the workers: Cameron's laborers "were not disposed to pick what I know they ought to pick"; "Your hands are very indifferent pickers"; "Your hands are slow pickers"; "If I attempt to pick clean cotton, I shall never save it."[17]

When Cameron returned to Alabama in November 1845, he discovered what the overseer had omitted from reports that focused on weather, insects, and quantities of cotton picked. Under the gun from the absentee owner to make the best crop he could, Charles Lewellyn had done what most Black Belt overseers did with enslaved workers shifted from the East: he sought to break them in. Some southwestern overseers believed that laborers from Virginia and North Carolina were soft and spoiled, requiring blustery threats and repeated whippings to bring them to heel.[18] Charles Lewellyn seemed more military and matter-of-fact in his drive for discipline and output. He compelled the entire force to appear at his cabin at noon every Sunday, there to be inspected for cleanliness of garb and person. Cameron found the overseer "a very rigid man too much so for me. But he says no man had a harder set to deal with," he added, rationalizing the climate of fear he found. "The negroes fear him a little more than I wish." Yet however the overseer had induced that fear—here Cameron felt no need to provide details to his father—Lewellyn had achieved results. He had "made a very decided impression upon the habits, manners, and customs of our people, improving their capacity and disposition to labor, making the rude orderly & respectful and the idle uniform and attentive in their efforts." In backhanded admiration of the increased effort that the overseer had wrung from the transplanted people, Cameron observed that "we don't but half work back in North Carolina."[19]

Those asked what they thought of Charles Lewellyn reported that he was "kind in the main and just." At least that was the view, Cameron added, of "that portion of the family who are disposed to do well"— implicitly dismissing dissenters as ill-disposed.[20] It's not known where Paul Hargis and other members of the Hargis family appeared on the planter's spectrum.

Sensing that their owner would side with the Alabama overseer—as he had ten years before sided with the Carolina overseer who nearly killed the man Jim—most took care not to express dissent or anger to the visiting planter. But not all. The enslaved man Toney hated work in the cotton field. In the midst of Cameron's visit to Alabama in November 1845, Toney ran away—a brazen statement to the owner that at least for one of "his people," all was not well. Toney didn't get far. He had the misfortune of crossing the path of neighboring whites out on a fox hunt. The foxhounds forced Toney to take refuge on top of a fence. He surrendered to the hunters, who the next day, with the hounds baying all the while, returned Toney to the plantation. As Cameron reported the incident, Toney's fellow workers were horrified at the episode, perhaps fearful that the hounds were ferocious dogs trained to capture runaways—and, if uncontrolled, to maim or kill. Cameron hoped it would be a lesson, presumably about the futility of escape. Cameron himself chose to draw no lessons about the enervating fieldwork or demands of the overseer that drove Toney to flee.[21]

Cameron was more perceptive about the message sent by the enslaved woman Rosezetta. At the age of fifty, she was one of the older women taken to Alabama, there to look after her daughter and granddaughters, and to be the companion of fifty-four-year-old Lewis. Rosezetta did no field work, but rather was expected to sew and oversee the sewing of garments from the yards of cloth Cameron bought and had delivered to the Alabama plantation. Sew she did—as badly as she could. The overseer left it to Cameron to decide what to do. The owner felt "obliged to punish her for her mean sewing on thè Negros' clothing," even though he realized what was behind it: "She would give her head to be back in N. Carolina."[22]

If the Hargis siblings and others felt deceived by their owner, if they too stood ready to give their heads—or Cameron's—to be back in North Carolina, they kept their fury to themselves. It was well that they did so, for Paul Cameron's six weeks in Alabama from mid-November to the end of December 1845 inflamed his own sense of betrayal. He was the man swindled. He was the "victim."

Less than a week after Paul Cameron returned to Alabama in mid-November 1845, he wrote the first of four livid letters to his father, each one seething with anger and shame. He'd looked to his wife's uncle for "*disinterested* counsel and advice" and had gotten instead lies about the land. "I regard myself as a deluded man, blinded by misplaced confidence and unsuspecting friendship," he wrote. Paul Cameron had hoped for more than honest advice and a good investment. The Alabama place was to have been his proving ground—the chance to demonstrate his "manliness" to himself and his worth to his father. Instead it became "the *theatre of my sacrifice.*" "Had I come to the country an utter stranger my chances for success would have been far better," he lamented. Not only had Cameron bought an inferior place, but he'd paid well "beyond the usual price for *such land.*" Consequently, "no one has a better right to exclaim 'save me from my friends.'" He had "now but one hope or wish"— to undo the harm from "your indulgent confidence in an erring son." With each letter, his indignation grew. He would rejoice if he "could leave it today never again to set my eyes upon it. That I have been 'wronged'—& deceived there can be *no sort* of 'mistake,'" he wrote angrily. "We should have to work on I fear a many long day if ever we could get rid of 'this folly.'"[23]

Duncan Cameron had to have known his son was disappointed in the western plantation before he ventured back to Alabama. But the father was nonetheless startled at the ferocity of the letters he received, and urged—indeed demanded—that his son pull back: "I regret that you cannot forget, or get over what you regard as a wrong done you in the abuse of your confidence." The father hoped his son was mistaken, "but if you are not, what good does it do to indulge . . . so unpleasant a subject. Let us agree for your own sake" and for family harmony "to dismiss it from your mind."[24] In reply, Paul Cameron assured his father that he would be "prudent."

> But at the same time I see no harm in disclosing to you the troubles of a devoted son. If I have been wronged, grossly wronged, why may I not tell you of it! If injustice—gross injustice has been done me, why conceal it from one who has ever been so kind and liberal. Pardon me dear Father. I meant not to disturb your peace. . . . To *waste* your means and to make myself an object of derision—it makes me weep alike in sorrow and in anger. . . . Less than this I cannot say.[25]

The son accommodated his father's directive by focusing on the place rather than its perpetrator. "If I had a deed of Gift from you tomorrow for this Estate, I would let it go to the highest bidder," he wrote. Besides, "I should be removed from a place perfectly *detested*," a plantation where "we must *look for no increase of yield*" but rather "look for a *very steady falling back*—in quantity and quality."

With no evident awareness that he might be giving voice to the sentiments of 114 enslaved people he'd uprooted from North Carolina thirteen months before, Paul Cameron concluded the response to his father: "I know not how, where or by whom the day of my ~~redemption and~~ emancipation shall come around, but I shall shout with a new born joy to know that I am not again to see this spot of earth."[26]

Shards of evidence offer clues that the four Hargis siblings in Alabama also thought of home and family. Cut off from contact with parents and their brother Squire, all left behind in North Carolina, and at best only able to fantasize a return to their birthplace, they expressed their family connection through names given their children. Not long after the move to Alabama, Sally Hargis started a family with thirty-three-year-old Green, who had come from the Eno quarter back in North Carolina. Nancy Hargis had made a household with thirty-four-year-old Peter. Over the course of the next several years, the two sisters had children named after family members left behind: George after their father, Agnis after their mother, and Squire and Jim after their brothers. Not until 1850 did Paul Hargis, the youngest of the Hargis sons, start a household with Dicey, a woman seven years younger than him. The two children Dicey bore died in infancy; their names went unrecorded. Back in North Carolina, Squire Hargis named an infant son after Paul, his exiled youngest brother.[27]

Unlike Paul Cameron, the Hargises of Alabama recognized that for them there was no alternative. They had to make the best of where they were. Reports of the pounds of cotton they picked at harvest time found their amounts mostly in the middle—well short of the 200 pounds a day picked by the worker Carolina, well above the lowest day's haul of 93 pounds. Jim, Paul, Sally, and Nancy Hargis doubtless were among the ever-multiplying number who fell sick at later harvest times. First a handful, then ten to fifteen, then fifteen to forty were reported sick by the overseer as August gave way to September and October and the crush was on. But almost never did the illnesses of the Hargises reach the point where they or their ailments were mentioned by name, or where overseer Charles Lewellyn felt obliged to call in a physician for treatment. Paul Cameron had observed on his trips to Alabama that younger workers looked well (and the children fat as pigs). The Hargises were among those favored in the process of acclimation by their youth. It's also possible that they were looking after the health of each other, partly by sharing workloads when pressure mounted.

Nothing changed on the plantation during the year that passed before Paul Cameron's winter visit to Alabama in December 1846. The overseer's reports in early 1846 had begun with buoyant forecasts of the largest crop ever, but descended as hopes for a good crop gave way to blasts of bad weather and to rust, worms, and rot in the cotton. Illnesses multiplied, keeping hands out of the field. One week he reported ten hands out, another nineteen.[28] Yet Cameron's response to the reports, conveyed in letters to his father, was tempered. Was there a fatalistic accommodation on the part of all parties to the place, the crops, and the manager?

So it seemed when Cameron returned to Alabama in December 1846, a month later than he had come the year before. He had traveled by coach for much of the trip, including the last 120 miles from Montgomery to his Greene County plantation. He got there at eleven at night and found all asleep, and so he blew the driver's horn at the gate to signal his arrival. The overseer and "two boys" hurried to greet him, and despite exhaustion, he chatted with the overseer until one in the morning. While the two men talked, Rosezetta—the woman whose "mean sewing" of the year before had revealed fury at her exile and gotten her punished—fixed a tub of hot water for Cameron to soak his feet and legs, swollen from the trip. When he finally settled into bed, also prepared by Rosezetta, he found it clean and welcoming. The next morning he woke late, refreshed, and was swarmed by people. Some told him that they had dreamt of his coming. Others professed despair that he might never return. Whether from relief that they'd not been abandoned or from a conscious effort to flatter their lifeline to news, supplies, and support from home, those who greeted him conveyed more warmth than he'd known before. "I have said 'how'dy do' to *all*," he noted, "and have had to answer a great many questions about home and friends."[29]

If Paul Hargis and Rosezetta and others decided to put the best face on their lot, their affirmations masked tension under the surface. One man in particular declined to join the lovefest of greetings for the owner. As Paul Hargis probably knew, and as the overseer unequivocally knew, the enslaved man Milton was deeply restive and resentful over the exile to Alabama. Milton had spent his early years on the Person County quarter owned by Duncan Cameron and had been part of the household of the Camerons' only black overseer, Jim Ray. At Person, Milton had worked with and for a black man with authority, who in turn didn't hesitate to affirm his loyalty and gratitude to the senior Cameron for entrusting rule to so black a man. Moved with his family from the outlying Person quarter to the Fairntosh home place by the mid-1830s, Milton himself became one of the trusted men. He worked in the field and was summoned from time to time to be a courier and a wagoner. It appears that he came to know the ways of side trade and barter that covertly went with those roles.[30]

Accustomed to latitude in North Carolina, Milton bridled at subordination in Alabama—to the discipline of the overseer, to the demands of the crop, and to the extremes of the climate. In 1847, he watched while older men sickened and died, and he witnessed the death of one younger man. More frequently than any other laborer on the place, Milton reported himself too ill to work.[31] There is little doubt that he and the overseer clashed. Before Cameron left Alabama to return to North Carolina, the overseer warned the owner that "Milton intended to run away."[32]

As it turned out, the two most troublesome men on the Alabama place—Milton and Toney—had in 1846 found a temporary outlet for their restiveness. They engaged in the barter and sale of clothes to enslaved people on nearby plantations. On places above and below the Cameron plantation, workers had owners who sought to boost effort with bonuses of suits and material rewards. Those workers had wherewithal over and above the rations and garb distributed by their overseers. Milton and Toney acquired their booty in other ways, including theft. It was rivalry, and theft of clothes from each other, that led to an unruly quarrel between the black-marketeers. The overseer had them both handcuffed. Either with help or on his own, Milton got free of the handcuffs and fled the plantation.[33]

Milton was gone more than three weeks and, remarkably, made it 150 miles to the east. One can only imagine the grit and guile that enabled him to cross almost the entire width of the state. He was captured and jailed in Tuskegee, Alabama, where he told the jailor he was headed back to his master in North Carolina. The overseer hired a man to retrieve the runaway. Word came that he and Milton were en route back, and that the overseer should meet them in Greensboro. At two o'clock in the morning they arrived, and at daybreak overseer and fugitive returned to the Cameron plantation. Supposedly for Milton's benefit, the overseer reported that he would wait to whip Milton until he had recovered from his trip.[34]

Capture, return, and flogging subdued thirty-three-year-old Milton but did not settle him. In May 1847, the overseer reported that Milton's "carelessness and laziness" had come close to causing the death of Paul Hargis. The overseer did not detail what happened or why. The twenty-year-old member of the Hargis family had never reported ill, had picked acceptable weights of cotton without fail, had never been named for any infraction. It's possible that the episode was entirely an accident. Yet it might have been something else: an eruption on the part of a man brought low, aimed against Paul Hargis, a younger man—little more than half his age—who was trying to navigate rather than fight the plantation's demands. In Milton's angry eyes, was Paul Hargis's compliance identical to capitulation? For his nearly lethal "carelessness"—perhaps an act of reprisal—Milton was whipped again.[35]

If contrasts in the conduct of people in Alabama revealed a range of strategies among blacks on the Cameron place—some exhibiting attachment, others resentment—Paul Cameron himself seemed the picture of calm at the end of 1846 and throughout 1847. No more was he the flustered and furious man of two years before. His letters about Alabama were matter-of-fact, even when he learned that the cotton output, once promising, had reverted back to the disappointing levels of previous years.[36] There was reason for Paul Cameron's equanimity: he had won his father's consent to try again.

Duncan Cameron realized that his son was not to be placated by reminders that his workers brought better returns in Alabama than in North Carolina, or by the knowledge that other North Carolinians had also met disappointment in their western ventures.[37] The father knew his son well enough to realize that no call for family comity would quash his sense of humiliation, no reassurances would satisfy his need for redemption. So Duncan Cameron agreed to back a second chance for his son.[38] For Paul Hargis, a second chance for the planter portended another uprooting of Cameron's workers.[39]

Paul Cameron held off on a new search until the end of 1847. Not only were there crops and a grain harvest to oversee on lands in North

Carolina, but in June 1847, his uncle Thomas Bennehan died at the age of sixty-five, bequeathing the bulk of his land and majority of his enslaved people to his nephew Paul, who also acted as the agent for bequests to his sisters and brother.[40] There was a deeper family complication as well. In 1844, Cameron's sister Mildred came down with a mysterious affliction that rendered her an invalid, unable to walk. No physicians in Raleigh could find any physical cause for her paralysis. Nor were any prepared to diagnose it as hysteria, a somatic response to the traumatizing deaths of four older sisters in four years from consumption and to further grief at the death of her mother in 1843. Absorbed by his daughter Mildred's illness, Duncan Cameron had taken her and his healthy oldest daughter, Margaret, to Philadelphia in the summer of 1846 for medical treatment at the best medical school of the day, the Jefferson College of Medicine. In mid-1847 they were there again, still in vain search of a physician who could ease or cure Mildred's symptoms.[41] Meanwhile, discouraging news came once again from Alabama. Illness had confined dozens of Cameron's workers—and this time had laid low the overseer as well. Paul Cameron knew that at the end of 1847, when he did travel west, he would have to replace the overseer, which he did on-site.[42]

When Paul Cameron left Greene County in January 1848 and headed west to replace "the *theatre of my sacrifice*," much had changed since his deployment of families for Alabama in 1844. For that departure, he had prepared with meticulous care. He selected the individuals and family groups to go south, he staged the reassuring presence of his father for the departure, and he accompanied the caravan for two days and nights to the edge of the Blue Ridge Mountains—all to settle his workers for the rest of the journey. For that trip and on subsequent visits to Alabama, he continued to refer to "our people" and "our black family," as had been the custom for his mother and uncle. In letters home from Alabama, he had written of individuals by name, as he continued to do in North Carolina. But unmitigated *"disappointment"* had alienated him from the Alabama place. There was "nothing I *more wish* than to get clear of what we have *here. And the sooner the better."* He found it hard to keep separate the place from the people: "I wish to God a fair sale could be made of both land & slaves."[43] By the time he began his tour of plantations in early

1848, Paul Cameron's relationship to his workers had changed. As always, he supplied provisions—cloth for their garments, shoes for their feet, food for their sustenance. But as he primed for a second removal, and readied to redeem his error, detachment replaced the intimate engagement of 1844.

⁓

For Paul Hargis, his family, and the survivors of the 1844 move to Alabama, that detachment augured ill. So did the places that Paul Cameron chose to scout in 1848. He decided not only to include but to focus on Louisiana sugar plantations. In considering a switch to sugar, Cameron was looking at a crop that was known equally for its payoff to planters and its toll on workers. Sugar was notorious for its intensity and debilitating demands on labor—sugar cane had to be harvested and the sugar refined and extracted at a pace that sometimes killed or maimed.[44] That said, sugar might be the best and quickest means to make up for the disappointment of Alabama. Only at the end of his reconnaissance did Cameron look at cotton lands.

For a time, outside events in 1848 dampened everyone's ardor to buy or sell. Conflict broke out in Europe in the middle of 1848. Britain held steady, but upheavals shook the continent; revolution convulsed France. Cotton exports and cotton prices fell.[45] Most distracting for the Cameron family in 1848 was the ongoing condition of daughter Mildred. Again in Philadelphia with her father and sister, the invalid experienced incremental improvements, followed by regression to familiar or even new symptoms. During the summer of 1848, the prolonged months away, the brutal Philadelphia heat, and the dubious results tested the patience of all, but especially frayed the nerves of seventy-one-year-old Duncan Cameron.[46] Paul Cameron, knowing how draining the year had been for his father, backed off discussion of Alabama or the timing of a new settlement. He hoped that after Duncan Cameron returned to North Carolina in August 1848, he would regain his stamina and be ready to confer by the time his son planned again to depart for the West.

For forty-year-old Paul Cameron, the fall of 1848 beckoned as the time to act. Reports from Alabama had gone from bad to worse. The new

overseer was ineffective; the cotton crop had been poorly cared for; returns would disappoint again. In public affairs, the presidential election
looked good for the candidate favored by the Camerons—Zachary Taylor,
a victorious general in the war with Mexico, and a Louisiana sugar planter.
For the seventh time in the nineteenth century, it seemed likely that a
slaveholder would become president.

"Now what do you think of this matter," Paul Cameron wrote on November 2, 1848. Cameron had spent the previous week visiting his father
in Raleigh but waited until he was back at Fairntosh to give "utterance
to my thoughts. Indeed I have hardly had any *plan* until I left Raleigh
last week."

> What think you of my sending out a wagon & team with some
> fifteen hands from my stock of People, to the Plantation in Ala-
> bama, to be joined by some 10 or 12 more of the most efficient
> hands from that stock, & them to be taken to a settlement of
> unimproved lands on the bottoms of the Yazoo or one of its
> tributaries.

Paul Cameron proposed to purchase a "really fine body" of totally un-
cultivated land and to assign twenty-five "hands" the work of removing
the bamboo cane and cypress trees on 1,000 acres "*for 4 years*"—"250 a year
& make good crops of corn. I would then have a perfectly good *fresh*
Cotton Estate, free from all insects and diseases incident to *long culture*."
Cameron would have "the slaves from N.C. to follow me out" and remain on the Alabama plantation until he went over to Mississippi and
made the purchase, and then he would go with them the 200 miles to
the new place. Cameron had earlier discussed the possibility of a sugar
plantation with his father; he accepted "your advice to *Stick to Cotton*."
He intended at the "end of the 4 years to place all the slaves remaining
on the Alabama plantation with other additions from here on the *New*
settlement," and then to sell "the Alabama concern if I can—or if not
then sold to quit it."

If Paul Cameron succeeded, Paul Hargis and the remaining Alabama people would be moved to Mississippi by 1852. And not just them. As Paul Cameron outlined his plan to his father, he no longer spoke of "our people" or "our black family." Rather, the Cameron workers, in Alabama and North Carolina, had become "hands," "stock," and "slaves."[47] The son made it clear to his father that his ambition had broadened. In Mississippi, he wished "to get at least 3000 acres, in which 200 hands might be worked & 2000 bales of cotton made with a plenty of food." Cameron was no longer thinking of Alabama "hands" alone. The *"New* settlement" was to be a destination for North Carolina "stock" as well. Their laborers would be far more profitable for the Camerons when growing cotton in Mississippi than wheat in North Carolina. "Our interest in the *security* of the property & our own *comfort* will induce us to keep here only enough to keep our plantations in order & make them grain & clover plantations," he wrote.

Burned by the buy of a worn-down plantation in Alabama, Cameron hardly needed to explain "my reason for purchasing unimproved lands." The purchaser of already-cleared lands "is made to pay an enormous price for poor improvements—& on new lands every lick we strike, we enhance the value of the property & then we have the *Virgin soil* with its *purity.*" The "we" who would strike the licks and enhance the value of the property were, of course, different from the "we" who would then possess "the *Virgin soil* with its *purity.*"

Eager, almost breathless, to make the new start, Cameron sought his father's approval as he always did, with a mix of urgency, entreaty, and deference. He was ready to go, he noted: "Should *you* approve *of this thought* I can have the emigrants shod & clothed & under way in 5 days from the time I go about it." In his one mention of the move's impact on their workers, Cameron declared that their laborers would be well served: "by introducing the slaves in this way to a new settlement, we should have less sickness" and get them acclimated more easily. But most of all, the purchase and the "emigrants" would be the means of Paul Cameron's vindication. "If I take this step it is to cost me many an effort," he predicted, but "I shall take some pride in working out a more ordered establishment on a large scale, & if fortunate reestablish my self-confidence & perhaps *grieve* some of my friends." That said, the son, as always, had *"no wish* to make a *single* move" without his father's approval. "Tell me in plainness what you wish, what you think I should & should not do."[48]

On Duncan Cameron's answer hinged the fate of Paul Hargis, his brothers and sisters, and hundreds of fellow workers in Alabama—and in North Carolina.

Four ✍ Held Back

HAD PAUL CAMERON had his way in November 1848, he'd have sold or surrendered his entire plantation in Alabama and eventually moved Paul Hargis and all the enslaved workers upon it to newly cleared land in the Mississippi Delta. Paul Hargis and his fellow laborers would plant cotton on fresh soil with a new overseer, with the prospect of returns that would reverse the young master's mistake in Alabama. Given a second chance, Paul Cameron would prove to his father—and to real and imagined skeptics—that he could add to his inheritance, and be more than its dutiful custodian. But Paul Cameron did not have his way—and Paul Hargis was held back in Alabama.

The delay was short at first, at least as the younger Cameron initially envisioned it. Two days after receiving his son's November 2 proposal to buy a place in Mississippi and then move "hands" from North Carolina and "stock" from Alabama to clear land for a "perfectly good *fresh* Cotton Estate," Duncan Cameron replied. His response put a damper on any sudden move. "The *principal* subject contained" in the plan "has taken me somewhat by *surprize*, and does not allow me *time* (even if I was more capable of forming a *proper* judgment than I am at present) to give you a reliable opinion about it." The father questioned whether the season was "too far advanced to carry out the plan . . . with comfort to yourself and the People to be removed." He acknowledged that the wisdom "of the measure is apparent," and he would—"if you can see your way *clearly*" to undertake it—back his son. "I would have you do in this matter what your judgment formed with *deliberation* should lead you to do."[1]

Duncan Cameron's message to guard against impulsiveness reflected decades of experience with his forty-year-old son. Paul Cameron acquiesced, writing back, "I shall not make any move . . . , fearing I might get myself surrounded by difficulties from which I could not make a retreat if I wished." "This I can & will do," he added. "I will go over and make the purchase" this winter, "& send slaves to it in the spring. But of this when we meet."[2]

When the two Camerons did meet in Raleigh later that month, Paul Cameron learned that there was far more than timing behind his father's ambivalence. Duncan Cameron was a shattered man. The deaths of four daughters between 1837 and 1840, each of whom wasted away from consumption; the death of his wife in 1843; the subsequent paralysis of his youngest daughter, Mildred, which three successive summers of medical treatment in Philadelphia had failed to cure—all these had combined to bring on a nervous breakdown. Face-to-face, he revealed to his son that his collapse had obliged him to resign from the presidency of the Bank of North Carolina. Nor was his father's breakdown the only family setback to the expansion plan. Paul Cameron's two-year-old son, Duncan II, named after the family patriarch, became ill in mid-November. The only son—he had five sisters—young Duncan was a delightful and buoyant child. He reported a stomachache just before his father's planned departure for the west. The stomach ailment worsened into excruciating pain, and chills and fever followed. Doctors, called in, could detect nothing and do nothing. Within a week of his first symptom, Duncan Cameron II died. Father and grandfather were heartbroken.[3] An old friend of the senior Cameron reported that "his domestic misfortunes have completely broken him down. He is now, in mind & body, as weak as a child"—"not a vestige is left, of his high commanding character." Paul Cameron put off his trip to the west and the search for a new settlement.[4]

The delay stretched out for years. Not until November 1856, eight years after he first proposed the plan for a second chance to his father, did Paul Cameron buy the western cotton plantation he had envisioned. By then much had changed. For Paul Hargis, the changes would ultimately mean that he and his siblings in Alabama would again be spared—this time from removal to the bottom of the Mississippi Delta. Only in time would Paul Hargis learn what he'd escaped.

Paul Cameron put his expansion plan on hold while his father and sister remained unwell. Strokes followed Duncan Cameron's 1848 breakdown; despite further trips to Philadelphia for treatment, his daughter Mildred continued as an invalid.[5] Paul Cameron resumed scouting trips in 1850, continued to make and receive inquiries about a western place, and made one offer that was refused. But he made no buy.

Instead he concentrated on Alabama. He hired a new overseer in 1849 to replace James Stephenson, who in the opinion of a trusted neighboring planter had produced an inexplicably poor crop in 1848 despite good weather and the good health of his workers. The new overseer, John Webster, was a nearby small farmer who was highly regarded as the best manager in the area. There was no doubt about his ability or conscientiousness; Cameron hoped that he might grow more cotton. Webster fared little better than his predecessors, however. When Cameron complained that other planters with the same number of workers had produced far more cotton, Webster responded with characteristic straightforwardness. On comparable land—black soil—his hands had done equally well; on sandy and red clay soils, the crop had succumbed to vicissitudes of weather and worms. So Cameron turned once again to the possibility of selling his land in Alabama. He asked Webster to sound out neighboring planters on what they might offer for his plantation. He placed the deed to his property in the hands of a fellow planter, ready to convey should he find a seller. None was willing to bid unless and until Cameron himself set a price.[6]

Unable to extract an offer for the land through long-distance haggling, Cameron prepared to take a bolder step. On June 4, 1852, he instructed his overseer to specify a monetary value for each and every person he owned in Alabama. The valuation was not a list for tax purposes, which in any case would have been estimated only for persons over twelve and under fifty, and not be due until the end of the year. Far more likely was Cameron's wish to know the price to ask were he to offer the people as well as the land for sale. Valued at $900 each, Paul Hargis and his brother Jim stood at the top of the list.[7] Cameron's agents found no taker.

The one Alabama offer that Cameron did receive was for neither land nor workers. Through an intermediary, the overseer of a nearby plantation offered to take over the Cameron place free of charge. The overseer, John Hampton—who from time to time had visited Cameron's land—declared that Cameron's plantation had been badly managed. He proposed to run the place without a salary. He would produce as much cotton as the place had averaged the last four years. All cotton grown over that would be his commission. He believed he thereby could make his reputation as an overseer.[8] Silence was Cameron's response. The planter knew that while he might not pay a price, his workers would.

So John Webster remained Cameron's overseer into the early 1850s, doggedly struggling to make the best crop he could with the force he had, contending with cotton that thrived on one part of the plantation and languished on others. Webster had to cope as well with the owner's absence and long silences, commenting at one point that it seemed as if "you have lost sight of this place out here as you never write." In June 1852, Webster received permission to visit his ill mother back in Virginia, and en route back, stopped by to see Cameron in North Carolina. It was on that occasion that, for the first time, the overseer realized that the planter knew exactly what he and his predecessors were up against. "I have thought of you a thousand times . . . , of you saying that we had the most uncertain land for cotton of any for this is the only place that I have heard of the crop was short." From that moment on, Webster hoped that Cameron would "be out in early fall for now is a good time to put your plantation in market for I want to see you put your hands on a better place."[9] Unsaid was that John Webster no longer wanted to be in an impossible spot. He too wanted out.

For Paul Hargis and others in Alabama, there could be little doubt that their owner wished to find a new place. Cameron's workers were not hermetically sealed on the plantation. Some went to the river landing with wagons of baled cotton, to see the cotton safely on a steamboat down the Black Warrior River to the broker in Mobile. Others traveled to the post office to pick up the mail in Greensboro. Word of mouth about landowner bargaining almost certainly reached Cameron's people from workers on adjacent places. If rumors weren't confirmation enough, it was clear from the comings and goings of the number one worker on the place—carpenter and gatekeeper Sandy Cameron—that he was accompanying Paul Cameron on scouting trips to the west.[10] Even if Sandy had been sworn to silence about those trips, his long absences spoke volumes. It didn't take two weeks of travel to pick up mail in Greensboro fifteen miles to the north, or a month to accompany Master Paul to the train depot at Selma, sixty miles to the east. Something was in the offing.

In November 1856 came word: Paul Cameron had bought himself another place. The "new settlement" was in the northwest corner of the Mississippi Delta, the richest cotton-growing land on the continent. Cameron instructed his overseer to pick three dozen people from his Alabama plantation to be taken to Tunica County, Mississippi, a place three miles east of the nation's greatest river, thirty miles south of Memphis. They would be the ones to clear the 1,811 acres of its immense stands of cypress trees and bamboo cane. They would be his advance force to convert the semi-swamp into a "making bank," as one of the land promoters touted the Delta. They would be the ones brought, as blacks termed it with foreboding, "to the bottom of the Mississippi."[11] Enslaved people saw it as the bottom of bondage.

Paul Hargis, his brother Jim, his sisters Sally and Nancy, and their spouses and children were not among the thirty-five people designated as the first force to go to Mississippi. Cameron, preoccupied with politics and business back in North Carolina in December 1856, left it to overseer John Webster to choose who would go and who would stay. Webster's picks included all but one of those who at one point or another had attempted to run away from Cameron's place in Alabama. Paul Hargis's sister Nancy, her mate, Peter, and their two children had been on Webster's first list; the overseer struck them off at the very last.[12] When or whether members of the Hargis family would be next remained to be seen.

There was no way for Paul Hargis to know that Paul Cameron's idea for a "new settlement," as the owner called it, had been long in the making, or that over the eight years since he had first proposed it to his father, his goals had altered. In 1848, Paul Cameron had sought the chance for redemption from his purchase of "so detested a place" in Alabama, and for the restoration of "confidence in an erring son." His father's breakdown in 1848 and declining health thereafter had kept the project at bay. On January 3, 1853, Duncan Cameron died. The death of his father made Paul Cameron the inheritor or guardian of all the land and enslaved people accumulated by his father, uncle, and grandfather since 1776—and opened the way for him to act.[13]

The passage of years had reordered Cameron's goals. Gone was Cameron's obsession about betrayal in Alabama; elevated was his focus on the promise of bonanza profits in Mississippi. That prospect was promoted by letters that came to him from planters who learned he was on the lookout for a large quantity of fresh land. One offered a place called Nitta Yuma, a name that the writer said had been compounded from the Choctaw language: "Nitta, bear, and Yuma, mixed; mixed with bear, or as *we* would say, *greasy*, rich as cream, rich as oil."[14] All seemed to think a minimum return—once land was cleared of trees and stumps and dense thickets of bamboo cane, and then prepared for cotton—would be a bale per acre. Each bale of cotton weighed 500 pounds. Each pound brought 10¢ or more. The numbers dazzled. Five hundred bales added up to 250,000 pounds of cotton. At 10¢ a pound, the harvest promised $25,000 a year. No wonder Cameron heard, and hoped, that his initial outlay would quickly pay for itself and thereafter, as one writer promised, put him and his family on a course of perfect independence.[15]

Nor was there a way for Paul Hargis to discover that Paul Cameron was thinking of more than one plantation in Mississippi. In 1859, Cameron put out word that he was looking for still more land, where he could duplicate the formula in Tunica: clear, plow, grow. He sought another large plantation as close as possible to his initial purchase in the Delta, perhaps thinking to aggregate adjacent lands in Mississippi as his forebears had done a generation before in North Carolina. Cameron didn't seem to blanch at the mention of $50 an acre as the soaring new rate for land, or at a proposal to sell him 4,000 acres at a bargain price—$20 an acre. His was an imperial vision.[16] Though late to the Delta, he'd arrived at a time when cotton prices were rising to their highest in history. No matter how much cotton the South produced, more was sought by manufacturers of Great Britain and New England. For Cameron and others with the land and enslaved labor to make the most of the boom, the white gold of the cotton South was every bit as lucrative as gold ore was to the miners of the Far West.

What Paul Hargis may have learned, if only incompletely and in an unguarded moment from overseer John Webster, was what happened to that first batch of thirty-five people taken from Alabama to the "new settlement" in Mississippi in mid-December 1856. If Paul Hargis and his siblings were next, the future boded ill.

"My slaves from Alabama I have no doubt are now quartered at their new home in Mississippi," Paul Cameron wrote to his father-in-law, Thomas Ruffin, a week before Christmas, 1856. Quartered with them was a new overseer, hired before they left Alabama. Samuel Jeter was a single man, twenty-eight years old, who had worked for a large planter a dozen miles below the Cameron place. Having tried but failed to get a family man to go to Mississippi, Webster decided that Samuel Jeter would do, even though his previous employer had reported a flaw, namely, that he was "too tight for him."[17] "Tight" could mean strict, which Webster took to be acceptable. "Tight" might also mean severe, which could lead to trouble. Samuel Jeter accompanied the people for the entirety of their 200-mile trip to the Delta. Webster caught up with them halfway there. By candlelight, he wrote Cameron from mid-journey: "All had kept well and gone on well."[18]

But on Christmas Eve, back in Alabama, John Webster wrote again: "I thought your slaves was very much dissatisfied overseer not much better."[19]

What had gone awry? The Alabama overseer affirmed right away Cameron's choice of location. "You have a rich plantation there. . . . It is as rich land as I ever saw." But he added immediately that "it will [take] a great deal of labor time & money to fix it." The land was wet, Webster reported, surely wetter than when Cameron had scouted and walked it; "you must have come in the dry season." Without ditching, it would stay a swampland, its footing unreliable. If no outside workers were hired, his workforce would have to ditch it themselves. Cabins? Cameron had been promised suitable cabins for his people, but as one would expect in a swampy setting, they were clammy, and hardly fit to live in. Hogs, cattle? Cameron thought he'd bargained for half of those on the place, but the seller's manager, still resident, knew nothing of the arrangement. Drinking water? Groundwater was unsafe; no wells could be dug in the swamp. The answer in the Delta was to build cisterns to catch and hold rainwater. Described as adequate by the seller, the cisterns seemed corroded and undersized to Webster. Finally, Cameron had assured Webster that he would find 200 acres of the place ready for planting cotton and corn—cleared of the cane and giant cypress trees, unburned logs and massive tree stumps that covered the rest of Cameron's 1,811 acres. The Alabama overseer of course didn't wish to contradict the claim of the seller or the buyer, so he hedged. It was hard for him to judge, he wrote, but it didn't look like 200 cleared acres to him.[20]

Of greater concern to John Webster was the response of the Alabama exiles to their new overseer. They were hostile. Webster's wording was discreet: the hands seemed "very much dissatisfied." Almost all of the adults sent from Alabama had previously worked under four overseers— three in Alabama and one or more back in North Carolina. Some, including Old Jacob, had even worked under the supervision of Jim Ray, a black driver in North Carolina who, though enslaved, received and acted with the authority of an overseer. Now they were in Mississippi, on a barely cleared section of dry land with decrepit cabins and contested cattle and hogs, in the dead of winter, under the governance of an overseer who was "tight." More than tight—in the view of a neighboring planter who later met him, Samuel Jeter was deficient in "the upper story."[21] The Alabama people didn't need long to size up his competence. With him on the trip out, with him as he surveyed the challenges before them, comparing him to overseers past, they did something never done before by Cameron workers: with "Old Jacob" in the lead, they said they wouldn't work for him.[22]

Webster's advice to Cameron focused on backing—and keeping—the overseer. "There are men in there that has been there for several years that want your business," he wrote. They "will talk to him in such a way as to dissatisfy him so as to get him to quit." They might tell Samuel Jeter he wasn't getting paid enough, or that he had an impossible task, or that he could do better on the next plantation. With a vacancy created, the owner would be desperate, and forced to hire a man prepared to whip the workforce into shape. If Cameron pushed his overseer for fast results—a big cotton crop, rapid clearing of the land—the only harvest would be trouble. Webster didn't elaborate on what the workers might do, surely surmising that Cameron could guess. After all, four of those who had attempted escapes in Alabama were part of the contingent sent to Mississippi. Rather, Webster focused on treatment of the overseer, advising, "Hard driving will not do there. It will take a long pull and a pull all together."[23]

John Webster's apprehension about the combustible mix of hard driving, a tight overseer, and dissatisfied workers proved prophetic. Days after Webster returned to Alabama, Old Jacob attacked the Tunica overseer, got him to the ground, and with others began to flog him. Samuel Jeter's hidden knife helped him repel the rebels, who fled but were captured with the aid of the overseer's dogs—and for a time, subdued.[24] Nevertheless, Jacob had made his point. For a time, the overseer backed off.

In bits and pieces, in evasions or telltale silences, Webster may have disclosed to the attentive in Alabama where he had left things with the people he took to Tunica. Or he may have just left Paul Hargis and others to wonder—and to imagine for themselves—what it meant to be sent "to the bottom."

When Cameron himself finally made it out to Tunica in March 1857, he found "all well here." He saw what the overseer and his workers were up against—piling up huge logs and burning them; coping with heavy rains, which drenched the fires and brought down more trees; planting 100 acres of cotton and 200 of corn; building new cabins. With only twenty-eight adult workers, Cameron recognized, the overseer had "a force hardly equal to his undertaking." Cameron thought the overseer was "full of energy and quite equal" to the task. But given the "difficulties" behind and demands ahead of Samuel Jeter, Cameron urged him "not to press the hands."[25]

"Don't press the hands" was an instruction that fit with Cameron's wish to preserve the health of his workers and peace on the plantation. But it left open the question of how and when he would realize the princely returns promised from cotton grown in the Mississippi Delta. As it turned out, Cameron expected both preservation and profit from his overseer. When those goals conflicted, as they did repeatedly, the overseer heard and heeded the owner's displeasure, and the enslaved people—and one worker in particular—bore the brunt of pressure from them both.

For the better part of 1857, Samuel Jeter welcomed and followed Paul Cameron's directive to go easy on the workers brought out from Alabama. The resulting pace proved far too slow for the owner. By the end of the year, he wrote Jeter to complain about the "quantity of work . . . done on the place this year." The overseer's defense? "You requested me not to expect too much of your Negroes and still write me the same . . . in your last letter." Cameron's exasperation spilled over into insult. He wrote the overseer that he wished for his letters "to be filled with facts or what I think to be facts." Jeter responded: "If I have ever written otherwise I do not know it." When a neighboring planter, Andrew Polk, visited the Tunica place on Cameron's behalf in January 1858, he confirmed that the overseer had "gotten on very badly with his business." When "I urge him to work faster & turn out better results, his reply is that he is following your instructions not to press the hands." Andrew Polk "assured him that he had misconstrued your instructions and that he must push" ahead. Polk got to the heart of the matter: Cameron's overseer was not only incompetent "to manage your affairs" but was "afraid of the negroes."[26]

When Cameron made his second visit to the Tunica plantation in February 1858, he came with an emphatically different message for his overseer. He wished him "to make head way on the forest and enlarge my crops rapidly." Cameron was spurred by the report of a different neighboring planter, who claimed that he made ten bales of cotton to the hand. In 1857, Cameron's twenty-eight adult workers had grown a meager

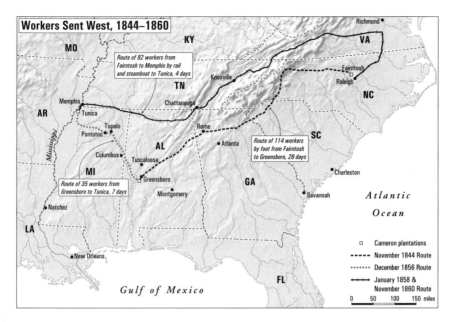

Workers Sent West, 1844–1860

Route of 82 workers from
Fairntosh to Memphis by rail
and steamboat to Tunica, 4 days

Route of 114 workers
by foot from Fairntosh
to Greensboro, 29 days

Route of 35 workers from
Greensboro to Tunica, 7 days

MO
KY
VA
Richmond
Fairntosh
Raleigh
Knoxville
TN
NC
Memphis
Chattanooga
AR
Tunica
Tupelo
Pontotoc
Rome
Atlanta
SC
Columbus
AL
Tuscaloosa
Greensboro
MI
Charleston
Natchez
Montgomery
GA
Savannah
LA
New Orleans
FL

Atlantic

Ocean

Mississippi

□   Cameron plantations
- - - -   November 1844 Route
••••••   December 1856 Route
⊢━━➤   January 1858 &
        November 1860 Route
0   50   100   150 miles

Gulf of Mexico

Workers Sent West, 1844–1860.

thirty-five bales of cotton on a hundred acres of land. There was a second reason that Cameron expected better results in 1858: he had added forty more people to his Mississippi workforce.[27]

Paul Hargis was not among them. Nor were members of his family, or indeed any of the people left behind in Alabama. The forty new workers brought to Mississippi all came from North Carolina. They had not trekked across the South by foot, nor taken a month to walk and wagon the distance of some five hundred miles. The evolving southern railway system had made it possible for Cameron to transport them by train. They had made the trip in four days.

⌒✎

By the time Paul Cameron launched his Mississippi venture, he had arrived at a new view of his Alabama plantation and the people remaining on it. Thanks to good management, good weather, and the temporary decline of insect invaders that stunted the crop, Alabama's cotton harvests had spiked. In 1853, Cameron's workers had grown 236 bales of cotton; in

1855, they'd picked 395 bales. The harvests reinforced Cameron's decision, made earlier, to use his Alabama workers and the proceeds from their cotton harvests to build a cash reserve with his brokers in New Orleans and Mobile. The brokers would sell the Alabama cotton, keep the money, pay him interest while they held it, and have cash ready when he decided to buy more fresh land in Mississippi.[28]

There was no more talk of selling the place or people in Alabama, nor a plan to send more workers from Alabama to Mississippi. Instead, Paul Hargis and the 106 other people left in Alabama confronted a new overseer and heightened expectations. John Webster had bought a small place of his own not far from Cameron's plantation and left at the end of 1856 to farm it full-time, but before he left Webster picked the new overseer. Wilson Oberry was fifty-three years old in 1857. Born in Virginia, he'd come to Alabama with his wife; they lived with their daughter. Oberry had worked for a nearby planter for a number of years. When that owner died and his widow remarried, Oberry decided to leave. On Webster's say-so, Cameron hired the new overseer sight unseen. In his first directive to Wilson Oberry, Paul Cameron had a simple instruction: he wanted a large crop of cotton. "You said that you wanted me to make you a crop," the overseer replied, promising to make Cameron at least as good a crop as Webster had been making. "I am second to no man in making cotton."[29]

That same expectation came through to Cameron's overseer in Mississippi in 1858, and led Samuel Jeter to reverse course in dealing with the forty newcomers from North Carolina. Leniency disappeared. The owner wanted his overseer to push, and push he did. What happened in Mississippi from that point on is something that Paul Hargis and others would never have known had it not been for a reversal of fortunes that none foresaw in 1858.

"I will keep a look out for your lost negroes." So wrote Paul Cameron's longtime friend and fellow Mississippi planter Archibald Wright in early October 1858. Both workers had been brought from North Carolina earlier that year. Both were listed on slave inventories, and identified in planter and overseer letters, by their first names only: Len and Phil. Len would be named many more times. The two men had fled the Tunica plantation in September 1858 and were at large for more than a month. Somehow they made it almost a hundred miles to the north and east, until in Haywood County, Tennessee—forty-five miles east of Memphis—they were caught and jailed. Cameron had already received reports that Len was a troublemaker, and wanted him sold. But when Archibald Wright took Len to the "Negro Yard" of the leading slave trader of Memphis— Nathan Bedford Forrest—he was rebuffed. "Mr. Forest [sic] informed me that his health was so bad & he had been so badly cut with the whip that it was impossible to sell him for any thing like his value and advised me to take him [back] to your plantation."[30] The whip marks that crisscrossed Len's back were a tip-off that he was a recalcitrant slave, impossible to subdue, who would disrupt any plantation he worked on.

The marks on Len's back testified to the ratcheting up of expectations on Cameron's Tunica plantation. For the next two years, Len became the emblem and barometer of pressure facing all the hands—and the leader of flight from those demands.[31]

Len was still on the Mississippi plantation when Paul Cameron returned to Tunica in January 1859. By then, Cameron had endured more than enough of Samuel Jeter. He fired Jeter on the spot and replaced him with a first-rate "bottom fellow."[32] That man was William Lamb, an experienced overseer who had a wife and children. Cameron directed his new overseer to continue clearing hundreds of acres of land and, at the same time, to have his enslaved workers grow and pick all the cotton they could. Lamb's task was to deal with Cameron's expectations, with the workers who were compelled to carry them out—and with Len.

Over the spring and summer, the overseer sent detailed reports about the immense work done by his sixty-four prime laborers—cutting, rolling, and burning logs; clearing undergrowth in brutally hot weather; and picking cotton as fast as it opened. So as not totally to exhaust his hands, Lamb hired Irish laborers to dig 1,425 cubic yards of ditches to drain the boggy soil. Cameron, in his letters back to the overseer, focused on cotton and pressed for results. Lamb responded that he thought the planter should make an allowance for picking clean cotton, which would sell at a higher price: "I can't get the hands up to high figures if they pay attention to how to handle it."[33] Lamb knew, however, that the Carolina planter would not be satisfied with excuses. Cotton was selling for the near-record price of 11¼¢ per pound, bringing over $50 per bale. If the overseer could duplicate his neighbor's alleged feat of ten bales to the hand, that would be $500 per worker. William Lamb pledged to "try to carry out your instructions."[34]

Carrying out Cameron's instructions compelled all the Tunica workers to meet the owner's "high figures"—or receive punishment for falling short of his quota. Those who reached a breaking point, under the strain of work or pain of the lash or both, turned to Len, who stood ready to run with any who wished to escape. When the plantation blacksmith, Meredith, and his wife, Evaline, reached their limit in July 1859, Len guided them up to Memphis before they were captured and returned to Tunica. In early December 1859, when Betsy Cooper wanted out, Len stole a dugout canoe below Memphis and got them across the Mississippi River to Arkansas. The river's width and strong current made it a highly "dangerous undertaking for them," since neither could swim. Caught again, Len was brought back. The overseer was certain "he will run away again the first chance after he is turned loose." Exasperated, Lamb wrote Cameron that "you would save money by selling Len and by that means get shut of a very trubelsom negro one that you might possibly lose by being drowned or meet his death in some other way."[35] The overseer did not specify the "other way" Len might perish. In the meantime, William Lamb put shackles on Len's legs and confined him every night "by a chain fastened to a large staple" in the house of a trusted black worker. In the spring of 1860, Len seemed to capitulate, asking for release from his chains. The overseer got three collaborating workers—"trusty fellows"—to agree to act as "his securities that he will not run away again in twelve months."[36] He set Len loose.

In the fall of 1860, Len once more became the target and symbol of Cameron's demands on his Mississippi laborers. The overseer reported in September that a huge cotton crop was in the offing; his hands could barely keep up with the bursting bolls of cotton. They were picking 160 to 170 pounds a day, he wrote Cameron on September 16, "but will not be able to reach your figures (say 200)."[37] On the next day, Saturday, at noon, Lamb went to the field and totaled the weights brought in by each hand. Len was short—and was punished. He took off on Sunday with fellow worker Nat. The overseer, who had promised Cameron a year before that he would manage Len firmly "but not cruelly," saw himself as blameless in the matter, for he was carrying out Cameron's orders. Lamb speculated that Len and Nat "had rather try the woods than pick cotton. Len is the leader as usual. He was whipped Saturday at noon—for not having cotton enough. Is the only cause I know of. I suppose he was offended for being whipped." Otherwise "all is well."[38] In fact, all was hardly well. For the time that Len was out, Lamb was "not able to get as much cotton picked as I would like to have, for some cause."[39] Len, who before had tried going east to Tennessee and west to Arkansas, this time had gone straight north and had made it to Osceola, Arkansas, almost a hundred miles from the Tunica plantation and apparently en route to St. Louis. Again captured and chained, Len was returned to Tunica at the end of October 1860. Two days later the overseer reported that the "hands were picking better than they had done for some time"—155 pounds a day.[40]

Len's escape had prompted a work slowdown, and forced the overseer to accept a lowered quota.

Paul Hargis would have known nothing of Len, or the struggles of those Cameron workers under mounting pressure in the Mississippi bottom, or what eventually might have been his fate, save for two pivotal events of the first week of November 1860. The first was the arrival in Tunica of forty-two additional workers, brought out by train from Cameron's place in North Carolina. In the group was Squire Hargis, the one Hargis brother left in North Carolina in 1844, whom Paul Hargis had neither seen nor heard of in sixteen years. The second event of that week was the election of Abraham Lincoln as president of the United States.

Five ✑ Reversals

WHAT WOULD THE FUTURE HOLD? That was the question in the first week of November 1860. It was the question for the country. It was the question for Paul Hargis and those in Alabama, as word spread of Lincoln's election and threats of southern secession. It was the question facing Paul Cameron, as reports from everywhere signaled that he would have to freeze additions to his empire of cotton. In a quite different way, it was the question for Squire Hargis and the forty-one other enslaved people who arrived that week at the Cameron plantation in Tunica County. None could anticipate the scope and sweep of the reversals ahead.

All the way up to the week of presidential voting that began on November 6, Paul Cameron had sought more land in Mississippi. In June he had visited Memphis and left word with brokers there of his interest in another plantation. In August he sent letters to those he'd not seen, reaffirming his wish for a large plot of land. More letters followed in October, including one that arrived at the desk of Jacob Thompson, a Mississippi planter, lawyer, former congressman, and in 1860 the secretary of the interior.[1] By the time of his October inquiry, Cameron recognized that victory was likely for the "Black Republicans" and their presidential candidate, Abraham Lincoln.[2] He pursued a purchase nonetheless. Those who responded recognized that they were living in limbo. Eager to promote a sale, they also knew that land sales might be overwhelmed by what was to come. Jacob Thompson had received Cameron's letter on November 3. In Washington, sitting at his desk in the Capitol, the outgoing secretary of the interior and owner of thousands of acres in

Mississippi described in enticing detail the best place Cameron could buy—4,000 acres of unsurpassed fertility. He couldn't help his promotional language: "If you want to put yourself in a position of perfect independence, this is the land for you." Political reality compelled a bleak caveat, however. With Lincoln's likely election, Thompson wrote, "I fear the beginning of the end is upon us."[3] Could any planter—could the South itself—achieve a "perfect independence"?

For Paul Hargis's brother Squire and the other people who arrived in Tunica in that first week of November, there was a more immediate issue. What would it be like to be in the Mississippi bottom, 500 miles from home, cultivating a new crop under a new overseer? The one thing that seemed certain, for them as for others taken to the Deep South, was that the change was permanent. For them, Mississippi was to be a land of no return.

Overseer William Lamb hoped that his drivers, and the people he had designated as trusty fellows, would be the ones to break in the new hands. The North Carolina arrivals had to learn how to pick cotton. They had to adjust to their new regimen. Lamb knew there would be hurdles ahead; his reports on the new workers were positive but provisional. "All easily managed so far—so far as I can see," he noted. The new hands were "trying to give satisfaction," "picking as fast as might be expected."[4] The unspoken reality was that the North Carolinians were not quick about it. Sooner or later, his pace—which was Cameron's pace—and the newcomers' limits were destined for conflict. Paul Hargis's brother would witness the results.

On February 12, 1861, Paul Cameron received a telegram from Mississippi. There had been an attempt on his overseer's life. The telegram gave no details of the attack, nor whether William Lamb had survived. It simply called for Cameron to come to Tunica at once.[5] Cameron hastened by train to the Delta. There he found his overseer alive but wounded by an axe blow from Zack, one of the new workers brought from North Carolina the previous November.

William Lamb, coming as was customary at the end of the week to check on work done under the supervision of drivers, had found Zack's

work deficient. Lamb may well have warned Zack earlier, when the overseer had made allowances for workers trying—but not yet succeeding—
to give satisfaction. The overseer apparently had decided it was time for
a lesson: a lesson for Zack, for the plantation drivers, and for all the newcomers from North Carolina. Their owner had a quota; William Lamb
expected them to meet it; his patience was gone. Zack, like Len the year
before, was to be made an example. Whether the whipping was to come
from one of the drivers or from the overseer himself, Lamb ordered Zack
to take his punishment.

Zack, too, had reached his limit. What William Lamb allowed as latitude in Mississippi—a Sunday free to roam, trusty men to do his bid-
ding, perhaps rewards on the side for bondsmen willing to take on extra
work to cultivate cotton on the overseer's unauthorized private plot of
land—could hardly compare to what Zack had known in North Carolina. There he'd been a courier, trusted to drive a wagon and carry goods
between quarters and even between Fairntosh and Hillsborough, fifteen
miles away. His father, York, had known the same privilege. In North
Carolina, he'd been a perfectly good field hand, working grains and
tobacco as he had for years and as his father had taught him to do. In
Tunica, he was a cotton picker, and not a good one. But he was not about
to take a lashing for what his overseer deemed deficient results. He
picked up an axe.

A fight ensued. Who attacked whom, and who got the better of whom,
is not clear. The axe gashed the overseer; wounded, the overseer fought
back. Into the midst of the struggle stepped another bondsman, Ned, another of those sent in November 1860 from North Carolina with his wife
and children. At Fairntosh, Ned had been the first man on the list of enslaved workers, one of Paul Cameron's trusted men, but in Tunica he,
too—like Zack—was reduced to the role of field hand.

From William Lamb's vantage point, Ned joined Zack in the attack.
From the viewpoint of the enslaved man Washington, one of Lamb's
"trusty men," Ned jumped in to protect Zack, or to separate the fighters,
or perhaps to stop the fight. Possibly with help from one or more drivers,
the wounded overseer subdued Zack and Ned. Lamb flogged Ned and
shackled him at the plantation. He had Zack taken to the nearby jail at

Hernando, Mississippi, ten miles away. Both men were charged with attempted murder.[6]

So things stood when Cameron arrived in Tunica after three days of travel by train and a short steamboat ride to the dock three miles from his plantation. His first job was to restore calm, to convey to both the workers and the overseer that the owner cared about all. Cameron long since had learned to back the overseer in a dispute with a worker, no matter who first attacked whom. Yet he also realized that there was more than one side to the story of what happened. So he asked a fellow Mississippi planter to take a hand in the matter. Archibald C. Wright was a prominent lawyer and state supreme court judge from Memphis who had a plantation twenty miles away near Senatobia, Mississippi. Wright lived close enough to look after Cameron's affairs in the owner's absence. He was also a friend.[7] So Cameron asked Wright to handle the case for him. The request solved two problems: it meant that Cameron didn't have to linger in Tunica if the case dragged on, and, more important, that Wright could arrange to have an attorney represent the accused men—so Cameron himself didn't have to question the account of his overseer.

In early April, acting for Cameron, Wright hired a lawyer. James Alcorn was not just any attorney. He was the best in the region, the best in northern Mississippi, and destined one day to be governor of the state. Under the law of Mississippi and all southern states, courts barred testimony from enslaved persons. If the trial went on the overseer's testimony alone, both Zack and Ned were doomed. Wright had talked to black witnesses about what happened, and in particular to a trusty man, Washington. He instructed James Alcorn to hear out Washington. It was a delicate matter, and Wright put it delicately: "Not that one doubted Mr. Lamb—but that [Washington] might know & see what the other did not." Alcorn understood. He was to get the other side of the story from Washington and, without calling the slave to testify, use his legal skills to insert the account into the trial record.[8]

The two bondsmen's cases came to trial separately. On April 4, Zack was tried, convicted, and sentenced to hang. On April 5, Alcorn argued successfully that Ned, though he had taken part in the struggle, had not intended to kill the overseer. Ned was acquitted of attempted murder. But since Ned had laid hands on the overseer, the jury deemed him guilty of assault. Alcorn contended that his client had not been indicted for assault and therefore could not be tried or sentenced for it. On a technicality, Ned walked.[9] Rather than await another trial or legal proceeding, townspeople made it clear they intended to "mob" Ned—that is, to lynch him; he was a marked man. Before a new indictment could be drawn up, James Alcorn sped Ned out of the Tunica County courthouse and took him under his wing.

William Lamb refused to take Ned back. Whether because the overseer was infuriated at the acquittal and the lawyer's craftiness, or because he thought Ned would be a bad example to others, or because he thought overseers in the area would finish what the judge and jury had not, Lamb did not say. What he did say was that he thought it best not to have Ned on the plantation, unless Cameron overruled him. Instead, he placed Ned with Byrd Hill, a slave trader in Memphis.[10] Saved from execution by the indirect testimony of trusty man Washington, Ned was sold away.

Squire Hargis and those who witnessed the attack and learned of the outcome could draw one of two lessons about their future in Mississippi. For some, the quick arrival of their owner, the hiring of a lawyer, the stealth testimony of Washington, and the sparing of Ned's life from the jury and then the mob could constitute proof that the owner who had had them carried to Mississippi still cared about them. He had not simply dumped them in Tunica and then abandoned them. For others, Len's scarred back, Zack's hanging, Ned's sale, and the presence of an overseer whose demands and whip could fall on anyone else who got behind confirmed their worst fears about what the Mississippi bottom held in store.

A clue emerged later of how at least one black witness felt about the clash. It was the custom in the Cameron black community, as on many plantations, for children born after the passing of a family member or cherished friend to receive the name of the person lost. In bondage, loss didn't mean death alone; when brothers, sisters, parents, or children were sold or sent away, they too were lost. So Squire Hargis had lost his youngest brother, Paul, in 1844, when Paul and his siblings were sent to Alabama while Squire remained in North Carolina. In the late 1850s, when Squire Hargis and his wife, Suse, had a son, they named him Paul, and the infant Paul traveled with them when they were taken to Mississippi in November 1860.[11] The same principle—naming to remember and honor one who was lost—seemed to be at work five years after Ned was acquitted but sold away. The young niece of Washington, the man whose evidence saved Ned from hanging, would name her second son Ned.[12]

Paul Hargis might have never known about events in Mississippi. He might have never known that his brother had arrived in Tunica in November 1860 in the second wave of workers brought out from North Carolina. He might have never learned that Squire Hargis had named a son after him. Paul Hargis and others in Alabama, as well as those left back in North Carolina, might never have known of all that transpired in Mississippi after Paul Cameron's purchase of the place in 1856, or what awaited if Cameron picked them as the next to go to the bottom.

But as events unfolded, Paul Hargis and those in Alabama would come to learn exactly what had happened in Mississippi—and of the adverse fate that, once more, he had escaped. Ultimately the Cameron plantation people in North Carolina would find out as well. The road to discovery began on April 12, 1861—exactly one week after the trial and acquittal of Ned. At four-thirty that morning, forty-three cannons and mortars at the waterfront of Charleston harbor opened fire on Fort Sumter.

"We are resolved—at every sacrifice—to protect the entire slave territory. . . . We do not intend they shall have access to our slaves—tho' in my opinion, a majority of negroes will be with us in the conflict." So wrote Mississippi planter A. C. Wright to Paul Cameron on April 21, 1861, nine days after the firing on Fort Sumter and the beginning of war. Southern soldiers, Wright assured Cameron, "will repel any army Lincoln may send, cost what it may, of life and money." Wright added that he would go down from Memphis to the Delta in a few days and "see the overseers in our neighborhood and assure them of [their] entire safety & protection."[13]

Sixteen months after Sumter, the Mississippi planter's bravado had given way to despair. "I am at a loss what to do," he confessed to Cameron on August 11, 1862, "whether to stand or run into the interior."[14]

The issue of whether to stay or flee was settled by Union troops. Immediately after the outbreak of war in 1861, the seventy-five-year-old Union commander General Winfield Scott had proposed a plan to squeeze the rebellious southern states from both west and east. The navy would blockade the Atlantic ports; troops and gunboats would seize command of the great rivers of the West—the Mississippi, Tennessee, and Cumberland; Union forces would attempt to take New Orleans. As a primary strategy, the president and his cabinet rejected the old general's plan, dubbed the "Anaconda Plan" for its vision of conquest by constriction. It was deemed too slow for a northern public eager for direct confrontation and a knockout blow. Nonetheless, while battles raged in the East and dreams of easy victories gave way to humiliating defeats, soldiers and sailors in the West fought for control of the rivers. By mid-1862, the Union controlled New Orleans and much of the Mississippi River. Union troops, in raiding parties and small skirmishes, roamed both the Mississippi and Arkansas sides of the northern Delta at will.[15]

A. C. Wright was paralyzed, uncertain how to counsel Cameron. So far, the Mississippi planter wrote on August 11, 1862, "your negroes [are] yet loyal; none had left and if let alone I think they will all be true." But Wright knew they would not be left alone. Three of his people had already "gone to the Yankees," and Wright looked for Union raiding parties "every day, when I fear the result. The prospect is that we shall lose all our negroes—and everything of value." Many had fled to Memphis, where, though still enslaved, they "claim to be free and do as they please." Wright disliked "to abandon our fine estates, supplies, etc. and go where it will be difficult to get food and shelter. At present I am holding on, hoping the war will be transferred North and that the enemy will leave our neighborhood." His fantasy? The South might yet regain the "territory lost—including, I hope, the rivers."[16]

Paul Cameron didn't need to hear more. He had his fellow planter order the evacuation of Cameron's "slaves from the bottom to [Cameron's] plantation in South Ala with the mules." On September 5, 1862, all passed through Wright's plantation at Senatobia, twenty miles to the east of Cameron's Tunica place, "in good health and spirits." Their overseer led the way east. By then, Wright had also moved out most of his people. "I was convinced if I did not remove the negroes most if not all of them would be taken by the Yankees and freed. . . . I think most of the negroes thought . . . that all they had to do was wait till the Yankees came." On other places, many didn't wait. Some "got on boats as they passed, others took canoes," and a few brazenly took plantation "mules (women children & all)" and "rode off openly, the owners and overseers being too alarmed to attempt to restrain or punish them." Though Wright had taken his own enslaved people to Georgia, he still hoped that "some event may turn up that will enable us" to return—before Christmas!—to "estates not surpassed by any to be found." Both planters left an overseer and a handful of "the most reliable slaves" to look after cattle, hogs, crops, and fences. Wearily Wright conceded that "it is uncertain at what time we can carry our slaves back. I think not safely till the war is over."[17]

Squire Hargis arrived in Alabama in mid-September 1862 with 110 other people brought from Mississippi. No account records the reunion of Squire Hargis with his brothers, Paul and Jim, and his sisters, Sally and Nancy. One thing is certain: for all of them—for the Hargises taken from North Carolina to Alabama in 1844, and for those taken from North Carolina to Mississippi in 1858 and 1860—this was a reunion they had never expected to see. Doubtless the Alabama overseer, Wilson Oberry, witnessed embraces and scenes of joy at the arrival. He most certainly knew that in the cabins, there would be months of talk about lost years and lost relatives—and revelations about the Delta and the war that had forced Paul Cameron to retreat. Whatever Oberry observed or surmised, he left out of his letters to Paul Cameron. The overseer focused singularly on the matter of how the Alabama plantation was to support a doubled workforce of 180 people in the midst of war.[18]

Even before the cannons at Fort Sumter had fired the first shots, the planters and overseers of Greene County had anticipated a massive cutback in growing cotton that would mark the years ahead. Overseer Wilson Oberry reported the earliest sign of curtailment to Cameron on January 2, 1861, two months after Abraham Lincoln's election. Prices for the hire of enslaved persons in Greensboro had plummeted. The year before, owners had paid $175 to $225 to hire workers for the year. On New Year's Day 1861, "choice field hands" went for $30 to $70, and "some are putting them out for their feed and clothes." From that, Oberry said, Cameron could "form some idea of the state of our Country."[19]

For Oberry, as for others in the Alabama Black Belt, secession and war forced a gradual but decisive turn to plantation self-sufficiency. Ironically, self-sufficiency rather than cotton was what Cameron's mixed soil was best suited for. Oberry's Alabama people would make one more full cotton crop in 1861 and the overseer would store the bales from 1861 and the year before in protected places. Otherwise, he had Cameron's workers shift to raising hogs and to growing corn and vegetables of all sorts, so as to have enough food without having to make purchases at hugely inflated prices. "It is a hard living in our county," Oberry wrote in April 1862. "God only knows how much worse it will be." Still, "we are making out a great deal better than a great many." "Most of your people can make out a good while without [new] clothes as yet, having been so well clad heretofore," Oberry wrote in May 1862, so Cameron should give himself "no uneasiness about their clothes yet awhile." Oberry overplanted corn, so even when the summer of 1862 brought drought to the Alabama Black Belt, "we will make a plenty anyhow." Other places "don't have a mouthful of meat to give their negroes"; Oberry had stored and rationed his pork. "Be assured about this place and your people here," the Alabama overseer wrote Cameron at the end of July 1862.[20]

Though Oberry had assured the owner that Alabama could support the Mississippi refugees, one would have expected that the doubling of the workforce in September 1862 would bring strain and complaint from the overseer, and indeed it did. "This is going to be a very hard year," Oberry wrote in March 1863, six months after the arrivals from Mississippi. "I will have a hard time for the next four months to feed my people." Nonetheless, a full year after the influx, the overseer reported that despite short rations, his people had "plenty of vegetables and bread" and "we have made out very well. All seem to be satisfied as they know it is the best I can do."[21]

"Satisfied" the Cameron workforce may have been with their rations. Insulated from the war they were not. Unlike in the Mississippi Delta, no Union soldiers menaced Greene County or the Cameron plantation through the year 1863. But evidence of war was everywhere. In March 1862, a Greensboro matron reported that the town was full of enlisted soldiers, with two more companies of men requisitioned by the governor and readying to march out. She couldn't see how any more men could be called. There "are but few left, & we have so many thousands of negroes in this section, who of course require white men to overlook them."[22] For a different wartime purpose, black men were also requisitioned. Wilson Oberry was compelled to supply men to work on the Alabama and Mississippi railroad that the Confederacy was building through the southern part of the county. Oberry arranged for "a good man who I know [to] take care of them," he wrote Cameron, saying that the man "will let me know if any are sick and I will bring them home." Oberry was able to keep eight requisitioned men working nearby, close enough to check on. Others were taken to Mobile; they came back with pneumonia. All witnessed that thousands of blacks were at forced labor to sustain the Confederacy.[23]

The ultimate uncertainty of the war for the Cameron people in Alabama was whether or not they would remain enslaved. Squire Hargis and those brought from Mississippi were well aware that Union soldiers had taken people off plantations, or encouraged them to flee, and given the impression that they were free. In fact, until 1863, fugitives from slavery remained in legal limbo. They were "contraband of war"—confiscated property. Though not emancipated, they were not returned to their owners. In Black Belt Alabama, where fighting and Union soldiers had not arrived through 1863, there was no such halfway house of liberation.

Yet even in the cocoon of the Cameron plantation and Greene County, enslaved people got word of the impending and momentous change in the Union war goal. Until the fall of 1862, the president had held to the mission of the war as one solely to preserve the Union. But on September 22, 1862, after a bloody Union victory at the battle of Antietam, Abraham Lincoln issued a preliminary Emancipation Proclamation. In all the states still in rebellion against the United States on January 1, 1863, he would as a military measure proclaim slavery at an end and enslaved people "forever free." Wilson Oberry had no doubt that the enslaved people of the Black Belt knew of the coming Proclamation. When Paul Cameron asked

Oberry about selling off some of the surplus mules, the overseer wrote back on December 8, 1862, advising Cameron to wait. Potential buyers were holding back until the first of January, he said, with planters and overseers waiting "to see how negroes will [work] before they will buy."[24]

In the midst of such a Revolution . . ." The phrase was Paul Cameron's, and it led off a letter to his brother-in-law on September 18, 1863.[25] By that month in the war, there was good reason for Cameron's language. January 1 had indeed seen the issuance of the Emancipation Proclamation and with it the enlistment of black troops in the Union war effort. Thousands of free people of color and ex-slaves responded to the call, supplementing another 100,000 white soldiers drafted into a war that was in its third year. Early hopes that the Confederate revolution would succeed, bolstered by victories on the battlefield in 1861 and 1862, had given way to staggering losses in the first week of July 1863—in the east with the defeat of Robert E. Lee's troops at Gettysburg, in the west with the surrender of besieged Vicksburg to the forces of Ulysses S. Grant. Nonetheless, the outcome remained unsettled. The Union and Confederacy were still, as Cameron properly put it, in the midst of upheaval—still far from the end of the war.

In September 1863, Paul Cameron's brother-in-law, George Mordecai, was looking to cut his losses. Though Cameron had been suspicious of Mordecai's motive in marrying Paul's sister Margaret, the two men reconciled during the crisis of war. From 1862 on, Paul Cameron and George Mordecai trusted and repeatedly turned to each other for advice and help. So when George Mordecai wished to give up the oversight of his wife's land and enslaved people, he offered to sell Cameron the property.[26] But Paul Cameron declined. "In the midst of such a Revolution and having the care of at least 800 slaves," he responded to his brother-in-law, "I . . . have about as much as I can stagger along with. . . . I do not see with what sort of propriety I can add anything to my cares and responsibilities."

Anticipating that Cameron might say no, George Mordecai had a backup plan, and wanted Cameron's opinion. What would he think of Mordecai's renting or selling his wife's land and slaves? Diplomatically, Cameron affirmed that the decision was "a matter for you and my sister."

But since Mordecai had asked, he offered his opinion, which was unequiv-ocal: hold fast. "I would by no means rent to any one. You will get your property back in worse condition." As to sale, "I would not sell one acre of land myself nor would I advise a friend to sell, unless I could invest in more desirable real estate." Even if the worst happened, "I am for holding on to the soil, as the most permanent property." He advised holding on to enslaved workers as well. He suggested that Mordecai hire out as many as he could for the construction of wartime railroads, and have the rest produce food. Of course, he added, "we may lose all that we have." In that case, the effort to feed, clothe, and employ enslaved people would be for naught. But "if we succeed in the great struggle the increased value of all this sort of property . . . will more than pay off the charge of holding—yet by a very large sum."[27] Hold fast.

It was with that commitment that Paul Cameron awaited a telegram from Alabama on February 18, 1864. Union troops had invaded Meridian, Mis-sissippi, less than thirty miles from Cameron's plantation in Greene County, and the soldiers appeared to be headed east.[28] "We fear all we have in that region is in peril," Cameron wrote a friend. At any moment he expected word from a neighboring planter. When the telegram ar-rived, it was brief: "Come at once." Cameron reached his Alabama plan-tation by the end of February. Realizing that he could not retrieve all 180 of his enslaved people and bring them safely back to North Carolina, he left behind the old, the young, and parents with large families, likely thinking that even if soldiers came to his place, his people would remain on the plantation.[29] On March 3, Cameron left for North Carolina "by Rail Road with some 65 of my slaves in families." Most were able men and women in their twenties and thirties. Cameron wrote his brother-in-law that he "shall not be able to feed this family," and he asked Mordecai for help: "Look about & see what is the best I can do for their comfort and my interest."[30]

Paul Hargis and his wife, Dicey, were two of the sixty-five Alabama people who arrived back in North Carolina in the second week of March 1864.

He had been away almost twenty years. The return was, at best, bittersweet. He and the others had been "run" 400 miles away from troops, once just 30 miles distant, who might have brought an end to their bondage. He was not only far from Union troops but had been parted from his family: his two brothers, two sisters, and their spouses and children had all been left in Alabama.

The retrieval from Alabama of Paul Hargis and the sixty-four other able-bodied workers was part of Paul Cameron's gamble that the slave states might yet succeed in the "great struggle" and that success would richly reward planters who held fast to their land and enslaved people. As late as the middle of August 1864, Cameron believed that "the day is not very far off when we shall be rid of the Yankee." His confidence came from the "temper & tone of the leading Northern papers. They are as anxious for peace as we are." In response to the president's latest call for a military draft of half a million men, the papers counseled "resistance in arms" with a "daring violence." Even "some of Lincoln's own Black Republican supporters" seemed ready to call a halt to the endless war. In the South, William Tecumseh Sherman's troops were stalemated in Atlanta—"he must fail," Cameron felt sure. In the East, Ulysses Grant had sacrificed 150,000 men in inconclusive battles, which Cameron labeled "the greatest failure of all." Cameron's conviction was "very strong that if the Yankee shall obtain no new successes" before the August 27 Democratic convention in Chicago, delegates to the convention "will set out a 'Platform' for instant & absolute peace" and sweep Lincoln from the field.

Paul Cameron was not living in a dream world. President Abraham Lincoln in late August sized up the situation exactly as Cameron did, believing that without immediate and decisive victories on the battlefield, his reelection and Union victory were doomed.[31] On the third of September 1864 came that decisive victory: Sherman conquered Atlanta. "Atlanta is ours, and fairly won," the general telegraphed Lincoln. In mid-November, Sherman's troops began their six-week "March to the Sea" through a fifty-mile swath of Georgia. With those Union triumphs, Paul Cameron recognized that Lincoln would win reelection, "enforce his draft—& will do pretty much as he pleases & will send us on in war until one of the sections cry out 'enough.' "[32] Two months later, with the president reelected, Cameron gloomily warned his son, "We are in the midst of a terrible revolution & no man can tell what may be its consequences to any one of us. We may be all plundered & deprived of our worldly goods— parents may not be able to continue the education of their children—& the rich may become very poor."[33] Cameron seemed most to have in mind the destruction and deprivation wrought by Sherman's troops as they for- aged and pillaged their way through the region. After a month in Savannah, Sherman's army had marched north into South Carolina, the state that had initiated secession, and then moved into North Carolina, approaching Cameron's own plantation. On March 21, 1865, Cameron wrote his father- in-law that "the enemy . . . makes his search broad and deep—and deprives all of the means of living." Unable to sleep, Cameron said, he was "unfit for anything."[34]

Having done all in his power to provide food, garb, and shoes for his hundreds of enslaved people throughout the war, the last thing that Paul Cameron was looking for as Union soldiers closed in was what was about to happen on his own plantation. In the weeks and months after their lib- eration in April 1865, the people whom Paul Cameron had once owned, including sixty-five he had dispersed and then brought back from bondage in Alabama and Mississippi, now made *their* aims clear. They intended not only to reclaim possession of themselves but were determined, Paul Cameron soon realized, "to hold on to *me* or my *land*."[35]

For both Paul Cameron and Paul Hargis, unforeseen choices lay ahead.

Part Two ☙ A Foothold in Freedom

Six ✐ Exile's Return

PAUL HARGIS HAD NO CHOICE when Paul Cameron moved him to a cotton plantation in Alabama in 1844, along with his brother and two sisters and another 110 people. Nor did he have a choice twenty years later, when Cameron hurried him and his mate, Dicey, and sixty-three others back to North Carolina in March 1864, to put distance between them and marauding Union troops. Cameron had brought them out for profits; he returned them to avert losses. Paul Hargis and 800 others on the North Carolina plantation remained enslaved for another year.[1] But in important ways, Paul Cameron had already lost the people he owned. He had long since forfeited any bond with his workers. That loss came from experiences that Paul Hargis had, for the most part, not undergone.

When the end of the war and the conclusion of bondage came to the Cameron place in April 1865, anger long under the surface erupted. Over the next twenty months, from April 1865 to November 1866, both Paul Hargis and Paul Cameron found themselves in the middle of an unfolding insurgency. Both faced choices about how they would cope. For Paul Cameron, dozens of letters chronicle his responses, and those of his overseer, to the ire and demands of emancipated workers. For Paul Hargis, only four words survive—a listing of his first and last name on two separate documents. Fragments though they are, the two entries reveal the choices he made amidst the upheaval.

✐

When Paul Hargis arrived back at Fairntosh in 1864, two decades after his departure from North Carolina, he was surely struck by changes at the plantation. The main house at Fairntosh had a new roof made of red tin, a decision made to protect it from weather that had rotted its shingled predecessor. A mile and a half down the road from the big house there was now an immense barn—an "architectural cathedral," in the words of a later historian. A hundred and thirty-three feet long, thirty-three feet wide, two stories tall, it had stalls that stabled mules used for plowing and hauling wagons, places to milk cows, and a vast upper level to store hay. Completed in 1860, the cypress-shingled barn encompassed the "'best stables' ever built" in the county, Cameron proudly informed his father-in-law.[2] Across from the barn, two hundred yards away and in plain sight, were four new dwellings for enslaved workers, at the quarter known as Horton Grove. These were no ordinary cabins, which customarily housed one or two families. Each house was a two-story building that had a tin roof, board and batten siding, and bricked interior walls to afford a measure of insulation. Wooden floors stood raised a foot off the ground; there was a two-story chimney on each side of the building, providing a fireplace in each of the four rooms. The structures had the appearance of rural town houses, and indeed the model had come from tenements built by Duncan Cameron in Raleigh, refashioned for the countryside.[3] Looking within, however, it became clear that each room of seventeen feet square likely housed a single family, bringing the total number of people in the four-room house to as much as two dozen.

To Paul Hargis, the fields of wheat may have looked most familiar. But the scale of the fields was far larger than anything he had seen twenty years before. A visitor coming through in the late 1840s was agog at the size and bounty of the place at harvest time. The "'plantation extends parallel with [two] rivers, a distance of fifteen miles, and covers an area of about sixty square miles. It . . . yields abundant crops of wheat, corn, oats, cotton, tobacco, potatoes, and other products. . . . It is probably the largest landed estate in the Carolinas, perhaps in the Union."[4]

It didn't take long, however, for Paul Hargis and others brought back from Alabama in 1864 to see what was missing: the Camerons. In 1856, Paul Cameron had moved his wife, Anne Ruffin Cameron, his four daughters, and his two sons to the town of Hillsborough, fifteen miles away. He had made the move for the health of his family and for the education and social cultivation of his children.[5] No more did Paul Cameron keep tabs on the health of his people, save by reports from his overseers. Only rarely did he ride from quarter to quarter, ministering to the sick, assessing the degree of illness, summoning a physician to care for those deemed at risk, and staying with the dying until they expired. The hands-on owner was gone. In North Carolina, as in Alabama and Mississippi, Paul Cameron had become an absentee planter.

Fairntosh and all the other quarters had become the bailiwick of overseers. For Samuel Piper, the manager of Fairntosh and the head overseer of the entire plantation, Cameron had built a large two-story dwelling within fifty paces of the unoccupied main dwelling. Except for occasional visits from Paul Cameron, and an appearance at the end of the year by his wife, Anne, to oversee the slaughter of hogs and preparation and storage of meat, the plantation was the overseer's domain. It was Samuel Piper who judged whether those who complained of sickness would work or remain in their cabins. It was the overseer who set the pace of work and punished the slack. How much the planter's absence became a point of tension for Cameron's North Carolina people can only be guessed. In 1850s Alabama, there were repeated complaints—from laborers and overseer alike—when Cameron failed to make his annual visit, and when intervals lengthened between his letters. "It looks like you have forgotten the place," wrote John Webster. In North Carolina, many might have thought the same thing about the owner who had decamped to Hillsborough and become a visitor rather than a resident at Fairntosh.[6]

Notwithstanding his removal of 196 people to Alabama and Mississippi and his own departure from Fairntosh, Paul Cameron kept a benign view of himself and his role as a planter. As he saw it, he provided for his people, keeping them clothed and shod and fed, even during the war, and bestowing favors when he thought them warranted. In 1865, looking back on his thirty years as a planter, he characterized himself as a benevolent master who had always maintained "a mild & humane care of the family of negroes" he possessed, rendering them "as docile & free from violence & vice as the same number to be found any where in the south . . . Supplies of food have been regularly distributed from the mills & store houses every seventh day," and "clothing suited to all classes [has been] distributed to all equally." He fed his people from infancy through old age, in sickness as in health, even though that meant "not one half of the entire population have been available in the field or house for any useful purpose."[7] Cameron's view of himself remained generous, doubtless reinforced by the affirmations of favored servants.[8]

One can only speculate what Cameron's people thought or said among themselves about their owner. What was it like for them to see others depart—114 people in 1844, 40 in 1858, and 42 more in 1860? What was it like for them to know that at any point, they or their friends or a family member might be next? How did they react when they actually learned, from the refugees returned from Mississippi, the fate that had fallen to Len, Zack, Ned, and others? For Paul Hargis, it wouldn't have been hard to detect rancor under the charade of calm.

Paul Hargis and Paul Cameron would see resentments burst into the open in the spring of 1865.

In March 1865, Union forces commanded by William Tecumseh Sherman arrived in North Carolina and steadily made their way toward the state capital, Raleigh. The reputation of Sherman and his troops preceded them. They burned, foraged, and pillaged, all part of the March to the Sea and the subsequent Carolinas Campaign, which included the burning of Columbia, South Carolina. Their actions were part of the "hard war" strategy to which Sherman and the Union had turned in 1863. For the Ohio general, the tactics were meant to destroy morale as well as goods—to punish, disable, and bring the war home. As word came of Sherman's unstoppable advance, Paul Cameron couldn't sleep.[9] No report came about the mood in the quarters. Whether anxious or expectant or silently exhilarated, all knew the end of their bondage was near.

Foragers came first, and arrived at Fairntosh in the second week of April 1865. The concluding events of the Civil War played out during that fateful month—the flight of Jefferson Davis from Richmond on April 3, the surrender of Robert E. Lee's army at Appomattox on April 9, the assassination of Abraham Lincoln on April 15. The commanders of the two remaining armies, the Confederate army of 21,000 led by General Joseph E. Johnston and the 90,000 Union troops led by General William

Tecumseh Sherman, agreed to a truce and provisional surrender on April 18. Over the course of the next eight days, further negotiations took place, shadowed by the assassination, the succession of a new president, and the replacement of Sherman by Ulysses S. Grant as the chief negotiator, until agreement was reached on terms of capitulation. Prior to the cease-fire and during the truce, troops milled about for almost two weeks. The negotiations and final surrender took place at a small farmhouse a dozen miles from the Cameron plantation. Well before the official surrender, however, emancipation had come jaggedly but decisively to the Cameron place.

As Sherman's troops neared, Paul Cameron remained in Hillsborough, and sent his wife, Anne, and his daughter Rebecca Cameron Anderson to occupy the main house at Fairntosh. Their presence did nothing to daunt the foragers. The men came in waves, ten and twenty at a time. Each gang of soldiers broke "open locks of trunks & doors rifling them of whatever they pleased," reported Cameron's daughter. "Some of them are drunk & they go from top to bottom of this house & have repeatedly threatened to burn it." Fearing the worst, the Cameron women had beforehand distributed surplus clothing among their servants—a last allowance. Rebecca Cameron Anderson, whose husband had died in battle the year before, asked one of the servants to hide a valise containing letters from her late husband. It was to no avail. The foragers raided the cabins of black workers as well as the big house, took the clothing, ransacked the suitcase, and burned the letters. The soldiers axed open the locked door to the meat house, confiscated the hams stored there, shared some with the freed people, and left with all the wagons, carts, and mules of the place. Only when the Cameron ladies appealed to the Union general in charge of maintaining order during the armistice did they get a guard—for one day—and relief from the foragers' "depredations & indignities."[10]

Paul Hargis was among the hundreds of once-enslaved people who witnessed the Camerons' fall from power. However unceremonious their emancipation, bondage was over. What lay ahead?

Soon answers came. Food dispersed among the people—including enough ham, bacon, lard, and flour to feed them for five months, in the Camerons' view—was consumed in weeks, "with much waste," lamented Cameron's wife, Anne, in early May 1865. Threats followed to slaughter and eat the plantation's sheep and cattle. Anne Cameron reported "all as idle and indisposed to work or return to their former duties." Black visitors came at will, one supposedly with the radical notion that the newly freed people had "a freehold interest in the soil on which they reside"—a claim to Cameron's land. In the view of Cameron's wife and his overseer, Samuel Piper, a bacchanalian holiday set in.[11] Order, as the Camerons understood it, and duty, as the Camerons defined it, disappeared. So too, in the words of Cameron's brother-in-law George Mordecai, did any semblance of "gratitude or the slightest regard for the interest of their former owners."[12]

The reversals on the Cameron place mirrored upheavals on plantations throughout the South. In a classic essay, "Masters without Slaves," written a half century ago, historian Willie Lee Rose identified a sentiment widespread among deposed slave owners: that their former bondsmen were *ungrateful*.[13] Like the Camerons, other planters had seen themselves as indulgent providers and humane masters. When "at least one of the negroes" denounced Cameron as "a hard Master—yielding short supplies of all sort & granting no indulgences!" the planter was indignant. Stunned by the chaos and by the report that even one of his people would give him "a bad name," he admitted to his father-in-law that "I don't know what to do. Nothing will damage my good name for humanity or else that is held in esteem by good men." For the time, he intended no reprisals or self-reproaches.[14] Indeed, *within* bondage, as Paul Hargis and his siblings could testify, the fair measure of "humanity" was comparative, and by comparison, the Camerons and Bennehans of the early nineteenth century stood high among their peers. What had most clearly changed behavior and belief was emancipation. Freedom ended the demonstrations of gratitude for provisions and indulgences that were the best one could hope for while enslaved. Flagrant new demonstrations of resistance and hostility suggested how little Cameron's former slaves had embraced his "good name for humanity." Bondage was bondage.

There was, however, a special intensity to the backlash on the Cameron plantation, as Paul Hargis would have observed. When it came time, as had long been the custom, to send milk and butter from Fairntosh to

Hillsborough, the freedmen refused.[15] In Hillsborough, when Cameron's daughter Maggie spoke sharply to her house servant Emma, Emma looked seventeen-year-old Maggie straight in the eye and proclaimed that "her skin was nearly as white as hers—that her hair was nearly as straight—& that she was quite as free!'" Emma and her family left Hillsborough and headed toward Fairntosh, where she could recount the story of what Cameron called impudence—to her, self-respect—to friends and the rest of her family.[16] By the end of 1865, the plunge from deference to defiance appalled Paul Cameron's wife, Anne, his emissary at Fairntosh. Treated rudely, with none of the obedience and niceties once due the mistress of the plantation, she came back from Fairntosh outraged. She said "without hesitation" to her husband that they should *"drive all off"* so that they would at least "have peace if you have no money."[17]

Was the suffering of Cameron exiles in Mississippi an additional goad to the unrest? Was there pent-up anger on the part of those who had *not* been sent away but had spent long periods of time fearful they would be next? Paul Cameron's workers had no knowledge of their owner's proposal to buy a large "platform" of 3,000 acres of *"Virgin soil with its purity"* in Mississippi, outlined in a letter to his father in 1848. Nor did they know of his intention "to keep here only enough to keep our plantations in order & make them grain & clover plantations," and to shift hundreds of North Carolina workers to cotton fields in the west, where their labor could swell the Camerons' wealth.[18] Rather, the ex-slaves' awareness came from successive disappearances of family members and friends who had been put on railroad cars and transported to the Mississippi Delta. If they had anticipated that it was not a matter of whether but of who would go next and when, they were right.[19] Accounts of those brought back from Mississippi had confirmed the worst fears of those still in North Carolina. It seems implausible that Mississippi exile—experienced or feared—had no impact whatsoever on the intensity of the insurgency in North Carolina. Paul Cameron himself thought that the mutiny was about payback—and possession.[20]

To be sure, on the Cameron place and on plantations all over the South, work disputes were central to the conflicts that emerged. Who would set the terms of work? To settle that matter, Paul Cameron agreed to the contract proposed by the agent of the Freedmen's Bureau in August 1865. With the urging of the government agent, the freed people finally signed. Overseer Samuel Piper doubted that Cameron workers, a large majority of whom were dissatisfied with the proposal, would abide by it.[21] He was right. Despite the contract, confrontations continued and escalated. In September, the overseer reported that Cameron's laborers couldn't be hurried: "If spoken to an impudent look and a slower gait is the consequence."[22] In November 1865, the people at the Stagville quarter abruptly stopped work. In the middle of the harvest, scythes in hand, they declared they would cut no more wheat, and allow no others to cut wheat, unless Cameron gave them three-fourths of the crop. A call to federal troops in the area brought soldiers to Stagville, and the workers to heel. So much did the officer—a Captain Freeland—side with the owner that he even altered the previous labor agreement. Instead of a third of the crop, the strikers would receive but a fourth. Other workers on other quarters, the overseer reported, got the message—and continued to work. A poor harvest it was, but at least they saved it.[23]

It was the Camerons' North Carolina overseer, Samuel Piper, who felt the brunt of the hostility from the workers. In charge of extracting labor and setting the pace during slavery, his efforts now were for naught. He confessed, "I am a sorry hand at begging a Negro to work." Ordered to save the fodder, they refused. Directed to mind the enclosures and fences, they dismantled them.[24] Even though Piper managed to complete gathering the crop, he admitted that "my authority with the hands is at an end." By the end of the year, confrontation had made the Cameron place an armed camp on all sides. Black workers no longer made their wills known by sidelong glances, insolent remarks, or work slowdowns. "They are armed and so am I," reported the overseer.[25]

Two documents give fleeting glimpses of where Paul Hargis stood amidst the turmoil. One is a work contract that Paul Hargis signed—marked with an X under his name—in November 1865. The other is the appearance of his name and that of his wife, Dicey, on a Certificate of Cohabitation, a record created by the Freedmen's Bureau to recognize and give full legal status to the marriages of men and women while enslaved.

Not everyone on the Cameron place was asked or allowed to sign a plantation work contract in November 1865. Far from it. By the fall of 1865, Paul Cameron was no longer sure he even wanted to remain a planter, much less to do so with free black workers. On November 27, he prepared an advertisement to sell the place, and told his father-in-law that if he could get an offer at half its value, he would take it, simply to secure peace and order and comfort, and to silence the complaints of white neighbors who protested the actions—one guesses poaching and bravado—of his workers.[26] Yet Cameron knew that no one had the wherewithal to buy his thousands of acres, even at half their value. An alternative to sale—an alternative that at least promised "peace and comfort"—was to shift from black laborers to white tenants. Renting his land to whites was the solution repeatedly endorsed by his overseer. Samuel Piper even gave the names of landless whites he was certain would leap at the chance.[27] Between these extremes, there was a middle ground. Cameron chose to order off the place those blacks who were the most troublesome. He contracted selectively, signing up those he viewed as of good service or of past good conduct.[28] Cameron reported to a fellow planter that "I will try those that remain this year and if not with fair results will give them up & out."[29]

Paul Hargis was one of the signers of the November 1865 work contract for Fairntosh and Eno.[30] By prior good conduct—and, presumably, by distance from the "troublesome" people and actions of 1865—he had been deemed worth the experiment of keeping him on. He chose to work, and was chosen for work, in part because he'd kept that distance. The question is why. In November 1865, he may still have seen himself as a man exempted from slavery's worst—exempted in 1829, at the age of two, when he and his family were spared sale to South Carolina; exempted in

1856, at the age of twenty-nine, when he was not among those from Alabama sent to "the bottom of the Mississippi"; exempted again in 1858 and 1860, when it was Cameron workers from North Carolina—and not from Alabama—who were added to the Mississippi labor force and made to feel the brunt of the planter's press for profits. Fortune had kept Paul Hargis in the eye of the storm as Paul Cameron pursued bonanza returns—as Cameron abandoned mastery "with feelings" for factories in the fields.

Faced with less traumatic currents of bondage, Paul Hargis had learned to navigate them well. In North Carolina, as a free man, he chose to navigate again—to see how far work and a work contract would take him on a plantation that still belonged to Paul Cameron. Paul Hargis chose labor over insurgency.

Working hard did not necessarily signal allegiance to the planter. By 1865, Paul Cameron had become dubious about fidelity from former slaves. In a letter to his brother-in-law, who had considered asking trusted black servants to bury treasured items, Cameron urged him to cease and desist, and above all to reveal no such plan to Thomas Cameron, Paul Cameron's impaired and too-trusting brother. "Our plantations are in my opinion the very worst places to deposit valuable packages. . . . The negro will on the slightest temptation expose both Master & overseer."[31] Throughout 1865, in addition to all his other worries, Paul Cameron felt despair over a wayward son, who lied to try to get into the Confederate army at the age of fourteen, who then ran away and sold clothing to make his way to Wilmington and Fayetteville, who befriended freed blacks, and who had become a chronic prevaricator. Repeatedly Cameron had to dispatch rescue parties to try to find, capture, and bring back the boy. By lecture and letter, Cameron warned his son about the perils of prevarication, and especially of association with freedmen, whom he regarded—as did his father-in-law Thomas Ruffin—as "model liars." "Have nothing to do with a negro," Cameron instructed.[32] For himself, as for his son, wariness was the safest course.

Paul Hargis, on the other hand, took a step beyond signing a work contract to signal his continued alignment with, if not allegiance to, the planter. On May 4, 1866, there appeared on the Cameron plantation a representative of the Freedmen's Bureau. Officially the agency was the Bureau of Refugees, Freedmen, and Abandoned Lands, and in large part its work was to help negotiate contracts between white planters and black workers and to referee labor disputes between them. The Bureau agent who appeared at the Cameron place on May 4, however, had a different mission. During slavery, black men and women took partners and remained together as long as their will and that of overseer and owner allowed. But marriage among enslaved people had no standing at law. The Bureau agent came around to make slave marriages official. Persons married in bondage gave their names to the agent, confirmed their union and the year they wed, and received a Certificate of Cohabitation. The recorder for the Freedmen's Bureau took the information orally and wrote down the names and marriage date of each couple.[33]

Paul Hargis gave his name and that of his wife, Dicey, and stated the date of their initial cohabitation as 1856. Then he stopped the agent, who had just written down his name, Paul Hargis, and asked that the last name be reentered. The Bureau man erased "Hargis" and wrote over it the new name requested: "Cameron."[34] In North Carolina in 1866, Paul Hargis declared himself to be "Paul Cameron." Was the name change an implicit pledge of fealty that went beyond the commitment to work, accompanied by an equally implicit expectation of benefits and patronage on the part of his former owner?[35] All we have is the overlay of his slavery-time name with the choice—his deliberate choice—of a different name in postwar North Carolina.

For the planter Paul Cameron and the freedman Paul Hargis both, the experiments of 1866 failed. For the planter, grievances mounted. Neighbors complained about theft by some of his workers, stealing foodstuffs and animals and selling the goods to buyers at the crossroad store of the tiny white settlement of Orange Factory, no questions asked. The fact that the workers soon appeared in Sunday garb, garments that Cameron found well above their means, satisfied him that the accusations were true.[36]

Though Cameron and his overseer thought they had rid themselves of the most troublesome workers, slowdowns and conflicts continued. By July 1866, well before the contract of November 1865 was set to expire, Paul Cameron had concluded that the only route to peace and comfort in the neighborhood was to rent all his places to white tenants and to evict every black person on his plantation. By September he had made the arrangements, and in October 1866, he gave notice to all the freed people that they were to leave.[37]

For Cameron, the expulsion served one other purpose. Cameron still had two western plantations that were worked by freedmen. Despite difficulties, the overseer in Alabama was holding his own. The great struggle was on the Mississippi plantation in Tunica County, which Cameron continued to regard as the most valuable place he owned. He had turned over management of the place to his son-in-law George Collins, who had married Cameron's daughter Anne in 1860. Collins was the son of an enormously wealthy planter from eastern North Carolina who had inherited the Somerset plantation—thirty miles from the port of Edenton. During and after the war, Somerset had fallen fast. So, albeit without enthusiasm, George Collins took up his father-in-law's offer to manage the place in Mississippi.[38]

The difficulty in Mississippi, as elsewhere, was labor—getting enough workers and managing those George Collins did get. On both fronts, in 1866, the son-in-law found himself in desperate straits. Dissatisfied, many of his workers announced they would leave after payment at the end of the year. Those willing to stay, he found unreliable.[39] So he turned to Cameron to see if his father-in-law could recruit hands among those he planned to evict. Understandably, Paul Cameron thought it unlikely: Mississippi was 500 miles away, and there was no love lost between the landowner and the freedmen. Nonetheless, he pledged to try, and in the end he did manage to get more than a dozen to agree to go.[40] At that point, George Collins decided to ask the Freedmen's Bureau to transport seventeen destitute freedmen, displaced by white tenants, from North Carolina to Mississippi. Needless to say, Collins did not specify that it was his father-in-law who had thrown the black people off. The Freedmen's Bureau agent responded cryptically: request forwarded, request denied.[41] Paul Cameron had to foot the bill for the trip out, made by train.

The day of the evictions, Cameron expected trouble. He doubted that the expelled freedmen would go peacefully when they had to abandon their cabins and allow white tenants to move in. Cameron brought his delinquent son with him to witness the expulsions, hoping that young Duncan Cameron III would be forever disabused of sympathy and association with black people, and be further convinced that his father was poor, without funds to "support his follies." No conflict ensued. Rather, the blacks who left, at least most of them, bragged that they had their sights on a new destination and that they fully expected to do better there. They were headed east, to Edgecombe County, where planters were raising big crops of cotton and paying good money to the laborers who worked their fields.[42] As far away as Alabama, word would soon confirm that Edgecombe cotton planters were making a go of it.[43] But Cameron's workers also had inside information. In 1859 Paul Cameron's brother-in-law had sold more than eighty enslaved persons, formerly owned by Duncan Cameron and inherited by his daughter, to four Edgecombe County planters. Former slaves of the largest Edgecombe purchaser, R. R. Bridgers, had trekked back toward Fairntosh in May 1865.[44] The Cameron people from and still in Edgecombe were most likely the source for the advice to head east. With good prospects ahead, the freed people being evicted refrained from a last clash.

And Paul and Dicey Hargis? Good wages beckoned from the cotton plantations of Edgecombe County. But they hardly knew anyone there. There was the promise of high cotton and good pay in Mississippi. Yet Paul Hargis may have heard quite his fill about "the bottom" from his brother Squire and others, enough to dissuade him from going to Mississippi whatever the windfall. What Paul Hargis did do was to seize an opportunity he saw in George Collins's need for workers and Paul Cameron's recruitment of them from North Carolina. He and his wife went out with that caravan of freed people. They traveled with the group, by train. Cameron paid their way. Then, at a train stop, perhaps at Chattanooga, Paul and Dicey Hargis got off.[45]

Their destination was Greene County, Alabama. They were going home. When they arrived, they retook the Hargis name. It was the first of many signs that eviction had opened the way for Paul Hargis's true emancipation to begin.

Seven ✒ "Against All Comers"

IT WAS THE THIRD WEEK of January 1867, and the manager of Paul Cameron's Alabama plantation was already worn down. During the previous decade, when Wilson Oberry had overseen Cameron's enslaved workers, January had been the time to resume work, plow the soil, and get a head start on the planting of cotton and corn. An early start meant a good spring and the chance to get to summer with strong stands of both crops in July. Not this January. It had been a trial to get his free workers to any agreement at all. At one point he thought about simply quitting the effort and breaking the place up. Finally, after "a long scuffle," he had managed to sign up thirty workers for the year, workers that he thought would make a good set of hands. He needed a few more men to bring his workforce to the size he wanted—still well below the forty-some freed people he had managed in 1866 and just a third of the number that he oversaw when bondage had given him sovereign power. At the end of Wilson Oberry's long report to absentee landowner Paul Cameron, he noted one matter he'd almost forgotten to mention: two arrivals from North Carolina. "Paul and Dicey is here," he wrote. "He says he will stay but has not assign no contract."[1]

The sight of Paul and Dicey Hargis must have startled the men and women who had decided to remain with their former overseer after emancipation. What were the two of them doing back in Alabama, and how had they gotten there? No less startled was manager Wilson Oberry, though for a different reason: Where did Paul Hargis get the notion he would stay—or could stay—but work without a contract?

All would learn that Paul Hargis had come back to Alabama a different man.

His fellow workers knew that Paul and Dicey Hargis had been among the sixty-five hastened out of Alabama to North Carolina in 1864, removed to keep them away from an anticipated Union invasion that never happened. Now, in January 1867, the two had astonishingly returned. Paul Hargis likely explained why they came back by telling of the mutiny he had witnessed in North Carolina and the decision of their former owner to eject all blacks from his Piedmont plantation. They'd been evicted. He surely didn't need to spell out why he chose to return to Alabama. His two brothers, Jim Hargis and Squire Hargis, had remained there during the war, as had the widowed husband of their Hargis sister, and all his nieces and nephews. Paul and Dicey Hargis had come back to family—and to the place where they had lived for twenty years.

Paul Hargis's relatives and friends must have wondered how a freedman without means had gotten himself and his wife from the Carolina Piedmont to the Alabama Black Belt, more than 400 miles away. He could explain that they had come partway with George Collins and the freed people he was bringing by train to Mississippi, had gotten off, and then had made it to Alabama on their own. Almost a half century later, Paul Hargis would say that he came out to Alabama by coach, and indeed came out on a stagecoach with Paul Cameron himself, crossing together over the Blue Ridge Mountains.[2] The story was an embellishment that telescoped two journeys into one. For the second migration to Alabama, the account had a basis in truth. Not only did Paul Cameron underwrite the Collins caravan of North Carolina workers to the West, but it seems almost certain that he also staked Paul Hargis to a coach or wagon ride from wherever he and his wife, Dicey, left the Mississippi-bound laborers and made their way back to Alabama. Obliged to sponsor Collins and his workers to get them to his plantation in Mississippi, Cameron seems to have done the same for Paul Hargis to get him to Alabama in January 1867. Not literally, but by sanction and support, Paul Cameron was with Paul Hargis on his return.

Paul Hargis's twentieth-century version of his return—that he and the planter had "come out together"—squared with the manager's 1867 report, a half century before, that "he will stay but has not assign no contract." Paul Hargis had seen what a contract meant to Cameron and his manager in North Carolina: *obedience*.[3] As long as he was on the Carolina plantation, he had complied, navigating its constricted freedom as he once had navigated bondage. He resolved to return on different terms. Initially transported west because his labor was prized and needed, he came back west a man who knew his worth. He stood ready to be a partner but not a pawn. He would work without a contract.

Whether he would remain depended on how events unfolded in the months ahead.

It didn't take long for Paul Hargis to find out what had happened on the Alabama plantation in the twenty months since "freedom come about," the term black folks coined when emancipation became reality with the Confederate surrender in April 1865. At first the Alabama overseer had reported that all was well, that all were working as they always had.[4] When the victorious federal government set up the Freedmen's Bureau to oversee the newly emancipated people, both whites and blacks awaited edicts that would determine the organization of labor. An initial answer came in late June 1865 from Henry Crydenwise, a New York lieutenant who had led a black regiment during the war and now was a Freedmen's Bureau agent in the area around Greensboro.[5] Crydenwise spoke to blacks and whites gathered in town. According to the approving editor of the *Alabama Beacon*, the white-owned newspaper in Greensboro, the government agent "told them they were *free*, but that freedom did not imply an exemption from labor, and liberty to do as they pleased." On the contrary, according to the editor, the Bureau officer said the freed people had "increased . . . obligations to labor assiduously and faithfully. . . . Labor was their lot, and those who expected to live in idleness would be made to work"—though no longer with the whip.[6]

Black workers at the gathering in Greensboro heard an emphatically more liberating message from Henry Crydenwise. What one person at the speaking recounted to her grandson—who recalled her words late in the twentieth century—was that "Cryden White" proclaimed, "You can do what you want to do, you can go where you want to go!"[7]

In a vivid letter home written just days after the event, Henry Crydenwise underscored the competing messages and divergent responses to his address by planters, by freed people, and by the Bureau agent himself.

> There were about five thousand present. You should have seen that vast crowd, that sea of eager faces. You may imagine somewhat the feelings which take possession of one standing before thousands of people (many of whom heard it for the first time) that *They were free* & of the new duties & responsibilities that come with this gift of Freedom. To listen to that deep murmur of thanksgiving that rose from that mighty mass as I said to them *"You are free"* would stir the dullest sensibilities & cause the most stammering tongue to grow eloquent.[8]

From his brother and others, Paul Hargis came to learn how the contrasting views of freedom had played out on the Cameron place in Alabama.[9] Wilson Oberry, now titled manager rather than overseer of the postwar plantation, had bragged in July 1865 about the contract he had reached with his workers. They were to get only one-eighth of the crop they produced. "They have to stick to the regular rules of the plantation—and if one deserts he forfeits his wages," he wrote to owner Paul Cameron, and crowed, "I have bound them up." Wilson Oberry's bravado and the workers' compliance didn't last. The manager's model of discipline crumbled when two freedmen of the place summoned others from the neighborhood to religious gatherings, where they prayed and preached—or as the manager saw it, pretended to preach. There was no regulating anyone when strangers freely came on the place. Oberry "could never break it up until I shot one of my neighbor's Negroes. I filled him full from head to foot." The lowest point came when seven or eight of his workers, in collusion with four Union soldiers stationed in Greensboro, tried to steal the cotton that Oberry had stored behind his dwelling. He caught them, and when they demanded his pistol and threatened to shoot him, "I told them shoot and be damned—that I intended to die by that cotton." They fled.[10]

All the troubles of 1865 might have been forgotten had the cotton crop of the next year come out well. Just the opposite occurred in 1866, on the Cameron place and throughout the county and the Black Belt. The harvest was a catastrophe. Some blamed the shortfall on the limits of free labor. As one writer to the *Alabama Beacon* later put it, in bondage one man with a whip could extract a good year's labor from a hundred. In freedom, he claimed, discipline vanished.[11] In fact, the disappointing crops in 1866 and subsequent years had multiple causes. "The Negroes have generally done fair work," judged a leading Greensboro planter in late July 1866. "The very unfavorable season has done more to produce this result than the want of energy on the part of the Americans of African descent."[12] The immediate lesson that Cameron's manager drew was to reduce his workforce and to tighten controls. "I never again want to work as many free Negroes as I had on the place before," he declared. Nor would he attempt, as he had throughout the previous decade, to work all of the cleared land—1,200 acres of Cameron's 1,600-acre plantation. He would work a smaller force "only on good land for a hundred bales of cotton." After he hired thirty-three people, he still had to fight off rival managers and landowners, who tried to entice his people away with offers of more money. He almost lost his hires when he banned religious gatherings "that had my quarters full of Negroes every night" and next dismissed all unmarried women from the place, as he believed they didn't carry their part of the load.[13]

"All the young people left him," wrote Cameron's son-in-law George Collins. Collins got that report from Paul Hargis's brother-in-law, who had come to the Mississippi plantation to reclaim his daughter. On the Cameron place, as elsewhere in the Alabama Black Belt, it was the young who most strongly felt their freedom, and who asserted it by moving to places where they had not been in bondage—to different plantations or to the town of Greensboro.[14]

As Paul Hargis learned of the "long scuffle" from his brothers and other freed people on the Alabama plantation, it surely confirmed his decision in January 1867 to begin work without a contract. If he and his wife couldn't get along with the man they had known as overseer until 1864—if Wilson Oberry still intended to bind them and others up—the two of them would be free to leave.

⸏⸏⸏

Paul Hargis chose to stay. Five months after his return to Alabama, manager Wilson Oberry declared that he never "knew a man try harder to make a crop." In June 1867, Oberry reported that he'd designated Paul Hargis as head of the hoes.[15] "I places Paul at the head of the hoes which has been a great advantage to me. . . . I have always said he is the best working hand I have. He carries his hoe and keeps the weak ones up and has done a harder year's work than any of them on the place."[16]

For whose benefit was Paul Hargis the "best working hand"? Clearly the plantation manager saw the return migrant as "a great advantage to me." In writing Paul Cameron, he sent the same message—Paul Hargis was a great advantage to the planter as well. For Paul Hargis himself, in the short run, his labors promised palpable rewards—a bigger crop to split and family members kept together. Was there hope as well for some more lasting gain—for land itself? To claim that as an ulterior goal of Paul Hargis's commitment goes beyond the evidence. To presume it never crossed his mind that persistence might bring a larger payoff goes against the signs everywhere that ownership of land was loosening and that land was starting to change hands.

At first glance, Paul Hargis's promotion by the manager appeared close to the slavery-time anointment of one of the bondsmen as the plantation "driver." The duty of the slave driver was explicit in his title—to force the pace and production of workers in the field.[17] Without question, Paul Hargis's ascent was about pace. But unlike the position of slave driver, Paul Hargis's role was not about compulsion. To be sure, his speed pressured fellow workers to keep up. At the same time, he was simultaneously enlisting them. If they pushed as he pushed, they could all come out ahead. As Wilson Oberry saw it, the appointment worked wonders. There were "negroes around me that don't do more than half work, which is a great disadvantage to the negroes that will work." Paul Hargis's model and urging energized the free riders. Despite having had but "half a Saturday off this year," there was "no grumbling." The results of freed people's effort astounded the former overseer: "I have cultivated the largest crop this year that I ever planted in my life, and other people may say what they will but I never had my hands to work better—I can say they have done the hardest years work they ever done since I lived with them."[18]

Paul Hargis had gained the latitude to push and persuade because the months before his elevation had taught the white manager that he could do better if he delegated some authority to a black leader, a lesson that other managers in the region eventually would also learn.[19] Before making Paul Hargis head of the hoes, Oberry had tried to sustain his control through a mix of payments and demands. When neighboring planters sought to lure his workers by offering "them big wages to induce them away"—$15 a month—"it cost me something to get them to remain," and the competition continued. Some planters or managers gave more of a share than Oberry; a few sold spots of land on long credit; widespread "undermining" left a "good many plantations close around ours . . . perfectly vacant [with] not a negro on them." Oberry weathered the challenges and emerged with what he regarded as "a set of good hands," only to see some begin to lag. He countered those slow to start the day's work by "eating my breakfast in the field. Some of them are not pleased at it. . . . I told them I intended to charge them for . . . all the loss of time. I['m] done doing any slack business with them."[20]

A deeper challenge emerged to Oberry and to the rule of white managers. Black workers in the region sought to know what their "rights" were. In April 1867, they called on the head of the Freedmen's Bureau to convene a public meeting in Newbern, Alabama, about eight miles from the Cameron place, to inform them of their rights.[21]

The growing attention to rights came home to the Cameron place in May 1867. Wilson Oberry got word that one of the leading men of the Alabama plantation—Sandy Cameron, the foremost man on the place in slavery times, the carpenter who made handcuffs for the recalcitrant and kept watch on the plantation entrance gate—had been appointed as a delegate to the "big meeting in Montgomery in the first of June," the convention to rewrite the state constitution. "It has been kept secret from me until a few days ago," Oberry wrote. "If he says he does go he will stay there for he shan't come back here." It turned out the rumor was wrong. The delegate was a Greensboro black carpenter with a similar-sounding name: Landy Charles.[22] But when another freedman proposed to go to the big speaking in town, Oberry repeated the threat. "I told him if he went he would go at his own risk. So no more came. I went out and gave them a talk and they all seem to be satisfied."[23]

By June 1867, however, Wilson Oberry seems to have realized that threats and talks had their limits. The manager needed someone inside the workforce to lead by example. That was the hardest-working man on the place, Paul Hargis.

The manager may have taken a cue about Paul Hargis from Paul Cameron himself. Cameron had made a quick visit to Alabama in March 1867.[24] The landowner knew that members of Hargis's family had served the Camerons long and well since their purchase by his father in 1829. He knew also that in 1865 and 1866, while a freedman on the Piedmont plantation, Paul Hargis had stuck to his work and his contract, steering clear of defiance by others. In slavery times, Paul Cameron had occasionally demonstrated his gratitude to favored workers—and sought to cement ties to selected "trusty men"—by giving a reward for exemplary service. It may be that he gave some such signal of partiality to Paul Hargis, and to his manager, at the end of the Alabama visit in March 1867. In later years, Paul Hargis's story of arrival in Alabama suggested such a special connection. Not only had the two Pauls ostensibly come out on a coach together, but before Paul Cameron left, he gave Paul Hargis "a bag of gold." Both men likely did journey partway by coach in 1867, though not together and not at the same time. And while a bag of gold did not pass into Paul Hargis's hands, perhaps a gold coin did, as a sign of favor.

With Paul Hargis providing a "great advantage to me," Wilson Oberry hoped that his workers would harvest the large crop that they had planted. All would be well for him and his foreman, the manager felt in late July 1867, "if I have no misfortunes."[25]

In the second week of August, uncertain weather and unsettled politics challenged the accord—and Paul Hargis's sway—on the Alabama plantation. The crops needed rain. Without rain, the growth of the cotton plant would stall, the bolls of cotton would be slow to open, and, disastrously, the plants would prove vulnerable to army worms, which devoured the green buds of cotton bolls. There were no worms yet in the immediate neighborhood, the manager reported. But "I hear a great complaint of them in Marengo County," just to the south. "I still flatter myself to make a very good crop of cotton," Wilson Oberry affirmed. But he knew that if the promise of high cotton vanished, the incentive for work would wane.[26]

A more immediate threat to the plantation equilibrium than drought and worms was the radicalization of politics in the region. In 1867, the state legislature had divided Greene County into two counties. Greene remained the county to the west, with Eutaw as the county seat. The eastern half became Hale County, with Greensboro as the county seat. Back in May, when Wilson Oberry's stern talk had deterred his workers from going to political meetings in Newbern and Greensboro, the county's black leaders were just beginning to organize potential voters in Hale. The tone of the two foremost Hale leaders was conciliatory. Alex Webb, an ex-slave who'd become a Greensboro saddle maker and who'd been appointed registrar of voters, and his colleague James Green, a former field hand who'd become a carpenter in Greensboro, urged blacks to keep to their contracts and to work industriously.[27] At the same time, they assiduously sought to register freedmen. Moderation disappeared in the second week of June 1867—a month before Oberry named Paul Hargis the head of the hoes on the Cameron place. On the main street of Greensboro, a white man named John Orrick killed black registrar Alex Webb. Different stories surrounded the murder—that the two were rivals for the same woman, that the white man said no black man would ever register him. The assassination and the escape of the killer incensed blacks and led James Green to call for freedmen to arm themselves. Rumors circulated that if the assassin or those who helped him weren't punished, the town would burn.[28]

Instead of arson, James Green channeled black anger into the mobilization of voters. Green became the new registrar of voters and struck a tone of defiance. At a political rally in nearby Eutaw, Alabama, when a local sheriff tried to knock him off the stage or shoot him, Green stood his ground. Armed blacks accompanied him back from the rally and fired their weapons in the air when he reached home—a salute that frightened some whites into thinking a "race war" had begun.[29] More important, James Green became the head of the Union League in the county. Planters and managers saw the very existence of the Union League as a menace. Certainly under James Green's bold leadership it was. Despite threats and intimidation, the registration of blacks as voters—and the schooling of them in their rights as citizens and workers—became the singular achievement of the Union League.

Voter registration and Union League meetings had a dramatic impact on the Cameron plantation. Every man on the place registered to vote on August 3, 1867. The prompt result, as Oberry reported, was that "the colored people have not moved as well as they did before." A week later, there was a great dinner and speaking in Greensboro. This time Oberry made no attempt to interfere—every hand walked fifteen miles to Greensboro and back. They "came home with a great many reports." Some "said they were to have the land and the growing crop on it. One or two said they understood no such things." All belonged to the Union League and embraced its message: "They say that they are in favor of the old flag, that the Yankee fought for their freedom." Oberry "talked with a great many of them," disputing whether League leaders and the Yankees were really their friends, but he concluded that "they will believe nothing our people tell them." A deepening slowdown replaced the rhythm that he and Paul Hargis had established. "There is negroes on the place that if you asked them to do anything, say to go to the gin house," they just turned away, Oberry said. "They talk of nothing now but Union League. . . . They say now they just begin to feel their freedom and equal rights with the white man."[30]

The plantation manager made no mention of where Paul Hargis stood on the "great many reports" that came back from the Union League meeting. Paul Hargis may have been one of the few who heard no promise of handing over land and crops to the freedmen, a promise that indeed most League leaders avoided making. What is clear is that by the end of August 1867, both the manager and the head of the hoes had a potential rival for leadership on the Cameron plantation. His name was Brister Reese, and he was one of the men Oberry had hired at the start of the year. Brister Reese was an organizer for the Union League.

Born in South Carolina in 1833, Brister Reese was brought to Alabama with enslaved relatives in the 1840s. In slavery times, his owner's plantation was adjacent to that of James Green's owner. It's likely that Reese and Green came to know each other while in bondage. By the summer of 1867, Reese had become a coordinator for James Green and the League in the rural southern part of the county. Literate, numerate, and ambitious, Brister Reese would become a teacher, landowner, and state legislator by 1874.[31] His start as an organizer began on the Cameron place, which he used as a base to mobilize freedmen from the area. When whites blocked League rallies in Greensboro, Reese sought alternative sites in the countryside. He met predictable resistance from planters who refused to have League meetings on their lands. Unexpected obstruction came from the local agent of the Freedmen's Bureau, who saw the League and its leaders as challengers to his authority. To no avail, Brister Reese and the county's most prominent white Radical Republican, physician William Blackford, "argued all day" with the agent, who "countenanced no League" or League meetings. Reese—whom Cameron's manager derisively called "Boy Brister"—"came home disgusted." Writing in early September 1867, the manager thought nonetheless that "the negroes will carry the day."[32]

As it turned out, on the Cameron plantation it was not the manager, his foreman, or the Union League organizer who gained the upper hand in 1867. It was the army worm. The "great misfortune" that Wilson Oberry had hoped to avoid came to the place and ravaged the cotton crop in the span of two weeks.[33] "I find it is no use in making any calculations on cotton crops," a deflated Wilson Oberry wrote in late September 1867. "It looks to me that we are never to get rid of the worm any more."[34]

Earlier in the summer of 1867, with his arrangement with Paul Hargis working well, the "hands never working better," and hopes high for a large cotton crop, Wilson Oberry had made a startling proposal to Paul Cameron. Would Cameron consider selling the plantation to the former overseer? Of course, even with a bonanza crop, there was no way that Oberry could afford the entire place on his own. Later he explained that his plan was to sell off the plantation in small plots. "I thought if you would sell the land, I could probably sell it off in pieces and have enough for myself." Oberry didn't say whether he'd market to black buyers as well as whites.[35]

Cameron wrote back in October to ask if Oberry was serious about the offer to buy. By then, the manager's expectations for the crop had gone from "good" to "tolerable" to "poor" to "ruined": "my year's labor is in a manner all throwed away."[36] Even with land selling for disastrously low prices that Cameron would never consider—$2 an acre, 10¢ an acre— Oberry backed off, writing, "I do not wish to buy the land and nobody at this time wishes to buy any part of the place." He doubted even that he could afford to rent—"it would cost me too much" to rent the whole place, and such an undertaking would wreck him if the cotton crop fell short again. "Now is no time for a poor man to get in debt. And this plantation you know is very poor," he noted, and offered instead to manage the place for another year. He wanted to know—and know soon—if the planter wished him to continue, as "I am compelled to have a home some where."[37]

Were freedmen and -women on the Cameron plantation, like the manager, looking for a home as well as a workplace? The people "on the place wishes to stay," Wilson Oberry reported in October 1867. Despite the disappointment with the crop, the Cameron people were "very anxious to make a bargain" well before the usual contract time at the end of the year. The manager didn't say why. Certainly there were reasons to remain. Ahead of his fellow managers, Cameron's manager had delegated authority, making Paul Hargis the intermediary who set the pace of work. Beyond that, Oberry made it clear that he would no longer ask those who stayed to cultivate all the cleared land, with its maddeningly inconsistent soils and results. He would have them work only "the good spots of land" that promised the best return for their labors. Paul Hargis and his fellow workers had to be aware that there were competing options. Some owners were renting land to blacks, others offering a third or even a half of their crop to acquire workers. Oberry proposed to counter those lures by planning to "work Negroes in families next year."[38]

Cameron went to Alabama in December 1867 to decide for himself what to do with his plantation there. The visit confirmed the worst. All debts were worthless, all land values had "sunk to a low point." With the second successive crop failure in 1867 and no assurance of a better outcome in the future, Cameron concluded he had to cease being an absentee planter. If he continued, it would fall to him to provide mules, tools, and plows for his place, and to supply money for his manager and meat for his workers. He rented his 1,600-acre plantation to Wilson Oberry for the sum of $2,000 a year. The trip and its results, Cameron confided to his wife, unsettled him so that he could "hardly write a letter my nerves are so out of order—as you will see by this hasty sheet." Never again would he "come out here for *nothing*." En route back, the misery continued, as he encountered strangers, Yankees, "soldiers, officers, merchants, and adventurers of all sort, men and women." Most disheartening were native white southerners in districts where he feared "the white man will come out & give it up to the Negro."[39]

In his harried notes about the trip to Alabama, Cameron never once mentioned the name of Paul Hargis or any other black worker on his place. As he later explained to his wife, his silence was deliberate. Stung by what he perceived as the ingratitude of his former slaves, he declared that "of the blacks we take no account as we have no interest in them outside of daily services."[40] Though he continued to receive letters with details about Paul Hargis and others, he declined to write about them in letters of his own.

Paul Cameron never returned to Alabama.

⁊

With full authority to run the plantation as he saw fit in 1868, Wilson Oberry immediately implemented the main element of his plan: working the land using families. The first bonus was the return of Jim Hargis, who had moved away from the Cameron place the year before. Paul Hargis and his older brother Jim were each put in charge of a small group of workers, consisting of their wives and other relatives. Two others were named "head men" of family groups.[41] Sandy Cameron had been the carpenter and gatekeeper of the Alabama plantation in slavery times; after the war, Oberry had reported, "Sandy had stuck with me like a man." Their ties had deepened in the fall of 1867, when Sandy Cameron was arrested and convicted of petty theft. The manager saved him from jail by paying his fine and becoming his "surety"—in modern terms, his parole officer. The next spring, Sandy Cameron publicly renounced the Union League and the Republican Party.[42] The other leader, Wesley, was identified only by his first name. A former "driver" on the Alabama plantation in the 1850s, Wesley in 1868 became the other head man, and did "not mind whipping them no more than he did in slavery times."[43]

Oberry called the family groups "squads," as did other planters and managers. The metaphor was military, echoing the soldierly language of the war just ended. The plantation manager was called "captain"—and indeed, the former overseer (who had not served in the war) now was called Captain Oberry. On the Cameron place, however, the reality was anything but military. Modeled after the system worked out with Paul Hargis as "head of the hoes," each squad leader was the head of family members and others under him. Authority was dispersed and delegated.

For the first half of 1868, the results astounded Wilson Oberry. The black families planted a heavy crop of cotton and worked zealously under the direction of the Hargis brothers and the two other squad leaders. "I have the best lot of hands in Hale County," Oberry boasted to Paul Cameron in early April. Each squad ditched its own portion of the plantation— "the best ditching that has been done on the place in ten years." Each head man "attends to his own mules, but Jim beats them all attending to his team." Now the de facto planter, Oberry wrote in proprietary terms. "My people" had good gardens; all were "behaving well and doing well— goes to work in due time and obeys all orders," he said, adding, "I have the best crop of cotton that I have ever had." When neighbors came over, they applauded the laborers. "There have been several of my neighbors over and they say they never believe[d] that free people would ever have cut out as regular a crop."[44] Report after report sang with optimism and confidence and pride.

Family leaders and the chance to work in families on the Cameron place provided the incentive to do well. With the prospect of a bonanza crop, Oberry wrote in mid-June 1868, they all had "no doubt of making a plenty."[45]

◡◢◌

It was not to be. Once again, the weather turned against the crop. In mid-August 1868, the manager reported that the plantation had endured eight weeks of drought, followed by "three weeks of as hard a rain" as he ever saw. The brutal combination caused the cotton crop to shed most of its bolls. Then came the scourge that had brought ruin the previous two years—the army worm. Swarming over the crop, the worms stripped the plants of leaves and remaining bolls in a single week. The manager and the black families saw the harvest and their hopes wiped out. Oberry assured Cameron that he had packed cotton "enough to pay all of my debts"—but "not enough to pay me for my trouble." Demoralization set in; work slacked off; a mule was stolen. Neither Paul Hargis nor his brother Jim nor other family leaders could hold the line. People tended their gardens and consumed their allowances of meat but made little effort to salvage what was left of the crop. "They have not worked for the last three months," Oberry bemoaned in November. "It is a tuff business now to farm it with free Negroes."[46] What workers could have done after the succession of plagues—drought, driving rain, worms—isn't clear. Good as the terms were at the outset of 1868—delegated authority, work on better lands, self-supervision, a fourth of the crop—they could not offset the bleak reality. At the end of the year, there would be little to divide.

By the fall of 1868, escape was on the minds of many. Planters began to think of abandoning the region and starting anew in the West. California was the fantasy of whites as they imagined a more remunerative world.[47] For the most prominent black leader of the county, still the head of the Union League, there was a more distant refuge—Liberia. James K. Green circulated pamphlets about Liberia and changed the name of the county's Union League chapter to the Loyal League and Liberia. Alabama blacks who left for Liberia, he proposed, would be better off in a nation that belonged to people of color. Those left behind, less numerous, could drive better bargains.[48] The exodus idea was far-fetched, but the impulse to depart was deep-seated.

For those going nowhere—the majority rooted by means and family to where they were—there was yet another way out: elections. The fall of 1868 was the presidential election, and Ulysses S. Grant was the Republican presidential candidate. It would be the first time that freedmen got to vote for a president of the United States. If Grant won that November, more than a few freedmen imagined, some great good would befall them.[49] They would not be the last voters to think that their ballots would bring a tangible gain.

In mid-January 1869, two accounts, a week apart, came to Paul Cameron on the state of affairs in Alabama. The narratives could not have been more different. Writing from Greensboro on January 23 about his two plantations located near the town, planter Allen C. Jones was pleased with the contracts signed by his 175 hands. The year before they had produced 590 bales of cotton. "At the prices ruling this season, that leaves cotton still the best business that I know of—or at least the best that I can engage in," Jones noted. Not only was the planter "entirely satisfied with the year's operations," but so were his workers: "The freedmen are greatly encouraged with their success & have gone to work with a *Will* that they have not exhibited since in their language *Freedom come about*."[50]

Wilson Oberry's report, written just a week before, was mired in gloom. Yes, his hands had just signed a contract—the first in the neighborhood. But there had "been no work done by the freedmen in a month and they have not gone to work yet." "People underminded each other" and used "all sorts of inducements" to lure workers away from their neighbors. A "great many persons have rented them their plantations and mules and it has turned them all fools." Some places were abandoned entirely. If the competition continued, the manager could imagine that "in about another year they will about take the Place and give a man the fourth." With successive crop failures fresh in memory and doubts about the future, Oberry expected to be hard pressed to work Cameron's place. The manager pledged to "try my luck again this year and hope for better luck." But he was edgy: "I will write to you when my mind is better sittle."[51]

Poor land and poor harvests had brought the Cameron workers and plantation manager to a crossroads. Two months earlier, in late November, some had wanted "to bargain now." It seems likely the number included Paul and Jim Hargis. It was the manager who delayed, "waiting to see what sort of bargain the neighbors are going to make." Oberry didn't say why some wished to stay despite the poor yield for their year's work and the widespread resort to renting. But in an unexpected postscript to his otherwise glum letter to Cameron, the manager shed light on why *he* chose to carry on—and perhaps hinted at why Paul Hargis and his brother persevered as well.

Oberry again asked about purchasing the plantation: "Mr. Cameron. What would you take for the Place, payable in Cotton, and how many years will you give me to pay it in, making a title when payed for. You know the place. You know there is a great deal of this land [that is poor] and I think you ought to favor me more so than any one else. I am getting old and I would like to leve my family a home."[52]

It was no secret to Oberry, and hardly news to the head men, that Paul Cameron was determined to sell his Alabama plantation. Oberry was blunt—when all was said and done about workers, weather, and worms, both the manager and the planter knew that the underlying trouble was the land. The mismatch of soils and preponderance of poor land made it a gamble for Oberry even to rent for the $2,000 he had agreed to pay. At the same time, ongoing losses and the plantation's declining value meant the place might be within striking distance to buy, allowing him to provide his family a home. The truly bold declaration was that Cameron *"ought to favor me more so than any one else."*[53] Oberry didn't feel the need to spell out the reasons. He had worked for Cameron for going on a dozen years, first as overseer and then as plantation manager. He had stayed doggedly loyal to the landowner through wartime and Reconstruction, while managers on other places had given up. Cameron had needed him, depended on him, and always been able to count on him. A year later, Oberry would become yet more outspoken: "Some say if I left the place that it would be abandoned."[54] As the manager saw it, Paul Cameron owed him.

Could Paul Hargis, Jim Hargis, and Sandy Cameron have put forth such a claim, or have dared to make such a veiled threat, to their former owner? They, too, might have felt that Paul Cameron owed them, that he ought to favor them for their years of "former good conduct"—as Cameron's son-in-law in 1865 delicately termed decades of unremitting work in bondage and thereafter in freedom.[55] But to *claim* such a debt surely would have jeopardized the chance to receive it. It was a dicey business to demand noblesse oblige. What the Cameron ex-bondsmen did share with Wilson Oberry, declared in actions rather than words, was a desire for permanence. Title or no title, the Alabama plantation was a place where they wished to stay.

The year ahead put that wish to the test.

From the vantage point of the plantation manager, things fell apart in 1869. No longer did Wilson Oberry praise the squad system. No more did he single out Paul Hargis, his brother Jim Hargis, or the two other head men for their leadership, or the freedmen under them for their good work. On the contrary, whether describing the weather, the workers, or the cotton crop, all was lamentation. Throughout the spring, rains mired the plantation and eroded all the understandings of the previous two years. In mid-January, Oberry reported that three weeks of incessant rain had made plowing impossible. Two months later, it was more of the same: "still having rain," "very little of plowing done." Unable to break up the mud-laden land, Oberry and most others had not yet planted their cotton. Exasperation had led a few neighbors to plant without plowing: Oberry thought them desperate. "There never was a country in a worse fix," he remarked. "God only know what is to become of us."[56]

Unsurprisingly, the plantation workers balked at trudging through the muck. Noted Oberry, "In the way of farming, you can't get negroes to half work this year. They have less notion of work than I have ever seen. They will sign a contract and work a while and get an allowance and of meat and run away."[57] In years past, Paul Hargis had been able to rally families with the promise that a good start and good effort would bring decent rewards, but not anymore. Why should they strain against the odds? Not only was the weather against them, but the successive crop shortfalls meant that the manager had no money to restock the plantation's mules or to replace its dulled plows and tools. At the end of 1869, after Paul Cameron's son-in-law visited the Alabama plantation, he reported that the place and manager looked exhausted. "Not half enough team on the place & what there is nearly all worthless. Twelve broken down mules on as many hundred acres of cleared land is a poor show, & looking at the team I wonder how they will make a crop at all."[58]

In fact, Cameron's son-in-law George Collins was doing more than passing through Alabama in December 1869. Collins was aggressively recruiting workers for his labor-hungry plantation in Tunica, Mississippi. He returned to Tunica with twelve "stragglers" from the vicinity of Cameron's Alabama place, and he received promises from "eight or ten" of Oberry's workers that "they will come out at Christmas." Collins thought "their promises are not to be much depended on." But a month later, when he sent the Tunica plantation physician to Alabama to follow up, the doctor came back with seven people and the report that "a good many Negroes left [Oberry] besides those that came here." Collins thought that "most of the desirable hands will come here eventually."[59]

There were two men, however, who made it clear that they were staying put: "Paul & Jim Hargis stick to Oberry against all comers."[60]

The Hargis brothers' commitment kept others in place. While the plantation manager did lose a third of the thirty workers he had in 1869, twenty signed on for 1870, with Paul and Jim Hargis as their squad leaders.[61] Sandy Cameron, too, was determined to stay. Paul Cameron's son-in-law didn't ask or say why. Nor did Wilson Oberry explain. His letters routinely focused on the state of the crops and performance of the workers. Certainly no one remained on the Cameron place out of satisfaction with the 1869 cotton crop. To Oberry, 1869 was the worst of his dozen years there as manager.

Paul Hargis and his brother and Sandy Cameron had a longer view of their time in Alabama. They were among the handful still left of the 114 people who had been marched 400 miles from their homes in North Carolina in November 1844. They had seen ten men and women die and be buried within twenty months of arriving, fellow expatriates taken in the prime of life. At the end of their first month in Alabama, they had learned that the young planter who had brought them out rued his new plantation and the relative who'd set him up to buy it. In 1856, they had seen thirty-five of their number removed to Mississippi, and in 1864, saw sixty-five others hurried back to North Carolina. Could 1869 have been the worst of their twenty-five years in Alabama? Hardly.

All the same, in that quarter century, they had made a life on the Alabama plantation. Paul Hargis and his brother Jim, their wives, their sisters and their sisters' families had been brought out together in the 1844 forced migration. Paul Hargis had chosen to return to Alabama in 1867 to reunite with his family. In deciding to stay on the plantation, forty-two-year-old Paul Hargis and his forty-six-year-old brother did more than "stick to Oberry." They stood by each other and by other family members rooted on the Alabama plantation. "Against all comers," they would stick to the land.

Eight ✑ "If They Can Get the Land"

Since 1845, Paul Cameron had seen his Alabama purchase as a grievous mistake, and been ready to sell it, even at one point to abandon it. After 1865, he'd received inquiries from whites who knew the land was up for grabs—his former overseer, two of his Alabama neighbors—but had never gotten an offer firm or credible enough to take. That Paul Hargis or other freedmen would have the wherewithal to buy the plantation surely seemed far-fetched. Even if they had the means, there was no indication that Paul Cameron was prepared to join planters he scorned in 1867 as ready "to give it up to the Negro."[1] For all the Hargis brothers' hard work, it would take more than "good conduct" for them to be allowed to acquire any part of Paul Cameron's land. Unexpected events—and unexpected advocates in Alabama—would reward their perseverance.

✑

Cameron felt stymied until the end of 1869, when he received and heeded advice he hoped would set the stage for selling out on favorable terms to white buyers. Asked for his advice, Alabama resident and fellow planter Allen C. Jones was candid. Under manager Wilson Oberry's rule, much of the land had gone fallow, abandoned to broomsedge when the manager decided to have his workers farm only the most productive parts of the plantation. Though not worthless, the abandoned portion of the place *looked* worthless, and could never bring a fair price if put on the market. Allen Jones thought that if Cameron ordered the recultivation of his abandoned lands, as well as the cosmetic relocation of workers' cabins and the manager's dwelling upon those lands, the worth of the whole place would rise. In the meantime, he believed, the prospective arrival of the railroad to the county would swell all land values. If made, the improvements he called for would get Cameron the price—and the riddance—he wanted.

The key to Jones's plan was labor—a labor force instructed to replant the fallow land and to relocate the cabins. Jones told Cameron that labor required rehiring the plantation manager, Wilson Oberry, though his deficiencies were myriad. Since 1866, the plantation's production of cotton had gone from bad to worse. Large numbers of his workers had left or were looking for other places. The lingering illness of Oberry's wife had turned him to drink. Nonetheless, Paul Hargis, his brother Jim, and the freed people who remained with them on the Cameron place were committed to Oberry. A neighboring planter, aware of their commitment, had made an offer to the manager to change plantations. The neighbor thought—and Jones thought—that if Oberry went, most of his workers would likely go with him. "I was really forced to employ him," Jones confided to Cameron. Otherwise, the plantation might be deserted.[2]

Allen Jones's plan for the plantation's improvement and sale might have worked but for unforeseen missteps. Before Allen Jones gave his counsel to Cameron, there had been another possibility for disposing of the land. Paul Cameron's son-in-law George Collins had passed through Alabama in December 1869 on his way back to Mississippi. Stopping at Cameron's place, Collins had also appraised the plantation, the manager, and the prospects for a sale. He learned that neighboring farmer John Webster, the onetime overseer of the Cameron place from 1849 through 1856, had proposed to buy the west side of the 1,600-acre plantation—1,120 acres—for $8 an acre, to be paid out over a number of years. The son-in-law thought that by far this was the best Cameron could do, and advised accepting the offer.[3] He told Webster of his endorsement. At a chance encounter, Webster met with Wilson Oberry, who wondered aloud why he'd not heard from Cameron about renewing Oberry's rental agreement for 1870. Confident of his impending purchase, Webster told Oberry that he "had better go and find a home," a comment that, Oberry wrote Cameron, "cut me very close." Allen Jones's proposal, which Cameron accepted, quashed the sale to John Webster. But Oberry learned how close he'd come to "being cut out of a home," and he felt betrayed. He realized that only the offer of hire from a rival planter had kept him from dismissal.[4]

In reality, those who had saved the manager's job were Paul Hargis and his brother Jim, and the workers and family members who labored in their squads—those who stayed with him "against all comers." The whole experience rankled Wilson Oberry. For many months, he was incommunicado, sending no reports to North Carolina. Cameron finally wrote in mid-1870 to ask if anything was wrong. The manager's candid reply revealed that he had learned the limits of friendship. He knew now, he confided, that longtime neighbor John Webster was not a friend. Colonel Allen C. Jones was not a friend. And Paul Cameron? "I acknowledge I was treated a little shabby," he wrote. "I thought it was [rough] of you to tell me to hunt a home," he added, and continued: "Friendship don't extend very far in the neighborhood, and it is more harder to have a friend a thousand miles away." Of course, he still wished that he and the gentleman from North Carolina could be friends. Cameron could still count on *him*. "It is believed by some people that if I was off the place that they could buy it for a little or nothing. I do not [say] that to flatter you for a home"— that is, to entreat Cameron to keep him.[5]

Oberry made no mention of how the Hargis brothers had stood by him. Had their steadfastness made them "friends"? He didn't say and might never have put it that way, at least to Cameron. But he and the brothers knew. Commitment had proved them true.

Once Wilson Oberry had learned of his near-eviction and had mistakenly identified the conspirators as his neighbor John Webster and planter A. C. Jones, he took action against them. Both of them had the right under his 1867 rental agreement with Paul Cameron to act as Cameron's agents and observers, and in that capacity could come on the land at any time. No more. He banned them. The only person to whom he would any longer extend that privilege was Cameron's son-in-law George Collins—a man who lived in northwest Mississippi and came to Alabama

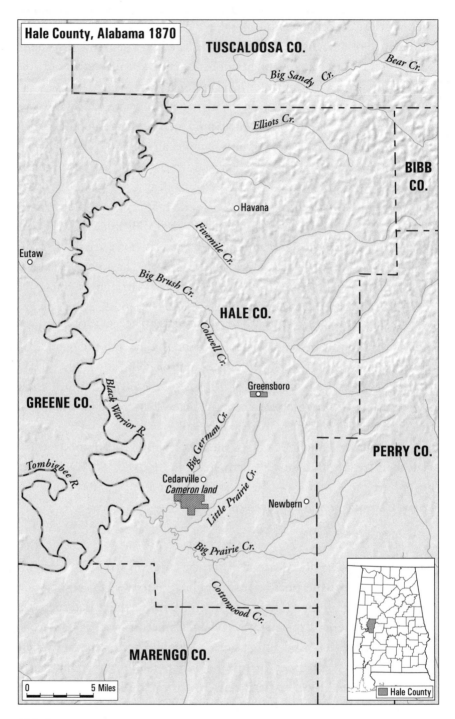

Hale County, 1870.

once a year.[6] Oberry didn't know that if one wanted to look for a culprit in the case, it was George Collins. It was Collins who had recommended the immediate sale of the western two-thirds of the Alabama place to John Webster. It was Collins's assurance that gave John Webster the boldness to tell Wilson Oberry—albeit at an unplanned meeting—that he'd better look for another home.

The banishment of Cameron's on-site observers put an end to the plan for the improvement of the land and its looks. Oberry continued to have his workers cultivate the better part of the land and let the rest go fallow. The cosmetic relocation of dwellings—the cabins of workers, the house of Oberry himself—never happened. The outcome for Cameron's 1,600 acres, with two-thirds in broomsedge and a dilapidated look to the whole, was more diminished value.

For Paul Hargis and his brother and their families, what was the gain of staying with Wilson Oberry? Measured by bales of cotton and year-end profits, Mississippi promised to be the better place, at least if the crop of 1870 there was the same as that for 1869.[7] On some places nearby, they might now rent land for a fixed sum or a share of the crop, with no manager to answer to. They declined the options—wisely, as it turned out. The crop of 1870 on Cameron's Mississippi place turned out to be a disappointment. Workers who had left a plantation near Greensboro to rent elsewhere came back to work on shares.[8] For the Hargis brothers and their families, the best bet seemed to stay in place and to work the most productive portion of Cameron's land with a manager who had long since delegated supervision to them. In the meantime, Paul and Jim Hargis quietly undertook a complementary arrangement. In the summer of 1870, they not only worked land managed by Wilson Oberry but also, as tenants or sharecroppers, labored on an adjacent farm. If worms or weather again crippled the crop on Cameron's place, they'd still have a chance to come out ahead.

The Hargis brothers may have been both sobered and heartened to learn that Cameron had declined to sell the property to Oberry for a sum payable in cotton over a number of years, as the manager had proposed in January 1869.[9] The Hargis brothers unquestionably would need a time arrangement to buy land, something like what Oberry had proposed. If

Wilson Oberry shared his proposal and Cameron's refusal with them, they were not deterred. They chose to remain on the spot. They would be among the first to know when Cameron's moment of decision finally came, and would be on-site if the planter changed his mind.

For a time it appeared as if a general elevation of land values would put the Cameron place out of reach to any buyers save fellow planters, despite the plantation's acres of broomsedge, its hands-off manager, and its record of worm-infested crops and erratic soils. The external catalyst was the prospect of a railroad coming to the county.

As with other southern states in the late 1860s, Alabama was swept by the hope that railroads would galvanize economic recovery from the devastation of war and defeat. Railroad promoters sought funds from counties as well as the state government in the form of bonds, which required approval by the electorate. The railroad promoted for Greensboro and Hale County was the Memphis and Selma line. The leading local supporter of the Memphis and Selma was the omnipresent Allen C. Jones.[10] The Democrat was joined in a striking alliance by the leading black Republican of the county, James K. Green. The Radical Republican Green and the conservative Democrat Allen Jones made speeches and appeared on the same platforms together, showing that they could collaborate in campaigning for followers to back the railroad. Green promised that he would bring "his people" on board for the county-wide vote on the bond. When the vote came, not all blacks followed their leader. Some rural blacks, including those in the precinct where the Hargis brothers lived, opposed it. But the bond passed.[11] With the railroad "slowly but surely" making its way toward Greensboro, lands were in demand and "the feeling in the country is rather buoyant," Jones reported to Cameron. For a time, too, it appeared as well that the region's cotton crop of 1870 would escape the plagues that had doomed harvests of previous years. Even freedmen were optimistic, Jones added, and "working well."[12] Merchants painted their stores and the county repaired its courthouse as the town of Greensboro expectantly spruced itself up to receive the railroad.

Once again, the bonanza was not to be. The Memphis and Selma Railroad had counted not only on county and state bonds but also on investment from Europe, in particular from Germany. On July 9, 1870, war broke out between France and Prussia. The Franco-Prussian War, which lasted eleven months, chilled German investors; they pulled out. The head of the railroad, Nathan Bedford Forrest, scrambled to replace German funds with money from New York.[13] He got none. Railroad construction, which had come within a few miles of Greensboro, with Chinese and Irish laborers and a hundred black convicts doing the work, slowed and finally halted.[14] Forrest, the daring general of the late Confederacy and in 1867 a founder and first head of the Ku Klux Klan, sought to sustain black and white support for the railroad with a call for racial cooperation. He wanted "every shade of politics and all colors to come together, to work hand in hand." The war "was the means of Providence to liberate the colored man, and he would not alter the result if he could. [This] was no time now to look to the past."[15] It was to no avail. Railroad construction froze, short of Greensboro. The state legislature refused funds to bail it out. When the crop of 1870 turned out no better than in years before, land values fell back.[16] The good news, at least for blacks who had aspirations to buy land, was that the setbacks kept land costs from soaring out of reach.

There was another way for landless people to acquire a farm in post–Civil War America: homesteads. First advanced in the late 1840s, the idea of homesteading was to offer public land to settlers at no cost. If a settler stayed on homestead land for five years and made improvements on it, he would acquire title to anywhere from 40 to 160 acres. Before 1860, the South had opposed the policy of homesteading, fearful that the majority of settlers drawn to "free soil" in the west would come from states without slavery. Unless southerners could bring their enslaved workers into the western territories, the territories would come into the Union as free states, and the South would inevitably be outnumbered in Congress and outvoted in presidential elections—and thus be unable to defend slavery.

Secession paved the way for passage of the Homestead Act in 1862. With overwhelming support from the Republican Party and the states that remained in the Union, the bill passed the Senate and then the House and was signed by the president on May 20, 1862. Public land in Kansas, Colorado, the Dakotas, the Nebraska territory, and the High Plains—millions of acres—drew hundreds of thousands of settlers, not just from the East but from Europe as well. While there were 97 million acres in the public domain in the South, much of the land was in forests or swamps. The best land was to the west. Men of all ages, and women and families as well, joined the exodus. Whether young or older, single or married, male or female, almost all of those who homesteaded in the 1860s and early 1870s had a common characteristic: they were white.[17]

How might people of color become homesteaders? The most drastic idea came from the most radical member of Congress, Thaddeus Stevens, who advocated confiscation of the lands of planters, breaking up their plantations, and dividing their property among former enslaved workers. The Stevens proposal gave rise to reports that each freedman might receive forty acres and a mule, or get some other "great benefit" from the federal government. Not just the opposition of Lincoln's successor— former slaveholder Andrew Johnson of Tennessee—doomed confiscation. Among more moderate Republicans, the principle of confiscation met firm opposition. If the government could seize the estates of planters, why couldn't it confiscate the property of corporations, bankers, and landholders in the North and the East, all in the name of equality or compensation? Confiscation proved to be a dead end as the way for ex-slaves to acquire land of their own.

Still, there was the vast public domain, millions of acres in the Midwest and the West—and the South—waiting for settlement and claims. But in every way, ordinary white settlers had the jump on freed people. They had means to travel. They had skill and experience in working land in more northern climes. They had political supporters to protect them from predators who might seek ways to filch from them. Advocates of homesteading for blacks proposed that land be set aside for former freedmen. The public land in the southern states would be a start, but since neighbors of those lands were white and implacably hostile, advocates also looked for set-asides in the Midwest.[18]

But none of the plans for black landholding came to fruition—not confiscation, not set-asides. How, then, could blacks who came out of the war with "nothing but freedom" hope to gain land of their own?[19]

To blacks in the twentieth century living on the 1,600 acres that Paul Cameron owned in the nineteenth century, the answer is clear: "Paul Cameron caused them to be homesteaders." It was not the United States government. It was not the Homestead Act of 1862. To descendants, it was the former planter himself who gave Paul Hargis, Jim Hargis, Sandy Cameron, and a half dozen other freed people the opportunity to homestead.[20]

Deed and mortgage records in the Hale County Courthouse in Greensboro, Alabama, bear out the oral tradition. To be sure, Paul Cameron *sold* his land. He did not convey it on terms available under the Homestead Act—free land for occupants who lived on public land for five years and made improvements. Nonetheless, almost all Cameron land was sold to black purchasers on terms that made it feasible for farm laborers with no capital. They put no money down, were allowed to pay over five years, and could pay in cotton rather than cash. When several purchasers went beyond the five years, Paul Cameron continued to carry them, extending the time of payment until they could pay off. Acting as both seller and lender, he made their purchases possible. By the 1880s, purchasers had farms ranging from 30 to 240 acres, with most purchases falling between 80 and 160 acres.[21] Without Paul Cameron as seller and lender, not one of the black purchasers would have acquired an acre of his plantation, and they knew it.

New calculations had entered the Cameron plantation picture in mid-1872. In May, manager Wilson Oberry wrote the North Carolina landowner after a long silence. He had lived through two years of "the hardest times I ever witnessed in this world"; his health had deteriorated; now widowed, he dwelt alone. For the moment he was well again. He was still Cameron's true friend. But he'd made no money in those two years. If nothing changed, he might have to move to Mississippi, "where I could make something."

Then the manager switched to an unexpected subject. He asked Cameron whether he would set aside an acre of land for a church and also a school for the black people. Wilson Oberry knew that Cameron's plans were fluid—he might again rent the land, he might try once more to sell. Oberry knew he might not be part of those plans. Still, he wanted Cameron to "see my reasons for it." It was a business proposition. On plantations which had a church and a school, it was possible to "keep hands in the neighborhood. Where farmers had done this they invariably can get a plenty of hands." Whether Cameron rented or sold the plantation, the acre would serve Cameron's purpose.[22]

Oberry saved the surprise for the end of his letter: "They will pay for it in cash." The manager was acting as an intermediary—as an advocate for a proposal from blacks living on the land. He named no names of those he spoke for. Paul and Dicey Hargis were childless, and therefore had no need for a school, but his brothers and others did have children. And all could worship at a church. The black people there were ready to commit. If Cameron accepted their offer, the acre would be home to their church, their school, and their community. They were prepared to do more than work in the neighborhood. They were ready to anchor their lives and futures where they were. "Let me know," Oberry concluded his letter, "if they can get the land."[23]

As it turned out, Paul Cameron was also pondering the future of his Alabama land in mid-1872. But the prompt came from a different offer, close to home. That offer set in motion a chain of events that would finally spur Cameron to act on his long-held eagerness to sell the plantation. Less than a mile from where Paul Cameron dwelt in Hillsborough, North Carolina, was the Hillsborough Military Academy. Started in 1859, it had gone defunct after the war, and postwar hardship had kept the school empty. In 1872, Cameron got word that an outside group was eager to buy the building and start a new school there for young black students in the center of Hillsborough. Rather than let freed people take over the site, Cameron agreed to buy the building, and he set about trying to recruit a supervisor to revive the Military Academy.[24] Cameron didn't pay for the school at once. He made a down payment with a promise to pay the rest over time. Cameron needed cash, much more cash than might come from the sale of a single acre of land. He now had a pressing reason to sell every acre in Alabama.[25]

There was one lingering reason to hold back. If by some remote chance the presidential election of 1872 brought the defeat of Ulysses S. Grant and the Republican Party, Cameron was confident that southern land values would rise. Grant's reelection in the first week of November settled the issue. On November 8, 1872, Paul Cameron and his wife, Anne Ruffin Cameron, conveyed their power of attorney to a trusted agent in Alabama. They authorized him to sell their entire Black Belt plantation.

The person that Paul Cameron turned to was a nephew for whom he and his wife had the highest regard. Thomas Roulhac was the son of Cameron's in-laws. His mother was Catherine Ruffin Roulhac, Anne Ruffin Cameron's sister. His father was Joseph G. Roulhac, a Raleigh merchant to whom Paul Cameron had become close, with Cameron writing him jovial letters that invited him to visit the Cameron home and enjoy their bounty of fresh strawberries. Joseph Roulhac's sudden death in 1856 had left a void. Catherine Ruffin Roulhac had a tempestuous relationship with her enslaved house servant, sometimes thrashing her, other times showering her with affection. The two sons who'd grown up in their parents' Raleigh household had both fought in the Civil War. The war over, they saw their future in law and business. Paul Cameron took a caring uncle's interest in his nephew and celebrated when Thomas Roulhac got his law license in 1867: "He is one of the most manly and correct youths in the county. We all have high hopes of him in his professional life."[26]

The nephew decided to make a fresh start for himself outside the South, and ventured to California. It's not known what brought him halfway back across the continent to Greensboro, Alabama, in 1870. Perhaps he met disappointment in the West; perhaps he hoped he might make a better beginning where he was not a total stranger.[27] In Alabama he knew a friend of his parents who'd moved to Greensboro from North Carolina in the 1840s and had become one of the most successful planters and prominent men of the town: Allen C. Jones. The planter and town patriarch made the young North Carolinian welcome, and was pleased when his daughter Julia and the novice lawyer courted, became engaged, and married in November 1870. Thomas Roulhac took a short turn at managing his father-in-law's plantation, then relinquished that role to start a law practice in town. The newcomer's marriage and connections brought immediate inclusion among the elite of the community. He broke bread and played whist with the best men of Greensboro.[28] To his uncle in North Carolina, Thomas Roulhac seemed the perfectly placed person to carry out his wish to sell his place in Alabama—and to sell it fast.

When Paul Cameron and his wife assigned their power of attorney to their nephew, they put no restrictions on who might buy the land. The document made no mention of race. The only stated requirement was that Roulhac should accept no less than $8 an acre for the land.[29] It is possible that Paul Cameron told Thomas Roulhac in a private letter to favor the black workers who had long stayed on his place. The preserved Roulhac correspondence is thin and contains no letters from his uncle. All other evidence suggests that not color but cash, not favors but speed, constituted Cameron's foremost objectives.

Cameron thought that at the low price of $8 an acre, the land would go quickly. After all, in previous negotiations with John Webster, his one-time overseer and now neighboring farmer, the neighbor had agreed to that price, though Webster had since found other property more to his liking.

Cameron's edginess surfaced when his younger son asked for a supplement to his allowance. Cameron responded that he was strapped for cash. He'd put everything into the preemptive purchase of the Hillsborough Military Academy and was waiting impatiently for money from Alabama. "I have been disappointed in selling my Alabama lands which will cripple me in my purchase of the H.M.A.," he wrote his son, telling him that he had "not one single dollar to waste until that property is paid for." He couldn't see what was taking Thomas Roulhac so long.[30]

From his close ties with those who knew about the Cameron property—his father-in-law, Allen C. Jones, and other planters—Thomas Roulhac learned quickly that the plantation was not an easy sell, even at $8 an acre. "It is poor land, as you know," manager Wilson Oberry had written Cameron in 1868. It is "worn and exhausted," John Webster had declared in 1869. It would need to be recultivated to achieve its true worth, Jones confirmed at the end of that year.[31] When Roulhac received power of attorney at the end of 1872, nothing had been done to improve the place, nor had general land values gone up in the county. Hopes for a good season in the spring of 1873 ran afoul of bad weather, rot, drought, and worms. By summer it was clear there was to be yet another short crop. In the past, a short crop at least had brought a higher price for the cotton that was grown. Not in 1873. During the Civil War, when the North's naval blockade had shut off exports of the South's cotton to Europe, Great Britain had found new sources of cotton for its ravenous textile mills. Egypt and India had become large suppliers. Even though the Black Belt cotton crop fell short, foreign cotton exports and surging cotton production elsewhere in the South picked up the slack. The falling price of cotton helped explain why Roulhac found no buyers through the summer of 1873.[32]

Then came financial disaster—the Panic of 1873. In September, the country's leading financier failed, and in rapid order trading houses and banks suspended payments, one after another. The bank in Raleigh that held the funds of Paul Cameron's sister was among the institutions that refused to pay out money to its patrons. In Greensboro as in rest of the South, all credit was suspended, all payments stopped, all debts deferred. To Cameron's entreaties about the land sale, Roulhac could only reply that things were as bad as he had ever seen them: "This country is in a terrible fix. I have not the heart to write fully about it." The price of cotton was so ruinously low that Roulhac had it stored rather than sold. Land sales were impossible. The best and only thing that Cameron's agent could do was to keep "collecting your rents."[33]

Thomas Roulhac had become the collection agent for renting Cameron's 1,600 acres. He did not name his renters, nor did he designate them by color. It's not known for sure whether the Hargis brothers or Sandy Cameron were among them. What is certain is that by the end of 1873, Thomas Roulhac knew those who were on the Cameron land, knew their work and ability to pay their rent—and knew who the best prospects were for buying the land, if it came to that. He also handled legal cases that involved black clients. Thomas Roulhac had the knowledge to judge his renters' and clients' ability to pay.

The financial depression in no way diminished Paul Cameron's impatience to have his Alabama land sold, or his frustration with his nephew. Cameron's son Duncan picked up on his father's frustration, writing, "That Thomas Roulhac is a rascal!"[34] For Paul Hargis and his brother, the good news was that if Paul Cameron had any residual reluctance about selling to black buyers, it likely had vanished by the end of 1873. A half dozen years before, en route home from his last visit to Alabama, Cameron had found himself disgusted by white southerners who were surrendering land to freedmen.[35] In the years since, Cameron's closest friend and fellow planter in Mississippi, Archibald Wright, had declared himself among those prepared to sell his plantation to blacks. To Wright, white overseers had failed and white purchasers were nonexistent. It was either sell the land to freedmen or abandon it. Wright rationalized that land sales to blacks would make them taxpayers and responsible citizens who would see the virtue of stability and sound government. Paul Cameron's son-in-law George Collins concurred: selling worthless "wild lands" to freedmen was "good policy." But by 1873, Collins himself was ready to abandon the Delta.[36] He had found it impossible to manage the Tunica plantation with free black laborers and, as he confessed to his wife, had lost his hair and his self-respect in the futile effort.

One thing was for sure: if Cameron had changed his mind and was now willing to sell to blacks who gave him his price, he had little compunction about offending acquaintances in Alabama. Alabama had long since been a place the absentee landowner simply wished to divorce.

The same could not be said for Thomas Roulhac, Cameron's nephew and land agent. If he sold Cameron's land to Paul Hargis and other black buyers, he would have to answer to the best men and best families of his adopted home, Greensboro. He had married into the most prominent family in the county. He had been welcomed to the convivial gatherings of its leading men, had won their trust as a friend and their patronage as a lawyer.[37] If they felt that he should hold the color line with the sale of the Cameron plantation, even if it meant keeping his exasperated uncle on hold, no doubt Thomas Roulhac would have complied.

As it turned out, both political expediency and personal inclination encouraged Thomas Roulhac's choice of purchasers in 1874, and the terms of purchase as well. Early on, the few whites who had sold land to blacks had suffered reprisals. White sellers were shunned, black buyers shot.[38] That continued to be the case in Greene County, adjacent and to the west of Hale County. Goaded by an incendiary newspaper editor in the Greene County seat, Eutaw, and backed by resentful planters and white farmers, violence had come to be the way that Greene whites responded to black enfranchisement and self-assertion. The Ku Klux Klan virtually controlled Greene County. One by one, assailants killed off local Republican officials and Union League leaders, assassinating some on the road and brazenly gunning down others in the middle of town. To forestall lawsuits against indebted planters, arsonists torched the county courthouse in 1868.[39]

Though the Klan was active as well in Hale County, the editor of the Hale County newspaper, the *Alabama Beacon*, decried the politics of violence. Klansmen attacked blacks. They frequently threatened the white Republican probate judge of the county, physician William Blackford. Rarely did editor John Harvey have words of praise for the Union League, for black leader James K. Green, for white Republican probate judge Blackford, or for other Radicals. But to him, killing was not the way.[40] Rather, he and others thought that the task of whites was to persuade black voters to follow white leaders: let them know that whites respected their rights, remind them that whites were their authentic friends. The planter "electioneers with the freeman to secure his labor, the merchant to secure his custom—and why not the politician to secure his vote?"[41]

The editor of the *Alabama Beacon* had advice for freedmen as well as for whites. "Heed your best friends," he wrote. "Your children must grow up in the midst of friends, otherwise they will be a hopeless people for generations. Whites will never sell homesteads to those who persist in being their enemies."[42] And if blacks *did* heed those "best friends"? The message was understood: whites would sell land to blacks who said no to the Republican Party.

It was in this setting that Thomas Roulhac felt permitted, indeed empowered—at least by leaders of the white community—to sell Paul Cameron's plantation to black buyers. In his circle, there was no need for

Roulhac to explain or hide that decision, if it came to that. Rather, he could exemplify the very bargain that the editor and other leaders were advocating. Tellingly, in March 1874, after only four years in Greensboro, Thomas Roulhac was chosen mayor of the town without opposition. He would have no resistance from his friends if he decided to sell Paul Cameron's land to freedmen.[43]

By the summer of 1874, the word was out: if blacks could come up with the money, Cameron's plantation would be sold in parcels to them. Paul Cameron's nephew made a trade-off. He sold most of the land for more than the minimum of $8 an acre.[44] But almost all the purchases were to be paid over time.[45] Cameron would get his money, but none immediately. Cameron's letters to family members from 1875 to 1880 suggest that either Roulhac didn't explain or the planter didn't accept that this was the way—and likely the only way, given the ongoing economic depression—for the nephew to successfully sell the Alabama land. Roulhac chose buyers who he knew had the will and skill to complete a purchase. Brothers Paul and Jim Hargis, who had stood by the overseer, the planter, and the land for seven years, together bought a hundred acres for $8 an acre.[46] Sandy Cameron, the carpenter and most valued man of the plantation since the 1844 trek to Alabama, acquired land down in Eddyfield. He was one of the first to gain a home place.[47] Other purchasers for the most part either lived near the Cameron place or had been among the renters of 1873 and 1874. For all, Roulhac knew their reliability as farmers and potential purchasers. Some had side trades—a wagoner who did hauling for the town, a repairman of cotton gins—which provided added resources to pay off their mortgages.[48]

The action of his nephew made Paul Cameron both the seller and the lender whose extended credit made possible the completion of the purchases by the Hargis brothers and a half dozen others. Most of the purchases were formally confirmed on the first day of January 1875 and detailed in a letter to his uncle on February 15, 1875. Paul Cameron was relieved at the sales but vexed when he came to understand that he would have to wait—and wait, and wait—for his money.[49] The deeds were not formally conveyed and recorded until paid in their entirety. For Paul Hargis and his brother, that was 1884. For others as well, payments lagged into the 1880s.[50]

Descendants of the black buyers recalled it rightly. In their words, planter Paul Cameron "had homesteaded them." Whether his heart was in it was another matter.

Was Thomas Roulhac's heart in it? A year before he became mayor of the town, Roulhac worked with his father-in-law, Allen Jones, and other planters and white farmers to form a Hale County chapter of the national Grange. Founded in 1873, the Grange agricultural movement was designed to create the Patrons of Husbandry, a fraternal organization for farmers, to boost morale and to enable members to collectively negotiate better deals from railroads and merchants. The Greensboro Grange, formed in September 1873, had an additional purpose: to create a common front of planters and landowners in constraining black renters and sharecroppers, something that previous efforts had failed to accomplish.[51] Until 1873, black tenants had been able to use competition and holdouts to get incrementally better terms for themselves. A consequence of the shift to renting and to sharecropping—and the resulting absence of daily white supervision—was the tenant view that they had the right to sell their share of the crop. In growing numbers, black renters marketed their cotton to independent traders on the road, often at night. At these "deadfalls," as they were called, blacks could sell for a better price than the owner would get or profess to get. To white landowners, the unregulated marketing was theft pure and simple.[52] In 1874, with Allen C. Jones as chair and Thomas Roulhac as secretary, the Greensboro Grange called on planters to pay in wages rather than shares, and for the county to shut down the deadfalls and to punish those who operated or sold to them.[53] When Roulhac became mayor, one of the city's first actions was to extend the policy of leasing out those convicted of crimes—including the crime of deadfall sales—to coal mines or to neo-slave plantations.[54]

On both fronts—the Grange agenda and the convict lease system—Thomas Roulhac was part of the effort to rein in renters. An 1876 law to set license fees for emigration agents, who enticed blacks to work elsewhere, found decisive support from the very men who campaigned as the best friends of the freedman. Back in control of the state legislature, conservative Democrats devised additional laws further to hem in renters and sharecroppers. Through policies that Roulhac endorsed and enforced, the gap widened between the mass of black renters and sharecroppers, on the one hand, and the few black landowners, on the other.

In 1880, Roulhac wrote his sister confidentially of his wish to escape Alabama and Greensboro, and to come back—were it practical—to his family in Hillsborough, North Carolina: "If I could dispose of my property I would not hesitate."[55] Even after his marriage ten years before, he had hoped to move to California and to begin a new life out there. When his wife became pregnant, however, her "dread of being away from home" created an "*inescapable* obstacle" to the plan.[56] They stayed and settled in Greensboro. After a decade, he admitted that what he'd seen done had not set well with him. He wrote that what "these indolent Southerners are going to do before . . . they can acquire better and more industrious habits, is more than I can tell." From all this, "you may infer that I am *disgusted* with the sunny South & I must confess I am. For, although in a modest way I have prospered here, yet for the most part I have *held aloof* from *them* . . . Some among them are excellent people and whom I much like, but with those exceptions, in supineness [and] rascality—from stealing a Negro's ballot up to stealing his mule, or anybody else's mule, and in the intolerance begotten by ignorance and retrogression"—they "are generally speaking '*solid*.'"[57] If he could move and start again, he would. As it turned out, he never left Alabama.

Nonetheless, Thomas Roulhac left a legacy. As Paul Cameron's agent, he helped a dozen black people and their families to homestead on a 1,600-acre plantation in Alabama. For Paul Hargis and his brother Jim, for Sandy Cameron, and for the others who became landowners in 1875, the Cameron plantation became their foothold in freedom.

Fairntosh plantation. Two-year-old Paul Hargis, his parents, and his siblings were acquired by planter Duncan Cameron in 1829 as part of a debt settlement with their former owner, Lawrence Hargis. Cameron moved the enslaved Hargis family to Fairntosh, the home quarter of his extensive land-holdings in Piedmont, North Carolina. Courtesy of Preservation North Carolina; photo by Tim Buchman, ca. 1972.

List of the Slaves Stock &c.
belonging to Judge Cameron
at his home plantation
1834
Decr.

	age
Anderson the foreman	58
George Hargis	50
Joe - the Carter	48
Minica	48
Luke	48
Henry the weaver	41
Abner „ do.	38
Toney	30
Dryden	28
David	32
Owen	22
John	24
Benjamin	21
Daniel	20
Milton	19
Joe - waggoner	26
Horris	18
Edmond	17
	Continued

"Home" slave register, 1834. George Hargis, father of Paul, was one of the few enslaved workers recorded with a first and last name. His placement between "Anderson the foreman" and "Joe, the Carter" suggests that he had a prime role on the plantation. Cameron letters reveal that he was a courier between quarters. Courtesy of the Cameron Family Papers, Southern Historical Collection, Wilson Special Collections Library, University of North Carolina at Chapel Hill.

Lawyer and planter Duncan Cameron bought enslaved families entire and kept them together as an inducement for their compliant work. By the 1830s, he found the role of planter "vexatious." In 1834, he accepted the presidency of the Bank of North Carolina, moved to Raleigh, and relinquished supervision of Fairntosh to overseers. Courtesy of the Southern Historical Collection, Cameron Family Papers, Wilson Special Collections Library, University of North Carolina at Chapel Hill.

April 26th 1835

I am truly concerned my beloved Husband to have such distressing intelligence to communicate to you. On Friday McNicols and Jim had a difference Nicols whiped Jim and at night Jim came over to see Paul after talking some time with him Paul told him to go home and conduct himself well and that McNicols would not trouble him again. accordingly Jim went over early on Saturday morning, and soon met with Nicols, who gave him a blow on the head which fractured his scull, and what is most astonishing before one breakfasted the poor fellow had walked over here alone. We sent off to Hillsborough immediately for a surgeon Doctor Webb came down and trepaned him last night, and says he thinks he will recover God grant that he may for many reasons —

About 11 o'clock on Saturday Nichols came over to the shop, I met him in the lane, and received from him an account of this most unfortunate affair — I give it to you in few words — In saying that they met in the yard about day light on Saturday morning — When N. said to Jim 'I suppose you went over to see your master last night; Jim said that he did — 'What did he say to you, — 'That is my own business Mr Nichols, — Thereupon Nichols, uttering some harsh and angry words got hold of a part of a rail and as Jim was walking off from him, his back turned he gave him the blow which brought him to the ground! But blow was given — the poor fellow has lost immense quantities of blood from his mouth and nose. I feel a deep solicitude that Jim should live — first on account of his thoughtless overseer —! and tho he has ever been a bad and ungovernable slave: I have ever felt a great regard for him, in as much as he

Letter by Rebecca (top) Cameron and Paul (bottom) Cameron. Paul Cameron wished to take the reins of his parents' plantation, but complied instead with his father's wish that he practice law. On an 1835 visit to Fairntosh, Paul Cameron and his mother, Rebecca, confronted the brutal beating of an enslaved man named Jim, who had defied his overseer. Their reports, on the front and back of the same letter, confirmed that such treatment violated the norms of the plantation. Courtesy of the Southern Historical Collection, Cameron Family Papers, Folder 748 : 1835 : Scans 28 and 30, Wilson Special Collections Library, University of North Carolina at Chapel Hill.

D. Cameron
Slaves sent to Alabama.

men	Boys	women	Girls
1 Charles	1 Thomas	1 Angy	1 Winny
2 Sandy	2 Gustavus	2 Rozetta	2 Leaky
3 Milton	3 John	3 Martha	3 Milly
4 Frank	4 Iuba	4 Peggy	4 Chaney
5 Little Joe	5 Jacob	5 Juicy	5 Diey
6 Orin	6 Lewis	6 Diley	6 Luse
7 York	7 Japhet	7 Moly	7 Betsy
8 Jim Hargis	8 Dave	8 Mary	8 Barba
9 Nathaniel	9 Simon	9 Mary I	9 Anne
10 Prince	10 Alexander	10 Nelly	10 Juicy
11 William	11 Anderson	11 Luckey	
12 Carolina	12 Eaton	1 Nancy	
13 Willie	13 Wesley	13 Poly	
14 Peter		14 Sally	
15 Anderson		15 Liny	
16 Tom		16 Eliza	
17 Nelson		17 Becky	
18 Eno Edmund		18 Chany	
19 Old Peter		19 Moly	
20 John L		20 Lylla	
21 Dave L		21 Sally	
22 Lewis		22 Nancy	
23 Iney Taylor		23 Delphia	
24 Green		24 Liny	
25 Paul			

Men 25
Boy 10
Women 24
Girls 10

Slaves sent to Alabama, 1844. Twenty-nine-year-old Paul Cameron took charge of Fairntosh in 1837, but setbacks undercut his plan to prove himself as a planter. In 1844, he persuaded his father to send 114 workers to the Black Belt of Alabama to grow cotton. The men sent included Jim Hargis, recorded with his full name, and his brother Paul, youngest of the men. Courtesy of the Southern Historical Collection, Cameron Family Papers.

Number two on the 1844 slave list, Sandy Cameron was the carpenter on the Alabama plantation. In the 1870s, Sandy Cameron became the first freedman to purchase part of the planter's Alabama land. Sandy Cameron's photograph was taken in the 1880s. Courtesy of Betty Hargress Washington.

Horton Grove. In 1864, Paul Cameron evacuated half of his Alabama workers back to North Carolina, with Paul Hargis among them. After twenty years away, Paul Hargis encountered many changes, including the two-story slave dwelling pictured here. Freed in 1865, Cameron's workers quickly challenged the planter's authority. In early 1867, Paul Hargis returned to Alabama. When he recounted his migration story, he telescoped his two journeys into one. Courtesy of North Carolina Historic Sites.

Born in 1906, Louie Rainey became the oral historian of his community. Paul Hargis and other elders shared their stories with him, which he retold to generations that followed. The most vivid account was of a "speakin'" in Greensboro in 1865, when his grandmother Elizabeth Rainey heard from a man whose name she recalled as "Cryden White" that "you're free, you're free." Photo © Sydney Nathans.

By 1872, labor difficulties and depleted soil had made Paul Cameron's Alabama place unworkable as a plantation. Many workers left. Paul Hargis and his brother Jim stayed. In mid-1872, the overseer relayed to Cameron this offer by the remaining freed people to buy an acre of land for "a negro church also for a school house." Courtesy of the Southern Historical Collection, Cameron Family Papers.

Paul Cameron refused the offer to sell a single acre to freedmen, wishing instead to find a white buyer or buyers for his entire 1,600 acres. The urgent need for cash at the end of 1872 spurred him to reverse course. He authorized a nephew to sell to whoever promised to pay. Cameron is pictured here in 1878. Courtesy of the Southern Historical Collection, Ruffin, Routher, and Hamilton Family Collection.

Thomas Roulhac, Paul Cameron's nephew, had become a Greensboro resident and attorney in 1870. As his uncle's agent in the 1870s, Roulhac sold almost all of Cameron's Alabama land to black buyers, including Paul Hargis, Jim Hargis, and Sandy Cameron. Most purchasers put no money down, made payments in cotton rather than cash, and paid over the course of several years. Courtesy of the Alabama Department of Archives and History, Alabama State Bar Association Photograph Collection, Montgomery, Alabama.

Cassimore school and church. In 1874, Robert Cabbil purchased 120 acres of Cameron's land. Twenty-five years later, in 1899, he deeded an acre for a church. The Cassimore AME Zion Church was built in the early twentieth century. In the 1920s, the community constructed a Society Hall and school. The old church was replaced in 1955. Photo © Sydney Nathans.

Forrest Hargress and Betty Cameron Hargress. Forrest Hargress was born on January 1, 1866. Family tradition held that his father was Confederate general Nathan Bedford Forrest, who had camped near the Cameron plantation in early April 1865, when his troops were in retreat from Union forces. He took his stepfather's last name, which became "Hargress" by the twentieth century. Betty Cameron Hargress was the daughter of Sandy Cameron. By the 1930s, Forrest Hargress had become the moral leader of the Cassimore church and community. Photo courtesy of Betty Hargress Washington.

The commitment to family land as a communal possession—as "heir land"—found its greatest exponent in Alice Sledge Hargress, who in 1933 married the grandson of Forrest Hargress. For Alice Sledge Hargress, pictured here in 1982, family land was not to be divided or sold. Rather, it was to be held in common for all the heirs. Photo © Sydney Nathans.

James Lyles, called to preach at an early age, became a man learned in the Bible and guided by visions that periodically came to him. A 1930s vision forewarned of evictions and land loss throughout the Alabama Black Belt. He urged fellow blacks to buy land as a refuge for those displaced. Skeptics rejected his proposal. Photo © Sydney Nathans.

Cattle farm. James Lyles's vision of the displacement of black farmers came true. In 1939 the plantation adjacent to the Cameron place was converted to cattle, and its tenants were evicted. Photo © Sydney Nathans.

Robert Cabbil, whose great-grandfather and namesake had donated land in 1899 for the community's church, was one of the tenants evicted in 1939. As black landowners saw it, when expelled tenants came out from under planter rule, they became "true men and women." After eviction, Robert Cabbil acquired his own home place. Photo © Sydney Nathans.

Lewis Black taught music and organized bands in several black high schools, including the Hale County Training School and, later, Sunshine High School in southern Hale County. He taught political activism as well. Photo courtesy of James and Eliza Lyles.

Mildred and Lewis Black. In the 1960s, the couple founded a credit union for black farmers who couldn't get loans from white-owned banks, and a sewing cooperative for black women as an alternative to domestic service. In 1965, they helped to mobilize the movement for voter rights in Hale County. Photo courtesy of James and Eliza Lyles.

Rev. Arthur T. Days came to Greensboro in the 1960s, and took the pulpit of the St. Matthews AME Church. When the Southern Christian Leadership Conference centered its 1965 voter registration campaign in the Alabama Black Belt, he became a leader of the Hale County movement. A.T. Days and Lewis Black helped to lead the movement in Greensboro. James Lyles rallied rural followers in meetings at Cassimore. Photo by Jim Peppler. Courtesy of the Jim Peppler *Southern Courier* Photograph Collection, Alabama Department of Archives and History, Montgomery, Alabama.

Demonstrators converged on Greensboro to march for voter rights in July 1965. After white night riders burned an outlying country church, protesters sought to march down Main Street to the Hale County Courthouse, with Greensboro leader Theresa Burroughs in the forefront. They were blocked by police and a barricade. Photo courtesy of Theresa Burroughs, Safe House Museum, Greensboro, Alabama.

Alice Hargress and friends from Cassimore joined the July 1965 marchers, expecting that the protest would be peaceful. Instead, troopers broke up the marchers with tear gas. Demonstrators regrouped and vowed to come back. Photo by Jim Peppler. Courtesy of Jim Peppler *Southern Courier* Photograph Collection, Alabama Department of Archives and History, Montgomery, Alabama.

When Alice Hargress and James Lyles returned to the barricade two days after the tear gas incident, they found troopers and busses waiting. Arrested, they were carried to jail near Selma, photographed with placards on which they wrote their names and dates of birth, and imprisoned for three days. Photos courtesy of Theresa Burroughs, Safe House Museum, Greensboro, Alabama.

Voting in Greensboro, August 1965. The summer demonstrations created pressure that President Lyndon Johnson used to win passage of the Voting Rights Bill of August 6, 1965. Alice Hargress's mother, born in 1890, had never voted. With others, she waited in line at the basement entrance of the Greensboro Post Office, walked downstairs, and voted for the first time. Photo courtesy of Theresa Burroughs, Safe House Museum, Greensboro, Alabama.

To Lewis Black, the right to vote was just a first step toward freedom. He predicted that whites would demonize black activists and seek to divide the black electorate. He widened his focus to gain funds for marketing cooperatives to help black farmers stay on the land. His efforts were undermined by state and federal officials. Photo © Sydney Nathans.

In 1968, Martin Luther King Jr. spoke at a daytime rally in Greensboro. Fear for his safety led him to stay overnight at the home of Theresa Burroughs, a leader in the Greensboro movement. The house subsequently became a museum commemorating the Greensboro struggle for civil and voting rights. Photo © Sydney Nathans.

On December 6, 2013, at the age of ninety-nine, Alice Hargress spoke at the Safe House Museum. To youngsters gathered there, she spoke about the 1965 demonstrations that won their right to vote. Then she added: "It's your turn now," and led them in her favorite movement anthem: "Ain't nobody gonna turn me 'round . . ." Photo © Sydney Nathans.

Alice Hargress's grandson, David Hargress, joined the navy, became a naval cook, and won the assignment to cook at Camp David, where he worked for President Barack Obama from 2010 to 2014. The Camp David wall hanging was a gift from David Hargress to his Alabama grandmother. Photo © Sydney Nathans.

Cassimore Road leads into the settlement acquired by African American forebears in the 1870s and circles around the Cassimore Church. The sign marks where Cassimore Road intersects with the lane curving up to Cameron Place, the Hargress family home. Further up Cassimore Road, the AME Zion Church mailbox stands across from the Cassimore Church. Photos © Sydney Nathans.

Founded in 1899, Cassimore Church fulfilled the aspiration of forebears first expressed in 1872—to stay on Cameron land, and to purchase an acre for a church and a school. In 1955, members constructed a new church building on the original site. For over a century, the church has been Cassimore's worship and community center. Photo by Sydney Nathans.

Part Three ✍ Beyond a Living

Nine ⤳ "Hallelujah Times"

By Paul Cameron's reckoning, his Alabama plantation had been a disastrous proving ground. He had come out in 1844 to add to his family's wealth; he'd failed and felt betrayed. Paul Hargis and others who bought Cameron's land did not seek riches from it. Clearly, none had his wherewithal. As one black contemporary put it, "We go entirely upon energy and self will and no capital." What's more, the soil proved no more fertile for them than for Cameron. But making a fortune was never their goal. For buyers of the land, there were altogether different sources of fulfillment in freedom.

⤳

When young Carrie Davis, born in 1906, sat on the porch of her great-uncle's home, she heard almost no stories about slavery. Nor did she learn that by the turn of the twentieth century, her Unc' Paul had changed the family's last name from Hargis—the name of the man who had once owned him and his parents—to Hargress. What she did learn, from Paul Hargress and others of his generation, was that they regarded the years after emancipation as their "hallelujah times." As a child and ever since, she was bewildered: How could the adults living in the hardscrabble world that surrounded her say that "this here is a good time"?[1]

Eighty-seven years old in 1914, Unc' Paul was still a commanding figure to his eight-year-old niece, with big shoulders, an erect head, and a gray curling horseshoe mustache.[2] Yet Carrie Davis also sensed his limits, and the vulnerability of others who had undertaken new lives for themselves as free people and landowners in the settlement. Paul Hargress, widowed by 1900, had lost a leg sometime early in the twentieth century. One account was that his drafty cabin, with a leaky unsealed roof and cracks in the floor wide enough for a quarter to drop through, hadn't held out against a snowstorm, and that his leg froze and had to be amputated.[3] Whatever the cause, by the time Carrie Davis knew him, Paul Hargress got around on a peg leg. Unable any longer to farm, he turned his cabin into a home-based store that sold candy, cheese, and crackers.

From looking at her aged uncle and at the dwellings and condition of others, Carrie Davis sensed that all was hardly well with the survivors of slavery. She surely did not know how unwell. Her great uncle, unable to make enough from his store earnings to sustain himself and pay his property taxes, had in 1912 turned to an arrangement to use the 100 acres he had bought in the 1870s to secure himself in his last years. With the help of a white lawyer, he devised a compact to bequeath equal portions of his land to eleven people, with the requirement that they support him for the rest of his life. Nine were relatives by blood; two were not. Each received nine and one-eleventh acres of land with the proviso that each must pay him $10 a year. The conditional bequests of land provided a home-grown annuity for Paul Hargress, who granted himself permission to dwell in his cabin as long as he lived. The others received the boon of an early inheritance—a home place of their own. But it was an inheritance with obligations.[4] Carrie Davis would eventually learn of the tempest provoked by her uncle's gifts.

From her vantage point in 1914 and after, Carrie Davis was right to wonder. How could the generation after emancipation see theirs as "hallelujah times"? Why might Paul Hargress, especially, look back on his years after emancipation as a fulfillment, even a victory?

Paul Hargress chose not to share with Carrie Davis that his family had been spared separation and the slave trade when in 1829 Duncan Cameron had acquired them from their ill and indebted owner L. V. Hargis. He did not explain that they retained the surname of their former owner as a way to sustain their connection with each other. Nor was she told that the Hargis siblings had kept their parents and each other in mind and memory when they bestowed names on their children. Above all, the one slavery-time story that Paul Hargress *did* tell—of coming out on the coach with Paul Cameron and receiving a gift of gold—obscured the fact that the youngest son had buttressed his kin in a more fundamental way. Paul Hargress had come back from North Carolina to Alabama in 1867 to re-join and reconstitute his family. Whether or not an award of gold was involved—certainly no more than a gold piece rather than a bag or a peck—he had used his labor and perseverance to acquire ownership of a portion of the old plantation.

As long as they lived, Paul Hargress and his brothers remained on what was now their home place and, year in and year out, made their living on it. As did other small farmers, they took out annual "advances" from mer-chants, and pledged livestock and tools as collateral for their loans. The Hargress advances were substantial—$200 to $500 each year. The prop-erty pledged as security included almost every possession. Paul Hargress mortgaged the forthcoming crop of corn and cotton, a red-spotted cow named Rose, a red-and-white cow named Strawberry, a mule named Buck, a dark bay horse named Bill, farm wagons, plows, and other tools.[5] Only twice, however—when obliged by a new lender—did Paul Hargress borrow against the *land*.[6] His goal remained unwavering: hold on to the soil, and sustain family members on it.

Like Carrie Davis, young Louie Rainey also went over to Paul Hargress's cabin and candy store. Born in 1906 and only eight years old in 1914, he hung back from getting too close to the man on the porch. The peg leg frightened him. He did get near enough to hear the story of Old Man Paul Cameron and Old Man Paul Hargress and the bag of gold.[7] In later years he heard plenty about the land division compact, too. For Louie Rainey, though, the views of that first group of freed people came less from Paul Hargress than from the tales of others who bought land from Paul Cam-eron. From those accounts, Louie Rainey could understand better than Carrie Davis why some of that generation could term the years since emancipation as "hallelujah times."

Louie Rainey grew up in the household of his mother, Louisa, and his grandmother Elizabeth Reese Rainey, known to some as "Elizabeth Ma" and to him as "Ma Vet." Both women farmed, and both did frequent out-work as domestics for white neighbors nearby. Louie was an inquisitive youngster and had a grandmother ready to answer his questions. So he learned that his grandmother Elizabeth Reese had several children while in slavery before she married freedman Wilson Rainey, one of the men to buy 120 acres of Paul Cameron's land in the 1870s. They were farming that land when she gave birth to their daughter Louisa. When enslaved, Elizabeth Reese had worked on a plantation ten miles to the north of the Cameron place, on land belonging to two brothers, Herb and Jim Locke. As Ma Vet told it to her grandson, the Locke brothers were relatively lenient slave owners who built a place of worship for their people.[8] It was from his grandmother that young Louie learned that she had gone to a speakin' in June 1865—to an outdoor meeting of thousands of newly freed people in Greensboro. From Ma Vet he got the name of the speaker—an agent of the newly established Freedmen's Bureau, former Union soldier Henry Crydenwise. It was a name that a century later Louie Rainey reported as "Cryden White." Ma Vet recounted vividly what she heard the Bureau agent declare on that unforgettable day: "You're free, you're free! You can go where you want to go and do what you want to do!"[9]

Louie Rainey's recollections extended beyond the stories of his grandmother. He remembered the time that the census-taker came by in 1910: "She rode a horse!" The white lady on the horse, with her oversized record book, rode from farm to farm to find the head of each household and record the names and ages and occupations of each person who lived there. She found young Louie in the field and asked him where his mother was. After the white woman left, he asked his mother, "Who was that lady?" "The census-taker." For years to come, Louie Rainey laughed, he wondered: "How could anyone take your sense?"[10]

Encouraged by his grandmother, and by the hours they spent talking in her cabin, surrounded by jugs of wine she made from home-grown grapes and aged for drinking the following year, Louie Rainey himself became a "sense"-taker and story collector for families in the entire community. In lore gathered by Louie Rainey, the aspirations of the new black landowners came to life. Those desires included—but went well beyond—making a living off the land.

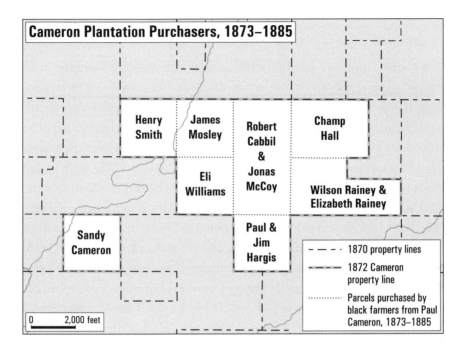

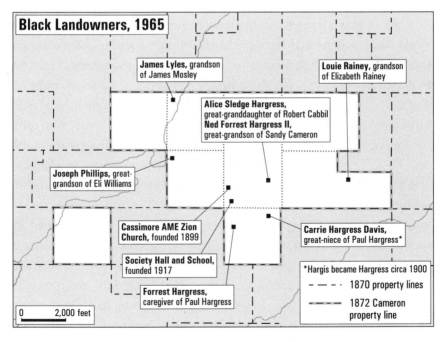

Cameron Plantation Purchasers, 1873–1885; Black Landowners, 1965.

For Paul Hargress and almost all those who obtained the Cameron plantation in the 1870s and 1880s, the first challenge was payment. How were they to pay for the land that many had bought on four- or five-year terms, and thereafter to make a living on it? Many of the new landowners had one strategy in common: they added non-family members to their labor force by sub-renting part of their land to other blacks. There were varied reasons for sub-renting. For several buyers, an income outside of farming had been crucial to their purchase of land, and they continued their outside work. Buyer Jonas McCoy continued to travel around to install or repair cotton gins, as he had before he and fellow freedman Robert Cabbil had become partners to buy 240 acres of Cameron's land. Purchaser Champ Hall continued to haul timber with his big wagon, as he had before he took a mortgage to pay for his 120 acres.[11] New landowners Eli Williams and Paul Hargress needed labor beyond what their family members could provide, so they too sub-rented. The new black landowners became not just individual farmers but small agricultural contractors.

A sub-rented farm needed supervision. Supervision came naturally to Paul Hargress, who had acted in the role of squad leader and plantation foreman after emancipation. Others had a distinctly more limited interest in day-to-day farming. For these new landowners, their wives came to play a crucial role. Black purchaser Eli Williams did the plowing and paid hired workers to do the rest, though it was Eli Williams's wife who took the lead hoe on his farm, working as the head of the hoeing crew and setting the pace for them.[12] A neighboring black farmer had an identical arrangement with sub-renters. The owner was a blacksmith who hated farming, so his wife insisted on heading the hoes. The husband protested—what was the point of his owning a farm if she worked herself to death in the field? She answered with a characteristic owner's view of tenants: if she didn't lead, they wouldn't work. The case of a wife who chose *not* to manage the farm in her husband's absence highlighted the emergence of a woman's managerial role. Jonas McCoy left farming to his wife when he traveled the countryside doing gin repairs. Oral tradition had it that his wife—far from tending the lead hoe—instead gave parties. "She partied away that plantation," Louie Rainey claimed. At best, the account was only part of the truth, but it did reveal expectations. In this community, the black landowner who supplemented his living off the farm needed an attentive woman to make it pay.[13]

Whether or not taking the lead hoe was a new "opportunity" for women, clearly landowning did boost egos and opportunities for men. The boost expressed itself vividly in the lives of two black purchasers of the Cameron lands. Eli Williams had been enslaved on the plantation of R. M. Johnson and had lived directly across from the Cameron place. The slaveholder had held his bondsmen in the strictest confinement. He gave no passes for his people to leave the plantation or for others to enter. He constructed no church to house black worship. When thirty-year-old Eli Williams bought 120 acres of Paul Cameron's land, he changed lives. As his grandson recalled, Eli Williams liked to plow—but only to plow, and even that, if possible, at night and by the light of the moon. He supplemented his income with hogs—he always had ten or eleven who ran loose in the adjacent swamp. To do the rest of his farming he hired folks and paid them in hog meat and syrup.[14]

During the day, Eli Williams visited. On a typical day, he could be seen all over the settlement riding his horse, wearing a black tie and a blue chamois shirt with an old-fashioned high collar ("a city-lawyer collar"), chewing on a turkey feather, and sporting a broad-brimmed sunhat. The collar, the tie, the horse, and the plumage all sent a message: this was a man putting distance between himself and his past.[15] Slavery had been on his master's terms. Freedom would be on his own.

Riding higher still was another young purchaser of Paul Cameron's lands. Champ Hall was recalled for his wagon—brand-new, sturdy, big, pulled by large animals. The wagon enabled him to do hauling for the county and get paid in cash by the county commissioners of Greensboro. Almost certainly it was thirty-year-old Champ Hall's performance as a teamster that brought him to the attention of Paul Cameron's sales agent Thomas Roulhac. Active in town politics, Roulhac knew who received jobs from the county. When the agent negotiated the sale of Cameron's lands, the confident Champ Hall looked like a good bet.

The same confidence led Champ Hall to compete with a neighborhood white merchant for the attentions of a black woman. The rivals were two tough men. The black teamster and landowner confronted white store-keeper and roustabout John O'Donnell. According to oral tradition, O'Donnell made his own bullets—and fired them with accuracy. O'Donnell lived a few miles above the Cameron plantation in the crossroad village of Cedarville, where he owned a store that sold goods to a black clientele. He lived with a black woman. As a merchant, as a justice of the peace, and as a constable, O'Donnell traveled. Champ Hall, attracted to O'Donnell's woman and reputedly one of the few men in the community who had no fear of the bullet maker, challenged him for her. While O'Donnell was away, Hall escorted the woman to a party. For the occasion, he took and wore John O'Donnell's greatcoat. When O'Donnell returned, he issued a warning to him not to talk to that woman again. Hall came right up to the gate and called for her. O'Donnell called back, telling him to get away. Hall replied that this road was public property, and went on talking. John O'Donnell took aim with his pistol and shot Champ Hall dead.[16]

Not all who rose to become purchasers of Cameron lands rode high or fell hard. Louie Rainey recalled stories of his grandfather as a man who liked to farm. In the summer, Wilson Rainey especially delighted in growing watermelons and giving them out to children. Robert Cabbil, transported in slavery times from Virginia to Alabama, likely worked on a nearby plantation owned by an absentee Virginia planter and operated after emancipation by his agent, Virginian Phillip Cabell. In 1875, Robert Cabbil, with his partner Jonas McCoy, jointly bought 240 acres and became the largest purchasers of land on the Cameron place. After McCoy fell into debt in 1884, the partners divided the land and Robert Cabbil kept his 120 acres out of debt for all the years he lived on it. Like Wilson Rainey, he modeled generosity to others. He exhorted his grandchildren to "live with an open hand. If you squeeze too tight, you'll lose it all."[17]

Robert Cabbil followed his own counsel on December 13, 1899, when he and his wife, Kizziah, deeded an acre of their land for the formation of a church in the center of the community. It affiliated with the African Methodist Episcopal Zion national church, and served not only the purchasers of Cameron lands but renters and sharecroppers on plantations nearby.[18]

Other landowners sought a middle ground between generosity to others and service strictly to themselves. For Eli Williams, indiscriminate sharing could—for someone who had got something or built something—become a hemorrhage. The man who kept his distance by riding horseback in a high-collared shirt and tie warned his grandson to keep clear of folks who "put a hand on you. If you've got something, people will touch you for it." He made it clear that his land was his own, his apple orchards were his own, even the quail in his thickets were his own. But having drawn the line, he let young Louie Rainey and his friends know that if they asked permission, he would share. His was a guarded mutuality.

A more quiet and unobtrusive confidence, and a careful combination of strategies, marked the man who would become the largest African American landowner in the county. Tom Ruffin appeared an unlikely man to become the buyer of close to 2,000 acres in the black prairie region of Hale County, land located five miles above the Cameron place.[19] Light-skinned Ruffin was disabled—one leg shorter than the other, both legs so bowed that the name given him behind his back was "Pothooks."[20] Tom Ruffin's owners were Alabama planter James Ruffin, the uncle by marriage of Paul Cameron, and Ruffin's physician son. James Ruffin had moved to the Black Belt in the mid-1830s with enslaved workers brought from North Carolina. It was James Ruffin's advice that had persuaded Cameron to buy the nearby 1,600 acres that became his Alabama albatross. Tom Ruffin, born in Alabama in 1843, grew up to become the enslaved livestock drover on the James Ruffin plantation.[21] When freedom came, his owners tried to entice the twenty-two-year-old drover to stay by offering him food, lodging, and a new suit. According to family tradition, he tried on the new suit, then took it off and bid the white Ruffins goodbye.[22]

Tom Ruffin moved just north of the Cameron plantation and by 1871 was farming as a tenant with his new wife, Molly, and his mother, Harriet, and brother Wesley. It is clear that he had the vision of a man whose handicap led him to look beyond the first windfall of independence—a new suit. Unlike those who bought the Cameron lands in the 1870s, he bided his time before making initial small purchases, and in the meantime he established a reputation among whites for enterprise. His trade was hauling timber. The onetime drover bought six oxen and used them to haul loads of logs to a nearby sawmill. He paid workers to plane the timber and then hauled the boards to market.[23] In 1880, he began to buy land in small quantities from neighboring white planters and merchants who were ready to sell out and trusted Tom Ruffin to make good on his payments.[24] Then, in 1895, he made what was likely the largest single purchase by any black man in the region, paying $11,200 for 680 acres of land, once known as the Stollenwerk plantation, named after the family that owned it.[25]

When white folks asked him how he accumulated enough to make those purchases, his answer was always the same, and wonderfully deflective: "I *worked* while others slept. And if you'd slept a wink more, *I'd have got it all!*" He bought more oxen, hired more workers, had timber hauled to his own sawmill. Ruffin knew how to use experts. He added expert drivers to gee and haw his oxen.[26] Unable himself to tell an *A* from a *B*, Ruffin employed a bookkeeper to tend his books. On a far larger scale than smaller landowners, he employed renters and sharecroppers to work his farmland. He opened a fully stocked country store where it was understood that his tenants would give him their trade. Ruffin's flourishing store was one of five at the Cedarville crossroads—the others were owned by white merchants. His store sold cloth, shoes, flour, sugar, groceries, candy, and even chamber pots, locally called "thunder mugs." A gristmill and a cotton gin made his a full-fledged plantation.[27]

Could Paul Hargress and other black folks take pride in Tom Ruffin's acquisitions, even rejoice in his singular achievement? That depended on Tom Ruffin himself, who, like black purchasers of the Cameron plantation, had to work out a middle ground between personal gain and generosity to others. On the one hand, he strictly regulated his workers. He rang a bell to wake them in the morning and to start and end the midday meal. He rode around the plantation in a carriage and to the idle called out, "Get to work, get to work." He had a reputation for tightness. Local folklore had it that when Tom Ruffin held a quarter in his hand, his grip "was so tight the eagle screamed."[28] Nonetheless he found ways to affirm a commitment to the community. He was a founder of the Mars Hill Baptist Church in Cedarville. He contributed to the creation of a black agricultural and industrial training school in Hale County.[29] Symbolically, he carried himself with humility. He wore plain clothes, patched pants, old rope suspenders. He made large loans to some neighbors, recorded in the deed books of the county courthouse, and arranged for a white merchant to extend smaller informal loans to others. Unable to read or write, he would give a borrower his pocketknife wrapped in a handkerchief and tell him to carry it to the Greensboro merchant, who took the knife as proof that Ruffin had authorized the loan on the borrower's behalf.[30] He was strict about repayment, and of course, a white middleman was involved. Tom Ruffin helped neighbors not so much through personal acts of kindness as through business loans and through support to institutions that would help the next generation to advance. "Get to work, get to work" may not have seemed very communal or loving, but it was basic to how he thought his family and the community could get ahead.

Louie Rainey could understand why some of that first generation in freedom could see themselves as living in "hallelujah times." But he also learned stories that warranted the bafflement and disbelief of Carrie Davis when she heard that term. There was the tale of Richard Virge and his brother, who went west for work and drifted into a Mississippi county that supposedly had an outdoor sign they couldn't read: "Nigger Read and Run." Chased out of the county, bullets flying, one got hit and told the other to go on; the wounded man was lost. Then came the "mob crew" hunting the brother who got away. In the cotton field, the mob surrounded a neighbor of the fugitive who they suspected knew where he was. Though he'd never seen the fleeing brother, the neighbor was "whipped unmerciful," and soiled himself in fear. Louie Rainey himself recalled being told by his mother to stay inside their cabin when the "mob crew" rode through the countryside, the hooves of their horses deafening as they crossed what locals called the Rooster Bridge just up the road, an iron bridge with thick wooden planks laid across it. When those riders were on the rampage, he recalled, "if anything was outdoors when that sun went down, it stayed there till the next day!"[31]

Less violent but more pervasive was the silent but steady assault on black rights at the ballot box. In the 1870s, white political leaders of Hale County proposed that in return for support for white candidates, blacks would be favored by whites willing to sell land or rent land to blacks on generous terms. Whites came to black political gatherings and spoke glowingly of that promise, none more so than young Greensboro attorney Thomas Seay, who in 1876 was elected state senator from Hale County, and would serve as governor of Alabama from 1886 to 1890.

A beneficiary of the momentary accord, Paul Hargress had gone to meetings in the late 1860s and voted into the 1870s. By mid-decade, his options and that of other blacks had narrowed. In 1875, the Alabama legislature passed new laws that increased the bond required for holders of local and state offices, bonds that guaranteed they would faithfully execute their duties. Bond amounts rose to the hundreds of dollars for all offices—state senator and state representative, sheriff, probate judge, coroner, and others. There was a further proviso: local candidates had to have *local* sponsors to put up their bonds. No outside persons or groups—such as the state or national Republican Party—could guarantee the money. So it was that Louie Rainey's great-uncle and his grandmother's half brother Brister Reese, who had in 1873 been elected to the state house of representatives, couldn't make bond for reelection. The oral tradition, passed on by Elizabeth Reese Rainey to her grandson, was that Brister Reese won election "but couldn't pass the test."[32] Unable to make bond if they won office, Brister Reese and other black candidates disappeared.[33]

When blacks ignored the promise of white favors and stubbornly voted as they saw fit for the "wrong" white candidates who could make bond, ballot boxes disappeared, as happened to the ballot box of Cedarville's black voters in 1875.[34] Or if counted, the votes were not counted as made. Such was the subversion of blacks in politics, and the consequent undermining of black rights, that the onetime Radical Republican leader of Hale County, James K. Green, left the county and moved to Montgomery in 1876. The erstwhile comrade of Brister Reese and former Alabama state senator became a building contractor, abandoned party politics, and declared that he would never buy property in the state. Green didn't want property to tie him to a place where he had no voting power to protect himself and his family—especially his daughter—from the whims of white men.

In 1883, James K. Green came to Birmingham to testify before the visiting Senate Committee on Relations of Capital and Labor. His reputation preceded him, and immediately Green found himself grilled by condescending committee member James L. Pugh, the Alabama member of the Senate committee, who became the state's governor in 1890. "You have got as much right to vote as anybody here, have you not?" Pugh asked.

"Yes, sir," replied Green.

Pugh went on. "Do you know of any way of taking that right away from you?"

"Only in the count," Green calmly replied. It "is just as well not to have the vote, unless it is counted fair."

When Pugh tauntingly asked Green whether he "thought the white people were going to take away your ballot and put you back into slavery," the onetime Radical Republican bristled back. "Oh, no, sir; I was never afraid of *that*."[35]

Momentarily the Alabama senator backed off and asked Green whether he had "any suggestion to make as to any means by which your condition would be improved." The former Hale County leader took the opening to sum up what he saw as the gains and limits for black people after freedom came to Alabama.

> I believe that the colored people have done well, and more than well, considering all their circumstances and surroundings. . . . I for one was . . . entirely ignorant; I knew nothing more than to obey my master . . . but the tocsin of freedom sounded and knocked at the door and we walked out like free men and met the exigencies as they grew up. . . . The Government said we were citizens and we accepted it and tried to make ourselves so to some extent. . . . But all the while we go entirely upon energy and self will and no capital: The white men have the capital. . . . I think

you have all had the benefit of us, and have got it yet, and if you want us to be good citizens of this country you ought to come out and help us—and you will find that our feelings are not as much one sided as you think.

Unmoved, and reluctant to have Alabama blemished by James Green's claim of voter fraud, Pugh hastened back to interrogation about the ballot. Have "the colored people been injured by what you call 'counting out'; how have their rights been injured?"

Green answered instantly: "We are injured that much in our rights as men to express lawfully and legitimately the wishes and will of the voter."

Thwarted, Pugh made it personal. "Do you think *your* vote was not counted?"

Green: "Oh, yes, it was counted; but not for my side."

"Why didn't you report that fact then?"

Green had the last word. "What good would it have done; I had no rights."[36]

Accompanying the loss of power and the vote was the rise of the convict lease system. When arrested for any reason—severe or petty crimes, vagrancy, or a dispute with a white man—blacks faced unsympathetic judges, all-white juries, and county officials eager for revenue. The outcome of trials was usually a fine, jail time, or both. Unable to pay the fine and not allowed to serve their sentences in local jails, convicts were leased to private companies for brutal labor in coal mines or unremitting toil on privately owned neo-plantations.[37] Attempts to challenge the system through the courts, through the state legislature, or through efforts to get blacks on juries met with failure. The Alabama constitutional convention of 1901 entrenched white supremacy with a host of provisions, including an annual poll tax, cumulative for those who missed any payment. Black voting ended for all but a handful.[38] In the Cedarville precinct that included Paul Hargress, the other Cameron land purchasers, and hundreds of others, only two blacks cast ballots after 1901. One of them was Tom Ruffin.[39]

By the time Louie Rainey and Carrie Davis came of age, most blacks could neither vote nor serve on juries. Any transgression could land a black in the snares of the convict lease system. Best to keep one's head down, pay attention to signs outside unfamiliar towns—and steer clear of conflict with white folks.

⌒

For Paul Hargress in the early twentieth century, personal setbacks more than civic losses diminished his prospects for a serene old age. In his eighties, he was widowed, childless, and an amputee. Having come back to Alabama from North Carolina in 1867 to look after his siblings and their children, having bought land where they could work together, he had expected their descendants to care for him when he could no longer make do for himself. They didn't. That failure prompted him at one point to announce bitterly, "I have no family." Care instead came from two more distant relatives.[40]

One can only speculate why "blood kin"—children of his brothers and sisters—did not look after Paul Hargress as he thought they should. A generation younger than their aged uncle at the turn of the new century, they too were living on the margin, trying to subsist on land smitten by disasters. The boll weevil reached Hale County in 1913 and infested the cotton crop for the rest of the decade. In 1914, the world price of cotton collapsed, brought on by the August outbreak of war in Europe and the subsequent interruption of trade across the Atlantic. Little wonder that in the first two decades of the twentieth century, one of every six black people left Hale County and the Cedarville precinct. Of those who stayed, not all were as tattered as Paul Hargress's nephew York Hargress, who, lacking shoes, walked around with his feet wrapped in burlap bags.[41] But none had wherewithal to spare.

For his welfare, Paul Hargress came to rely on two who were not blood kin. He turned to his late wife's niece, Dicey McCullough, to tend his household needs. He found in his brother's stepson, Forrest Hargress, a willing helper to keep his cabin repaired, cultivate his garden, and take on the other tasks the older man could no longer do for himself.[42]

That arrangement seemed to be tolerable to Paul Hargress and his relatives until 1912. That was the year that he decided that he had to have money as well as caregivers. He had taxes to pay, supplies to buy. That was when he deeded equal portions of his hundred acres to his nine blood kin—and as well to Forrest Hargress and Dicey McCullough—on the condition that each of the eleven paid him $10 a year. The compact was an ingenious final use of the land he had bought from Paul Cameron almost four decades before. Paul Hargress would secure an income, and his eleven beneficiaries would gain a home place.[43]

Perhaps in normal times the family members would not have given a second thought to the small payment in return for the boon of nine and one-eleventh acres—enough land for a house seat and garden plot. Even though they may well have believed that inheriting their uncle's land was their right—the right of his blood kin—in good times they might not have begrudged the inclusion of two more-distant relatives in their uncle's bequest. But these were plague times. Three years after the 1912 land grants, five of the recipients had made no payments to Paul Hargress. To recover the land from them, and as a warning to the others, he revoked the bequests in February 1915 and transferred their portions to a neighboring black farmer and businessman in return for a pledge to pay Paul Hargress $150—the cumulative sum of the payments due from the five delinquent relatives.[44]

For Paul Hargress, "hallelujah times" had come to this impasse. The use of his land to provide an annuity and security in his old age had exposed the vulnerability of all. No wonder Carrie Davis came to wonder, as a youngster in the second decade of the twentieth century, how anyone could view the era after emancipation as the best of times. Resources depleted, five relatives unable or unwilling to come up with $10 a year to meet their uncle's terms, others paying but grumbling—the Hargress descendants were divided and vexed. Discord over their inheritance came to center on the outside relative named in Paul Hargress's bequest.[45]

When Paul Hargress died on April 13, 1918, at the age of ninety-one, it seemed as if all that had gone into his striving—to acquire and keep land for family members—had dissolved into recrimination over who were its rightful heirs.[46]

Ten ⁓ "A Game Rooster"

"HE's YELLOW, but he's your cousin." So Carrie Hargress Davis's father instructed his daughter in how to regard mixed-race Forrest Hargress as she came of age early in the twentieth century. For young and dark-skinned Carrie Davis, the color of her elder cousin had to have been a puzzle.[1] Her father didn't explain to his daughter how he came to be her cousin, how the cousin came to be so fair, or how he came to be part of the community. The family link overrode origin and history. Not so for all. For other blacks in the settlement and for whites outside of it, Ned Forrest Hargress's name, color, and parentage all set him apart. Conceived in the last month of the Civil War and born in January 1866, he was for some a living reminder of what many wanted to forget—slavery, the violation of black women by white men, the ongoing intrusion of whites and whiteness in black lives. Well into his fifties, he had to confront those who questioned whether he truly belonged in the settlement of his birth.

Vexation about Forrest Hargress's share of Unc Paul's inheritance was about far more than nine and one-eleventh acres of land.

⁓

Ned Forrest Hargress grew up as an outlier. He was a stepchild in his family. For many years, he was a stepchild in his community. In multiple ways, he—and his first and middle names—embodied exactly what the generation coming out of slavery wished to put behind them: subjugation.

His mother was an enslaved woman named Dorsey. Dorsey was a child when she and her parents were sent from North Carolina by Paul Cameron to work his plantation in Mississippi in 1858. At fourteen, she gave birth to her first son, William.[2] In February 1861, Dorsey bore witness to one of the most traumatic moments on any of the Cameron plantations. Cameron's Mississippi overseer, pressed by the distant planter to extract more work and profit from laborers freshly arrived from the home plantation in North Carolina, brandished a whip to flog an enslaved man named Zack, who resisted. A fellow slave named Ned intervened, and both were tried for attempted murder. Zack was deemed guilty and hung, and Ned was acquitted—but nonetheless sold away. Five years after the acquittal and sale, Dorsey remembered the man caught in the middle. She named her second-born son Ned.[3]

Ned's other name had a different, though equally traumatic, history. In 1862, fearful that marauding Union troops would reach his Mississippi plantation and liberate his enslaved people, Paul Cameron ordered most of them sent to his less exposed place in Alabama, including Dorsey and her son William. Dorsey was on the Alabama plantation in early April 1865, when the Confederacy was in collapse, and its leading and most feared raider, in retreat. Hitherto always on the offensive, General Nathan Bedford Forrest had backtracked to western Alabama, desperately seeking to regroup after defeat on April 2 by a superior force of Union troops that had just taken Selma, sixty miles to the east. According to black family tradition, Forrest and his men camped for the night in the vicinity of Newbern, eight miles from the Cameron plantation.[4] That was when, according to family tradition, Dorsey was brought to the camp as a cook, and afterward taken to the General's tent. Nine months later, on January 1, 1866, Dorsey's second son, Ned, was born. She gave him the middle name Forrest.[5]

That Dorsey's son was fathered by a white man, there is no doubt. That he was the son of a soldier, Confederate or Union, is likely. That the father was Nathan Bedford Forrest is what Dorsey and later her son believed. Those in the community who also concluded that he was the son of the general presumed that "Ned" was an abbreviation of Nathan Bedford. Few ever called him Ned. Some occasionally called him "General."[6] All called him Forrest.

Sometime in the late 1860s, young Forrest acquired the last name—but not the attachment—of a stepfather. His mother, Dorsey, married Squire

Hargress, Paul Hargress's older brother. Squire Hargress had been taken from North Carolina to Paul Cameron's Mississippi plantation in 1860. Squire Hargress, too, had been in Mississippi at the time of the 1861 attack on the overseer; he likewise had been removed to Alabama in 1862. Unlike Dorsey, however, he had no wish to remember anything about Mississippi. His mate Susan, the mother of his daughter Cintha, likely died there, before the move to Alabama.[7] Nor did it suit Squire Hargress, when he married Dorsey, to have in his home yet another reminder of slavery—a stepson who was supposedly the offspring and namesake of a famous Confederate general. Squire Hargress gave his last name to Ned Forrest Hargress but was otherwise hard on him, finally spurring him to run away from the household when a young man.

The runaway didn't go far, but flight brought a lifelong lesson: he'd have to be what people in the community called a "scuffler," a scrambler who pursued every opening to make it in his world. Away from his stepfather, young Forrest Hargress found work from nearby white planters as a mule-tender. His skill in looking after mules aided him the rest of his life. He earned enough to acquire two mules of his own. He brought himself and his two mules back to his stepfather's household. That gesture seemed sufficient to forge a truce between the men.[8] Stepson Forrest rejoined Squire and Paul Hargress in farming the Hargress family land.

Marriage moved Forrest Hargress to a different part of the settlement, and to a more secure place within it. In January 1884 he married Betty Cameron. She was the daughter of Sandy Cameron, who in slavery times was the carpenter and most trusted man on Paul Cameron's Alabama plantation. He had become one of the former bondsmen to acquire Cameron land in the 1870s. Known as Eddyfield, his thirty acres constituted the richest but most flood-prone portion of the entire place. Sandy Cameron, sixty-nine years old in 1884, seemed more than happy to have his daughter and Forrest Hargress farm and start a family on that land, and to bring grandchildren into his life and that of his much younger second wife, Elvira—Betty's mother. Sandy Cameron may have schooled Forrest

Hargress in the basics of carpentry; it became another skill and lifelong side trade for the son-in-law, who came to build cabins not only in his own community but for miles around.

The trades of carpentry and mule-tending served Forrest Hargress well, for Eddyfield proved both a boon and a burden. In good times, its harvests of corn and cotton were bountiful. But in freedom, as in slavery times, the nearby German Creek flooded and often overflowed onto Eddyfield, ruining its crops. Forrest Hargress's wife, Betty, portrayed by her children as a "shifty woman," adapted by building a small skiff and had it always ready for rising waters. The recurrent floods and crop losses obliged Forrest Hargress to find work on white folks' places. After Sandy Cameron died, his widow, Elvira, urged her son-in-law to just let the lowland go and move permanently to higher ground. He took half her advice—he did move to higher ground. At the same time, he paid off the debts and taxes due on Eddyfield, and made the property his own.[9]

It was on the high ground of the former Cameron plantation that Forrest Hargress came to be the right-hand man of Paul Hargress, after his wife, Dicey, and brothers Jim and Squire all had died. Forrest Hargress worked Paul Hargress's field, repaired his cabin, even emptied the eighty-year-old amputee's chamber pot.[10] To aged Paul Hargress, Forrest may have reminded him of his younger self—the hardest worker around, a person who stuck by those who counted on him, patient, determined against all odds to root himself on the Cameron land. Nonetheless, when Paul Hargress decided to include Forrest in the partition of his 100 acres, his blood kin saw something else in all the energy and persistence that had gotten the white soldier's son—their "yellow cousin"—property on the low ground and then a house seat on the high ground. They didn't put a name on it—opportunism, calculation, cunning. All the same, they made their resentment clear. As community storyteller Louie Rainey recalled, "They kicked, but there was nothing they could do."[11]

Had the Hargress heirs known the full biography of Nathan Bedford Forrest, they might have done more than kick at his supposed son's presence among them. A few might have heard that Nathan Bedford Forrest had been the leading slave trader of prewar Memphis, buying and selling hundreds of people. It's doubtful that any knew that he was the commander at the 1864 battle of Fort Pillow, Tennessee, where Confederates—on the general's order to take no prisoners—had slaughtered a black Union regiment. Nor did any seem aware that in 1867 the ex-general became a founder and the first Imperial Wizard of the Ku Klux Klan.[12] What all did know was that the daring raider of the Confederacy was revered by whites in the Black Belt, and that his black namesake seemed to have a special standing among whites who credited the claim that the general was Forrest Hargress's father. Other whites scoffed at the story, perhaps aware that if true, the claim made the general a rapist.[13]

Even if Forrest Hargress hadn't been tied to the Confederate general, the other heirs would likely have challenged his right to the land. Both before and after emancipation, Africans as well as African Americans held contrasting beliefs about who could claim family property. To some, blood was all. If you were blood kin, you had a claim. If not, you had none. For others—including Paul Hargress—inheritance could be based on mutual assistance and care, on "built ties" as well as blood ties.[14] Of course, by American law, Paul Hargress's land was exclusively his and he could do exactly what he wished with it. But among blacks, from emancipation through the twentieth century and into the twenty-first, Anglo-American law didn't settle the matter. Black traditions of kinship and property claims had to be reckoned with. To Paul Hargress's blood kin, his brother's stepson was an outsider.[15]

Was there in fact nothing Paul Hargress's blood kin could *do*? Not entirely. What Louie Rainey perhaps didn't know, but what Forrest Hargress's children vividly recalled, was an episode when resentment did boil over into deed. The moment came around 1920. In his mid-fifties, Forrest Hargress was working down in low-lying Eddyfield while his young daughters were at his house seat on the high ground. Forrest Hargress had come through the hardships of the 1910s with two pieces of land, all paid for. The other Hargress inheritors had fared less well, still owing back payments to merchants and back taxes to the county. As some of the

Hargress beneficiaries were walking by, the daughters laughed and said something mocking, which the men took to be scorn. Infuriated, they summoned the other heirs. With pitchforks in hand, they all marched on Forrest Hargress's house. Ned Forrest Hargress was still in the field when the men shouted to the daughters and their mother, "We are full-blooded Africans and we're here to claim our land!"[16]

When Forrest Hargress returned and learned what happened, he acted. It's not known whether he confronted those who wanted him out. He did contact the white lawyer whom Paul Hargress had hired to do his trust in 1912, then to disinherit those who defaulted in 1915, and finally to devise a settlement after Paul Hargress died in 1918. Once more, the attorney intervened to confirm Forrest Hargress's full legal title to his portion of the land. Boil over they might. Shout they might. He was staying put.

The other heirs weren't done, though. Forrest Hargress's lot was set a hundred yards back from the center of the community—the church its residents had built on the acre of land that Robert and Kizziah Cabbil had deeded for that purpose in 1899. Forrest Hargress likely had a hand in the construction of the church, a one-story wooden building painted white on the outside with blue-colored wooden shutters over its open-air windows. Inside were hard wooden pews and above them an iron chandelier holding kerosene lamps lit when the service lasted past dusk.[17] All knew that Forrest Hargress, attached as he was to his land, was equally attached to the church at the heart of the settlement. A wide path from his home went straight to the church, and connected him as well to the red clay road through the settlement that led to the highway. The other Hargress heirs decided to hem him in. They moved fences on their lots right up to the lane from Forrest Hargress's cabin to the church, creating an alley barely wide enough for a wagon to get through. The narrow lane—dubbed "Hargrow Alley"—stood as a symbol of their resentment and reproach.

Undeterred, Forrest Hargress committed himself all the more to the church and ultimately came to reign as its moral leader. He was able to do this in part because its members constituted a wide swath of folks in the area, far larger than the number who had inherited Paul Hargress's land. The church that Forrest Hargress could see from his porch every morning had come to include dozens of renters and sharecroppers from a neighboring white-owned plantation. Before 1899, blacks who worked on the adjacent plantation had built a brush-arbor church on the property and named it Castleman Grove for the plantation manager, Lane Castleman, who let them worship there. Like many such designations, the naming was a sign of acknowledgment and a means of attachment. The name in time condensed to "Casmo" and ultimately evolved to "Cassimore." According to one account, when the Castleman Grove folk proposed to build a permanent place of worship on the white-owned plantation, the manager offered to sell them the land for $1. But "they thought they already had the land." Alertly, Robert Cabbil and the deacons listed on the 1899 deed adopted the shortened name of the brush-arbor church and welcomed its members to a black-owned sanctuary on black-owned property.[18] In Cassimore, Forrest Hargress found fellowship, neighbors who appreciated his drive and dedication, qualities that he channeled into the church. They viewed him not as an interloper but as a "Christian man." "Hargrow Alley" became his lifeline to Zion.

"Zion" was the term he and others bestowed on their church after the deacon board affiliated Cassimore with the national African Methodist Episcopal Zion denomination. Founded in the early nineteenth century, the AMEZ church had spread across the South after emancipation. It lodged its southern headquarters at Livingstone College in North Carolina, and there evolved the rules and protocol that governed its bishops, ministers, and members throughout the country. The AMEZ rules were codified, updated, and published yearly in a document called *The Book of Discipline*. Though unable to read, Forrest Hargress became a master of those rules. He had his literate wife, Betty Cameron Hargress, read the document to him aloud each year, and again when church disputes arose. He became an authority on the rules. Likewise, he had her read selections from the Bible that were to guide each week's Sunday service. He memorized the passages and parables. The unlettered farmer, mule-tender, and carpenter became, as one relative put it, "an ace on the Bible." To widen his home-grown knowledge—and to firm his certainty when differences came up—he hosted the traveling pastor who presided over the monthly service, got himself to meetings of the regional AMEZ conference, and made the acquaintance of church officials all the way up to the Bishop of Alabama. At home or away, he became a man of legendary fervor.[19]

His family, his church, and ultimately even his challengers came to see Forrest Hargress as a man who earned his way. A man who went to AMEZ conferences, who hosted visiting preachers, who had *The Book of Discipline* read to him each year by his literate wife, who'd "ask anybody anything"—in the admiring words of a great-granddaughter, he was "a game rooster."[20] There was no hemming him in.

Eleven ⌒ Sanctuaries

THERE WAS A PERIL greater than internal strife to the foothold in freedom achieved by Paul Hargress and the generation of blacks who acquired land after emancipation. The calamities that drained and divided Unc Paul's descendants had afflicted the entire South. The consequence was massive black exodus from the region. Departures during the 1910s began what came to be called the Great Migration—the ultimate exit of millions of blacks out of the rural South. There was no mystery about why so many left. The question is why some stayed, in the Cassimore community and elsewhere, and tenaciously held on to the land. Their reasons reveal the changing meaning of the land to those who came of age in the tumultuous twentieth century.

Cold numbers reveal the impact of plagues and pulls in the second decade of the new century. First by the hundreds, then by the thousands, men and women left Hale County and the Black Belt. Many sought work in coal mines in nearby Bessemer and Birmingham, others at mines as far away as West Virginia and eastern Pennsylvania. Some journeyed to cities, first to small cities of the South and then to big cities of the North, when the demand for labor in Detroit and Cleveland, hungry for industrial workers, turned to black laborers after war broke out in Europe in 1914 and stanched the flow of immigrants from the old world to the new. When the United States was drawn into the war in April 1917, black as well as white men from Hale County were among those drafted to fight. The impact of disasters at home and demands for soldiers and workers away, was to suction blacks away from a countryside that was ailing and failing.[1] In the Cedarville precinct, which contained the buyers of the Cameron place and black renters on adjacent lands, one out of every six residents departed between 1910 and 1920.[2]

Yet some remained. And others returned. They did not view the world away as the promised land. Rather, those who persevered came to view and value the homeland as their safe haven—as a sanctuary held for themselves, as a trust for those who departed. Two of the most tenacious of those who stayed were descendants of freed people who had bought the Cameron plantation in the 1870s. One born at the end of the nineteenth century, the other born early in the twentieth, in time they would come to be leaders of the community, every bit as determined to keep the land as Paul Hargress had been dedicated to getting it.

But that was in the future. No one could have foreseen at the start of the new century that both would emerge as models and champions of holding on to the land.

She would become Alice Hargress when she married, but she was born Alice Sledge on August 20, 1914, in a month and year that would prove to be momentous. She of course had no memory of the outbreak of war that occurred in the month of her birth, nor was any recollection of the fighting or the impact of the war passed on to her by members of her family. Conscription did claim at least one man in the neighborhood— he made it to the dock but fainted and was sent home. Other blacks from the county and state were drafted for service once America entered the lists in 1917. Ultimately the ripples of war extended far beyond the lives of the soldiers who served. The Great War opened the way for blacks to leave the South in droves and to find work and attempt new lives in midwestern and northern cities. Even though the migrants encountered barriers, antagonism, violence, and disappointments, most chose to remain rather than return to the South. Theirs was a migration that would continue for much of the twentieth century, as those who left summoned friends and family members to join them.[3] Why stay in the South when jobs and greater freedoms beckoned in the North?

For their part, Alice Sledge's parents seemed firmly rooted in the region where she was born, though her mother and father did not come of age on the same place. Her mother, Pinkie Cabbil Sledge, was born in 1890 and grew up on land bought from Paul Cameron in the 1870s by her grandparents Robert and Kizziah Lomax Cabbil. The grandparents had done well, rearing ten children on their 120 acres, gradually turning over the work of farming to their ambitious and prolific son, Cameron Cabbil. Cameron Cabbil—known by his community name, T'Lisha—farmed and fathered prodigiously. He had not one family but two. His wife and Pinkie Cabbil's mother was Laura Reese Cabbil, known as "Laura Mom." She bore ten children and was a churchwoman who would instruct her children, her grandchildren, and neighboring youngsters in the catechism of the Bible. Her husband also had a concubine—an "outside woman." Cintha Hargress was the daughter of enslaved people sent out from North Carolina. T'Lisha and Cintha—known by her community name, Cint—had thirteen children.[4]

The two women and two families lived in dwellings no more than a hundred yards apart. Cint cooked for both families. Laura Mom looked after the young. Youngsters from both families would go with Laura Mom when she made trips to the surrounding woods. While she went into the forest to collect plants for herbal medicines, the children gathered pecans—which they termed "scaly bark"—for her to store or sell.[5] As soon as his "inside" and "outside" children could go to the fields, T'Lisha put his offspring to work on Cabbil family farmland or on additional acreage that he sub-rented, some close by, some over in the next county. A large man with a booming voice, Cameron Cabbil used that voice to wake his sons each morning, summoning them to hitch the mules and prepare to go to field. "Get up, get up, get up!" he hooted. He was viewed by his two mates and his twenty-three children as a sire in the model of Old Testament patriarchs, and his rule and rulings went unquestioned.[6]

Alice Hargress, however, was not born on her grandparents' family land. She was born on a white-owned plantation—the home place of her father. By 1910, Pinkie Cabbil had married and moved. The marriage was to a young man nearby, and the move wasn't far. Most likely she had met Toney Sledge at the Cassimore church, which her grandfather had founded, which her grandmother and mother sustained, and at which she was called to Christ. Toney Sledge lived just to the south on a cotton plantation operated by the white Sledge family in Greensboro. In the 1850s the plantation had belonged to Dr. James Browder, a physician who had treated ill black workers on the adjacent Cameron place before the Civil War. After physician Browder sold the land to the Sledges, some of its black occupants called it Sledge's Browder place, while others kept the original title—the Browder place. Many formerly enslaved workers, including Toney Sledge's father and grandfather and cousins, took the name Sledge.

The black Sledges and other black families labored on the white owner's land, but as they saw it, the arrangement with the owner worked in their favor as much as his. Emancipation and Reconstruction had done away with the whippings that enforced slavery, and loosened the supervision that had sustained bondage. Former slaves now rented portions of the plantation for a preset amount of the cotton crop. Others sub-rented part of their allotted land to others. The complex arrangement made some of them tenants and employers simultaneously. The great advantage of working on the Browder place, as they saw it, was the quality of the plantation land. It was rich, without the variations and eccentricities that had driven Paul Cameron to exasperation on his place just to the north. It was the boss man's place, to be sure. But there was, in the view of descendants, "a living to be made down there."[7]

There was also music to be made. By day and during the week, Toney Sledge farmed with his father. By night and on the weekends, he was part of a brass band that entertained within the community and all around the area. Toney Sledge played the slide horn in the brass band and the guitar for his own amusement. Perhaps when he got religion, perhaps when he began to court Pinkie Cabbil, he realized the guitar had to go. In Pinkie Cabbil he found himself courting a woman for whom faith was central in her life. To the faithful of that day, the guitar was the devil's tool and guitar music the work of the devil. Many were the tales of fathers who thrashed their sons when they heard them singing or playing Satan's music. Toney Sledge understood. When he married Pinkie Cabbil, he didn't just give up or give away the guitar; he destroyed it.[8]

Six children were born to Toney and Pinkie Cabbil Sledge in the early twentieth century, with Alice Sledge, born in 1914, the next-to-youngest of the six.[9] Had nothing intervened, Alice Sledge, like other youngsters on the Browder place, would soon have learned the rules and the rhythm of farming on the plantation. Parents had to prepare the ground in January, plant in the early spring, and hoe out the weeds for the first months of summer, so that the cotton and not the weeds would get the nutrients of the soil. Then they had to hope that rain and sun would produce a strong stand of cotton by midsummer. Usually by late July people could "lay by" their hoes and let nature do its work of maturing the cotton for the next few months. When the bolls of cotton blossomed and the cotton bolls burst out, the harvest began.

As a child, Alice Sledge was too young to absorb the plantation ethos, or to be aware that the plantation included prompts that took the place of whips and overseers. During the winter and spring, when the cold precluded the raising of corn and foodstuffs, the landowner advanced money or credit at a store to buy necessities. Usually folks had stocked up on home-grown corn, pork, and vegetables. But there were clothes and shoes to buy, tools and supplies to purchase, and in harder times, food to pay for. People ran up debts and planned to pay them off, hoping to see some gain for themselves, if all went well when the harvest came in. Advances did not run throughout the year. Once the crop was laid by, advances stopped.[10] So part of the rhythm was that men had to seek paying jobs in mid- to late summer to be able to buy necessities at the country stores peppered throughout the rural areas. Usually men didn't have to go far. Planters and farmers nearby needed hay to be baled, fences mended, and other tasks done.

The year after Alice Sledge was born, however, her father and most others faced a seasonal migration that became more urgent. The boll weevil had first arrived in Hale County in 1913, bided its time in 1914, and wreaked devastation on the cotton crop of 1915. On the Browder place plantation as elsewhere, the weevil threatened to halve the harvest or worse.[11] Toney Sledge and his father could hold on as long as there were advances, and as long as planters were willing to "carry over" their renters and tenants, even if their harvests didn't pay off the debts of the year or years before. But there were voices, increasingly strident and public, that urged planters to put an end to the entire system. Let cotton go and let black laborers head north. There was a "crop" that didn't need labor at all, if only farmers would pay attention: cattle. Cattle needed only grass, and just a few tenders rather than a horde of them. The editor of the renamed Greensboro newspaper, the *Greensboro Watchman*, became insistent that it was time to use this providential plague of boll weevils to rid the land of cotton and tenants both, starting by curtailing advances.[12]

So things stood as folks on the Browder place and in neighborhoods nearby looked forward to the Fourth of July in the summer of 1916, seven weeks before Alice Sledge's second birthday. The weevil had yet to do its worst. Folks had come up with a homemade remedy for coping with the invaders by hitting the plants hard with sticks and knocking off the vermin.[13] Planters had stopped making advances, but plans were made to hit the road as soon as lay-by time came. Meanwhile, it was time for the holiday, which meant the summons to music for Toney Sledge and the brass band that was put together by Ambrose Hargress, the son of Forrest Hargress, who lived on his father's land just above the Browder place. By 1916, the rhythm of music was as set as the rhythm of work. There would be a party sponsored by the white Collins brothers on their plantation, ten miles to the south of Cassimore. There would be a gathering sponsored by black promoters, started by a dozen black men who ran stores or worked farms in the area. Barbeque, drinks, games were featured, and on the side, drinking and gambling and assignations flourished, all enlivened by Toney Sledge's slide horn and the mobile brass band that was the favorite of the area. Whites as well as blacks called for that music. On the way home, as they passed by the local justice of the peace, he too called for a song. Though it was early in the morning, and though loud music and drums had been outlawed by county commissioners, the brass band obliged with his favorite: "Dixie."[14]

The Fourth of July 1916 began with the usual preparations, but plans were dampened, then doused, then drowned by rain. All day it rained, rained as never before, and the next day and the next as well. A colossal hurricane, which had begun in the Gulf of Mexico, hurled itself up into the middle of Alabama and there, for more than a week, it stopped and parked, dropping twelve inches of rain. The Black Warrior River, a mile and a half from Cassimore, flooded all the way up to the road to Greensboro. "The rivers and creeks were converted into raging torrents," reported the local newspaper. Crops washed away, animals drowned. "There is no hope of anything being made."[15] Renters and landowners alike scrambled to bring what they could to higher ground—livestock, corn, clothing. It was the worst storm and worst flood on record. "The flood came and took everything," recalled Louie Rainey. With fields submerged, cows lost, "people had nothing to go on."[16]

The flood of July 1916 prompted a series of events that brought Alice Sledge and her mother back to family land. The move would reset her life course.

James Lyles was born in 1896. It was an inauspicious year, a year when the surge of laws hemming in black folks as a subordinate caste was confirmed by the Supreme Court. In May 1896, in the case of *Plessy v. Ferguson*, the Supreme Court ruled that separate but equal was constitutional. The 1896 decision ratified the segregation laws of Louisiana and a host of other southern states, and opened the way for the completion of segregation and for the disfranchisement of blacks in Alabama and throughout the South. In less blatant ways, northern states followed suit. As his life unfolded, James Lyles would find that his life's mission would be defined by segregation and the challenge of overcoming it.

James Lyles grew up on land that belonged to his grandfather and namesake James Mosely, 135 acres that his grandfather had purchased from Paul Cameron in 1884 for $1,950. To help pay for the land, James Mosely ran a gristmill, to which neighboring farmers brought their corn and wheat in season. According to family tradition, James Lyles's grandmother Nancy Mosely was part Native American and had red relatives who from time to time would come to visit her, her husband, and her descendants and speak "that backward talk." Her forebears may have been among Indian people who had never completely left the area, despite being compelled to sell their land and birthright to the white government in the 1830s. Well into the nineteenth century, they periodically returned to what locals called Indian Camp, a few miles from the Mosley place.[17] The Mosleys had a daughter named Rachel, who by 1880 had met and married Andrew Lyles, a mixed-race man. Andrew Lyles, as his son later put it, was "bredded around white folks," presumably including white relatives. After Rachel Mosley and Andrew Lyles married, they dwelt on Mosley land, where they farmed and started a family. James Lyles was their next-to-last child.[18]

Had all gone well, James Lyles might have followed in the footsteps of his father, taken over the family farm when he came of age, and never considered joining the exodus of those leaving the Alabama Black Belt. But all did not go well for Andrew Lyles. He was an ambitious man who sought to build upon what he acquired after part of the family property came into his hands in the 1890s. As Andrew Lyles sought to make his mark, he came up against a tangle of laws and practices that favored merchants, middlemen, and railroads, laws that were circumscribing the lives of farmers everywhere. In Alabama, those laws and practices met with resistance in the form of an insurgent Farmers Alliance movement. In the 1890s, the Alabama Farmers Alliance pursued cooperation by farmers and others across lines of race and region, and became part of a larger mobilization by farmers in the South and Midwest that took the form of the Populist movement. The key for Populists was the cooperative. Populists advocated farmer cooperatives to negotiate credit, purchase supplies, and market crops, all of which would reduce the control of bankers and middlemen who charged interest, bought cheap from farmers, and sold high to city dwellers.[19] Alabama Populists sought black support, but in the 1890s in Hale County, as in other counties of the Alabama Black Belt, many black voters had been pressured to vote the straight Democratic ticket. Counted out or used as pawns for what little benefits they could get, many blacks, intimidated or disillusioned, didn't vote at all. It's not known whether Andrew Lyles voted or did any differently.

But to him, the message of cooperation came through. In 1889, he and his brother Charles Lyles, and four others founded a cooperative farmers club in Hale County. The stakes of the Farmers Club in Co-partnership were miniscule—dues of 25¢ a month, with a treasury of $8.60 at the end of 1889.[20] What possibilities it had got crushed by the all-out assault of foes against cooperatives, cross-racial alliances, and Alabama Populist leader Reuben Kolb, who twice lost the governorship because of widespread fraud.[21] A massive economic depression that began in 1893 further sank farm prices without changing farmers' debts. By the time that James Lyles was born in 1896, his father's cooperative club had vanished. It's not clear whether Andrew Lyles ever shared the aspiration and vision of a cooperative with his son. James Lyles would much later say that it was not necessary for such communiqués to be direct. You get "the desire of your inheritance."[22] Known or unknown, directly or indirectly, he got that desire.

When farming revived in the early twentieth century, Andrew Lyles's ambition took a different form. Using his sons as labor, he got help from the wealthiest black man in the area, Tom Ruffin, the neighbor who lived just to the north and who had accumulated around 2,000 acres of land. In 1906, he took out a loan of $1,200 from Tom Ruffin. Was it for equipment? Was it for expansion? Was it to buy additional land? The goal was never stated, and by his youngest son, never known. What it seemed to signal was ambition for improvement, what his son would later call "betterment"—betterment in place. Why that aspiration fell short is not known. Had Andrew Lyles expanded, hiring others or planting more or buying added mules or equipment, his farming and his hopes would have been caught in the disaster of the boll weevil, the plague that destroyed cotton plants and which came to Alabama starting in 1913. Whatever the cause, he only paid back a fourth of the loan. For ten years, Tom Ruffin gave him extensions. Finally Ruffin sued and demanded payment or forfeiture of the land that Andrew Lyles had put up as collateral for the loan. By 1916, a portion of the inherited Mosley land was lost to debt, ostensibly transferred for a small payment to a neighboring white merchant, an immigrant from Ireland.[23]

What was left after his father's failures was more burden than birthright.

By 1916, as James Lyles neared his twentieth birthday, he could be excused for thinking he had precious little reason to remain on the family farm in Hale County, on the land that his grandparents had acquired decades before from Paul Cameron. His father was in debt and had forfeited a portion of family land to Tom Ruffin, who had transferred it to a white Irish merchant; the rest of his father's land was mortgaged. Prospects for successful farming were obliterated by the boll weevil, which for yet another year took the promise of bountiful crops and wormed its way into the core of each boll, leaving dead bolls littered all over the ground. No wonder that young Lyles, like hundreds of others in the neighborhood and thousands in the Black Belt, looked to seek a future in the bowels of coal mines, even as others moved to cities hoping, as poet Langston Hughes and author Isabel Wilkerson put it, for "the warmth of other suns."

Yet there was more to James Lyles's readiness for departure than the weevil and his father's debt. Twenty years after the Supreme Court's 1896 *Plessy* ruling, there was no escape anywhere from the reach of Jim Crow laws, which the Court had sanctioned. Ultimately his exodus was settled by a decision made by authorities in his home church.

As a very young man, James Lyles had come to see himself as a servant of God. A reader at an early age, he studied the Bible intently. He knew its passages by heart, able in an instant to cite them from what he called the "Master Book." That was where wisdom was, where the highest rules were, where one could find the vision needed to navigate the earthly world. As a youth in the Mars Hill Baptist Church, the church just a few miles north of where his family farmed and where Tom Ruffin and others were members, he accepted Christ as his Savior and received baptism. For many young people, that was an intense but brief moment, which brought joy to their families and membership in the church family. For James Lyles, his conversion experience was just the beginning of his opening to the Holy Spirit. In 1908, something remarkable happened. That Spirit spoke to him, telling him that it was time for him to share with others his understanding of the Bible and the lessons it revealed to him. He had a vision. It told him he was called to preach. He was twelve years old.[24]

Doubt was the response of those who could ratify or reject his claim of a call. The church deacons of the Mars Hill Church tested him, asking him questions. As James Lyles recalled it many years later, he didn't give them the answers they were looking for. His age surely made the deacons and pastor dubious, perhaps even hostile, and they denied him their sanction. It's not clear whether they encouraged him to pray more and return another time or dismissed his "call" altogether. He recollected only rejection.[25] If affirmed, his vision of himself as a sanctified preacher might have kept him at home, behind the pulpit as well as the plow. Yet it was not affirmed. He remained a young man of faith and studied all the more. But the Bible could go with him anywhere.

By the first of July 1916, James Lyles had made up his mind. He had a sister and brother-in-law in Bessemer, on the outskirts of Birmingham. The brother-in-law let young Lyles know that there was work for him there if he wanted it. With neither farming nor a church role to keep him at home, he was ready to go, to see what it was like to be man in a different and larger world. As he later put it, when he left Hale County for the mines and the city, he swapped the short pants of a boy for the overalls of a man, and boarded the train to Bessemer.[26]

He was with his sister and brother-in-law when, on the Fourth of July, the rains came to Hale County.

Their crops destroyed, their livestock lost, the men who had planned to celebrate the Fourth of July and depart for the seasonal migration later that month now collected what they could when the waters receded, and hit the road. With ruin all around, many would be searching for work far and wide to find those with jobs to do and wherewithal to pay. Toney Sledge was among the searchers.

There was one place that Toney Sledge might have gone at once to find a paying job. Fifty-five miles away, just east of the city of Tuscaloosa, the Holt Company in 1903 had opened coke ovens and a pig iron plant, and then a foundry for producing cast iron pipes. Black men flocked to Holt to undertake the hot work. They clustered in housing provided by the company and made do as best they could. The destination was well known to men of the Black Belt and Hale County. Numbers of men from the Browder place and Cassimore made their way to Holt in the year it first opened.[27] But that was not the work that Toney Sledge knew or wanted.

The crowds, the shacks, and the heat of the foundry intensified by the Alabama summer were not for him. He was a farming man. With so many rushing to Holt in hope of work, there was no certainty even if he went there that there would be a job for him. So with a friend he headed west, hoping to find farm work in places not decimated by the hurricane that had swamped Hale County. They walked, they hitched rides on wagons, they slept outdoors at night. Westward they traveled, first crossing the Black Warrior River, then the Tombigbee River, and finally into Mississippi, finding some work, but having to keep scrambling and moving. Finally they turned back toward Alabama and reluctantly headed for Holt and the pipe foundry, where they arrived to work in early 1917. By then Toney Sledge was ill. Working in the foundry with all the heat and dust, living in close quarters in dwellings with other men, his health deteriorated into pneumonia. They sent him home. On March 14, 1917, Toney Sledge died.[28]

The family and the community were so ravaged by the flood that there was no money to buy a coffin for the burial. Instead planks were pulled off floors and lumber was removed from the sides of abandoned cabins to improvise a casket. That humiliation prompted members of the Cassimore Church to do what other black communities had done earlier: create a burial society, with dues paid each year and surcharges levied with each new death, so that in the future its members could always decently bury their dead. The Cassimore Burial Society was the community legacy of the July flood—"the Big Water"—and of Toney Sledge's death.[29] The personal legacy was more desolate. Toney Sledge's passing left Pinkie Cabbil Sledge a widow and Alice Sledge, her sisters, and her brothers fatherless.

For a time, Pinkie Cabbil Sledge tried to sustain her family on the Browder place, farming along with Toney Sledge's father. Between 1917 and 1920, she picked cotton for a share of the crop with him, then moved to another plantation. With a family of six, it proved difficult to make ends meet. She gave away a daughter to grandparents who volunteered to care for her, and another daughter to a close friend. Around 1922, she and her remaining daughters moved back to the Cabbil home place of her father and mother, Cameron Cabbil and Laura Cabbil, and her still-living grandmother, Kizziah Cabbil. Deciding not to remarry, Pinkie Sledge lived there for the rest of her life. With the exception of a single year, so did her daughter Alice.[30]

Precipitated by the 1916 flood and Toney Sledge's death a year later, the move from the white man's plantation to family-owned land would shape Alice Sledge's view of her world. It became her original lesson in the fundamental importance of having a family home—heir land—to return to, no questions asked, none turned away.

By 1922, James Lyles had moved back to family land as well. Most who had left the farm and Hale County did not return, and for the longest time, it seemed that James Lyles would be among them. If life in the community looked bleak on the first of July 1916, when he'd left, there was even less left after the deluge. "What was there to go back to?" he reflected.[31]

Yet if the flood confirmed his decision to depart, his departure did not automatically mean that he could make it in the mines. It was not a given that a young man reared on the farm would welcome life hundreds of feet under the earth. Dark, dank, and dangerous, the mines offered pay, but with that came hazard and risk. At first he was afraid, but he overcame it. He learned that life below was like life above. People sang, talked, prayed, and ate. Most looked out for others, for indeed they knew they had to if they were to keep safe themselves. Others gambled and drank and played tricks, chancing that no harm would come. "You got used to it," he recalled. Good at the work, he enjoyed the benefits of making money, using his pay to buy fancy shirts with French cuffs for weekends on the town. Confidence and wanderlust propelled him to seek more distant work. Like others, he'd heard about prospects for blacks in West Virginia, where, far more than in Alabama, men were treated like men. He became a miner there. In the summer of 1920, he may even have spent a season in Detroit, rooming as a lodger in a household with others from Alabama.[32] By 1922, he was back in Alabama, working in the Dolomite coal mine, just outside of Birmingham.

Then came a vision: an explosion. He put it aside, unsure of whether it was an omen or simply the unbidden expression of suppressed fear.

However, on November 22, 1922, not long after he'd come up from working his shift in the Dolomite Mine No. 3, there was a huge blast. Four hundred and seventy miners were trapped; eighty-four died. James Lyles took it as God's will that he'd had the vision, and that he was above ground when the disaster occurred. He saw it as a sign—not the first one and not the last—that God had spared him for some greater work.[33]

James Lyles elected to go home. He didn't know what mission awaited him there, but he took it as God's message that home was where he would find it. And there was certainly family work to be done. His father, now sixty-six, and mother, now sixty-five, were aging on a farm that was in debt. Alerted to the risk of losing the home place, he scrambled to save it.[34] Then he sought to get back at least some of the land defaulted by his father to Tom Ruffin and transferred to an Irish merchant. He spoke to a lawyer who contacted the merchant, Pat Kelly, who said that for $25 his father could have some of the property back if he acted "damned quick." Act he did, "damned quick."[35]

Having saved his family's land, he never let it go.

Nor did he let go of the conviction that at times the Holy Spirit spoke directly to him, and provided him with understandings that he should pass on to others. His model for that role was his uncle, James Eaton, who sometime in the previous century had felt the Mantle of Christ bestowed upon him. For James Eaton, the Mantle of Christ meant that he could speak and share divine truths given to him to see. James Eaton's reputation as a minister was acknowledged in the notice of his death in 1925. Soon thereafter, in a vision, James Lyles felt the Mantle of Christ fall on him. This time he didn't seek the sanction of a deacon board or the elders of the church. As it had for his uncle, a capacity for prophetic visions had come to him directly. Nearing thirty years old, he awaited the Lord's word about the work he'd come home to do.[36]

While James Lyles was striving to reclaim family land from debt and save the home place from foreclosure, Alice Sledge was living on family land. But it was land already shrunken by debt and departures and—as family tradition had it—by a disastrous misstep of her grandfather Cameron

Cabbil. Family lore was that at the behest of strangers seeking a favor, Cameron Cabbil had agreed to put two of their mules in the lot with the many mules he owned and farmed with. Unbeknownst to him, the two mules had been stolen, and when they were found in the Cabbil lot, he faced jail as the thief or the accomplice to thieves. And in the early 1900s those convicted of crime could be hired out to other farms or sent to coal mines. As the story came down, Cameron Cabbil found whites who got him out of the scrape, but the cost was high: a huge chunk of the land acquired by his father, Robert Cabbil, in the 1870s.[37] It is clear that by the 1920s, a substantial portion of that original purchase was lost. Was it a quid pro quo for keeping Cameron Cabbil out of jail and the mines, or was it "bad management," or something else? Whatever the cause or causes, the family was down to a house seat and a small acreage by the time that Pinkie Cabbil Sledge and her children moved back to the Cabbil home place.[38]

Young Alice Sledge, eight years old in 1922, likely didn't yet know about the land loss or care about the shrunken size of the home place. Her formative experience was a personal encounter that would define for her the supreme importance of coming of age on family land and not on the white man's plantation. The traumatic experience came during an early visit to see her Sledge grandmother, who still dwelt on the Browder place. Pinkie Sledge outfitted her daughter in a Sunday go-to-church dress. As Alice Sledge walked the path to her grandmother's cabin, other children gathered round her, began to jeer, and then grabbed at her fancy clothes. As she recalled it, they left her dress in tatters. From then on, she dressed down for her visits, had a male cousin protect her as she walked, and took taunts as symptoms of the petty envy that went with plantation life. As she came to see it, plantation folk didn't want others to get airs. The next step was jostling for tiny advantages by seeking favor with the landowner, just as folks had sought boons from the master in slavery days. Baiting and tattling were the children's form of mimicking what adults did. As Alice Sledge came to understand it, that behavior was "plantation stuff," and the unavoidable outcome of living on land where the white man ruled and had always to be pleasured and pleased.[39]

In time, that early trauma and exposures that followed crystallized into a profound lesson for her: own your place, own yourself.[40]

In light of all the setbacks to farming in the Black Belt, the white Sledge landowners decided that they would no longer manage the plantation their family had owned in the nineteenth century. Nor would they sell it. Instead they turned the running of the place over to a nearby planter who had, with his brothers, systematically been acquiring ownership or control of lands for the first two decades of the twentieth century. By the early 1920s, the Browder place came under the management of James Compton, who grew up in adjacent Marengo County, and who by the twenties lived ten miles below Cassimore on a plantation near the crossroads hamlet of Prairieville.

From the vantage point of those who remained as renters on the Browder place—whether by choice or necessity—their memories of working on the white man's plantation were positive, and in stark contrast to the perceptions of Alice Sledge. First and foremost, the land was rich. Even after decades of growing cotton, going back to the 1840s, crops could grow there without the use of fertilizer to restore or buttress the soil.[41] Lessened supervision by the new boss man was another reason that families remained on the Browder place plantation. Both before and after management shifted from the Sledges to James Compton, descendants recalled that white supervision was minimal: "nobody watched over us." From time to time, James Compton did come through the place. But usually it was with men-friends on their way to a hunt. As descendants recalled it, the only watchman was the "see-see rider," a black employee who rode through the fields intermittently to check the crop on behalf of the boss man. The key to the lax supervision was the rental arrangement. On their allotted land, each family paid a rent of two bales of cotton. The rest of what they raised was theirs. There was a final benefit for renters on the Browder place, one that was widespread in the Black Belt: renters could sub-rent the land they contracted to farm. They sub-rented to those who didn't have the tools or mules enough to work out a full rental arrangement with the white landlord.[42] Good soil, lax supervision, favorable terms to rent—why buy when they could rent on terms like those?

Of course that was the rose-colored recollection of why renters stayed. The harsher reality was that even with the favorable rental arrangement, the Browder place folk had to take out advances in order to carry them through the months of the year when there was no income and no crop. Shoes, sugar, coffee, clothing—all had to be bought on credit. The condition of working on the Browder place and under Jim Compton was that you took your advances from him. You bought at his store, accepted his credit, paid his interest, and abided by his record keeping. You also sold your cotton to him, weighed on his scale, paid at his price. On settlement day, when Jim Compton totaled up the payment against the advances, the outcome was rarely better than break-even, and just as often the workers were told, "You *almost* made it," and remained in debt. In such a case, renters were "carried over" to the next year, when a better crop might allow them to accumulate enough to pay off the debt (with interest) and pay for the next year's advances.

Could they check or challenge the tally? Most of the men who farmed the Browder place could neither read nor write. Though there were grade schools to attend, parents as well as landlords expected the renters and their children to go to the field rather than to class. There was a deeper reason not to ask to see the record, namely that such a request implied that the record was flawed, tilted in the landlord's favor. No one could expect to challenge the landlord and be allowed to stay on the plantation he ran. Still less could one appeal to a local official who might call him to account. "Jim Compton was the law around here," as it was said. Even so, on at least one occasion, one of the Browder place men questioned the count and lived to tell the tale.

Unbeknownst to Gates Rainer, his literate and numerate son had kept his own account book of expenses and had brought it with him on settlement day. After the settlement, he took his father aside and said, "Mr. Jim has made a mistake." The father asked if he was sure, and when the son said yes, the father stayed until the end of the day and then quietly approached Jim Compton, likely with hat in hand, and asked if Mr. Jim could redo the tally, as his son had a question about how it came out. Compton, perhaps with bemusement, obliged, and when the recount brought the renter out ahead, took the correction with laughter rather than anger: "That son of yours must have spent his time *in* school rather than *under* it!"[43]

Not all sons in the 1920s, on the Browder place or on other plantations of Hale County and the Black Belt, were prepared to stay on the farm in a world of such mandatory deference, much less to risk challenging the landlord. One man who left explained that he had watched his parents bend time and again. He was not willing to bend to survive.[44] James Compton seemed to sense that unless he did something to keep the young on the farm, other workers might quit for the prospect of a freer and more remunerative life in the cities of the South and the North. He may have sensed as well the desire of fathers, for whom the Browder place arrangement was still "a living," to keep their sons on the farm. That dual awareness may explain an extraordinary proposal that Compton made a week before Thanksgiving in 1926. He told five of his renters that he had made an arrangement with merchant Isadore Bligh in nearby Demopolis to sell the men 1926 Ford Model Ts. If they could come up with $100 as a down payment, they could pay Bligh the rest over time.[45] The Browder place renters jumped at the chance. On Thanksgiving morning, they and their sons hopped on a truck, went to Demopolis, paid the $100 that each had scraped together, and took possession of their Model T Fords. Not a one of the men could drive, nor were there paved roads for them to drive on. Their sons took the wheels, and over rutted back roads and narrow gravel main roads, they made their way back to the Browder place, bucking and screaming all the way.[46]

The cars allowed the young men small freedoms their fathers and mothers hadn't had. They could drive the family to church rather than endure the jostling of a wagon or walk in their bare feet, shoes in hand, until they arrived at the sanctuary. They could travel up the road to see friends, court young women, or attend churches farther away. While racial etiquette required blacks to step aside for white folks on town sidewalks or paths in the countryside, road travel was a different matter. Obnoxious whites could and did force black drivers off the road, but for the most part the black driver didn't have to give ground to cars operated by whites. Having an automobile was a small victory in another way as well. Before the 1920s, cars belonged mostly to white people and to a few well-to-do blacks such as Tom Ruffin.[47] Now, in 1926, black renters had the status that came with owning a car—and a new car at that. Well might they ask, who needed the sanctuary of their own land?

Indeed, as Browder place renters drove up the road past their counterparts on the Cabbil place and other black-owned lands, they might be forgiven for thinking that they and not the landowners had the best of their world. They likely knew that to make ends meet, Alice Sledge's mother not only went to the field and farmed, getting what help she could out of her children, but also took in laundry for a neighboring white family. A single white man named Jim Simpson had moved onto Cameron land in December 1884; the land had belonged to Jonas McCoy until he lost his farm to a creditor. Jim Simpson dwelt on the 175 acres until 1919, when he sold it to Earl Compton, Jim Compton's brother, who moved there with his family that year.[48] Pinkie Sledge laundered for the Comptons. The white folks' clean sheets and bedclothes and freshly washed drawers and dresses gleamed in the sun as they dried on the clothesline outside the house where Pinkie Sledge and her children lived. The garb of the large white family was returned starched, ironed, and folded at the end of each week. The plantation dwellers surely did not know that on one occasion, when Alice Sledge was sent to borrow sugar from the white neighbor, she was chastised by the lady of the house for not saying "ma'am" when she made the request. Startled at the white lady's demand for subservience, Pinkie Sledge's daughter asked her mother "not to send me up there anymore."[49] Browder place people could have told her that you didn't need to be on a plantation to be expected to defer to white folks.

Sheltered from the commands of planters and neighbors, Alice Sledge instead looked to instruction from her mother and from the church founded by her great-grandfather in 1899. The refuge of a home place and the guidance of her mother would bring her into alignment with James Lyles. It was at the Cassimore AME Zion Church that Alice Sledge, like other youngsters coming of age, sat on the mourners' bench—sometimes called the "moaner's bench" for the sounds of supplication it produced. It was there that she sat while she and adults prayed that she, like James Lyles before her, might be visited by the spirit of Christ and feel her conversion to the faith of her forebears. She was out in the country on the day that the Holy Spirit came to her; she ran back to her family in joy to report that she was saved. In the Cassimore church, she and her sisters took up singing holy songs. From their mother, the sweet-singing Sledge sisters learned that they were to sing as one. There was to be no showboating, with one sister trying to outdo the other. There was to be no "greediness."[50] "No greediness" was a rule that Alice Sledge carried with her for the rest of her days.

Focused as they were on making the most of home ground and forging lives guided by God, neither Alice Sledge nor James Lyles foresaw the possibility that their sanctuaries might be threatened or their faith tested by changes in the outside world. Looked at from the outside, the twenties in American agriculture and in southern agriculture in particular was a decade of slow hemorrhaging. In cotton as in other crops, bumper crop followed bumper crop, each year's surplus drove down prices, and farmers sought to make up the fall in income by boosting the next year's harvest, only to have the cycle repeat and compound. When the stock market crash came in October 1929 and precipitated the Great Depression, the economic disaster that followed exposed the overproduction that had undermined cotton growing during the decade before.

For James Lyles and Alice Sledge, it was to be the upheaval of the 1930s that would clarify and intensify the utter necessity of holding on to the land—for themselves, for their heirs, and, in the Depression decade ahead, for those soon to be dispossessed from white-owned plantations.

Part Four ∽ Heir Land

Twelve ∽ "That Thirties Wreck"

IT WAS CHRISTMAS DAY, 1939. He called them together at the base of the hill, at the barn where his cattle were. He summoned the black men and women who had been farming there all their days, raising cotton and corn and sweet potatoes and peanuts and butter beans. They and their fathers and mothers knew the land, knew what it took to make a crop, knew where to hunt and fish during their time off, knew where children were born and love was made. Some surely knew what was coming. Others dwelt in denial. They were tenants, yet it felt to them as though they were tenants with tenure. Just as seventy years earlier their ancestors had felt that their toil entitled them to the fruits of freedom and, for some, a right to the land, so they felt now in 1939.[1] But that's not what they heard. What he told them, that man who had come there that year from a place 500 miles away—the "man from Missouri," as they called him—was that they had to leave. He would let them take their cabins if they could manage it. But for nineteen families, this would be their last Christmas on the Browder place. Still stinging in the memory of a man who was there, four words said it all: "We had to git."[2]

A different set of words to describe that moment came from those who were not there: "It was then that they became true men and women."[3] They lived nearby, but the difference was that they possessed their land. It had been bought from Paul Cameron in the 1870s and passed on to them by their forebears, mortgaged and atrophied but still in family hands. The landowners of 1939 had no way of knowing that seven decades before, eviction had set the stage as well for Paul Hargis's emancipation from plantation rule and placed him on the course that concluded with the purchase of land from his former owner. As had proved true for Paul Hargis in the unsettled 1870s, so for James Lyles and for Alice Sledge Hargress in the turbulent 1930s: self-possession was yours if you had your own land.

⁓

When thirty-four-year-old James Lyles married eighteen-year-old Eliza Pratcher in 1930, he had little idea that the decade ahead would be what he would come to call "that thirties wreck."[4] He had stabilized his father's farm, begun to repair the family home, taken up the slack left by his parents' aging and by the departure of older brothers and sisters. Just to the north of the family homestead, things had begun to break in favor of long-time tenants on the 2,000 acres belonging to the county's largest black landowner, Tom Ruffin. Tom Ruffin had willed that none of his land should be sold for at least five years after his death, which occurred in 1921. Ruffin made his daughter Hattie Ruffin Hudson, who lived 140 miles away in the small Alabama community of Union Springs, the executor of his will. Through the 1920s she'd come home to Cedarville each January to settle up with tenants.[5] But there was an understanding that eventually the land would be sold, and when it was, it would be sold to black people, with Ruffin's tenants getting first option to buy. Eliza Lyles's brother was one of the tenants who would buy in the 1940s, with land prices low.[6]

Times were hard, but at least James and Eliza Lyles could imagine that they and the family they would start could get by. They could hope that bad as things were, they couldn't get worse.

Worse they got. The price of cotton dropped to 5¢ a pound in 1933. Corn prices dropped, too, along with everything else. Even for those who raised their own crops, returns were barely enough to support them and their families.[7] For James Lyles in the first years of the 1930s, for those on the Browder place, and for Alice Sledge on family land, options narrowed.

In the larger world it was called the Depression. Kicked off by the crash of the stock market in 1929, it was marked by massive unemployment, which left millions jobless by 1932. Prices of all things went down in the great deflation spawned by the crash. But even with falling prices, millions could buy nothing. In the nation, the Depression brought a change in leadership, a new president who promised a New Deal, and a flurry of laws aimed at checking the free fall. For farmers, there was the Agricultural Adjustment Act, which sought to counter overproduction and rock-bottom prices for crops by paying landowners—and supposedly their tenants—for taking farmland out of production. Other massive New Deal programs put jobless people to work. In the rural areas, that work focused on road building. Crooked highways needed to be straightened and gravel roads paved. The Public Works Administration underwrote road-building projects that brought employment to men able and willing—and selected—to do the work. Selection in the Black Belt of Hale County was made by white landlords put in charge of the road programs. One could get picked if strong, compliant, and willing to take what the boss man dished out. If he didn't like you, or you couldn't take him, there was no work to be had.[8]

What the crash meant locally came out in the changing of the ruler and the rules on the Browder place. Folks who had grown up there in the 1920s remembered James Compton—"Mr. Jim"—as a benign boss man. He didn't look over the shoulder of his tenants. He rarely came down, letting his black "see-see" rider come through and report back. His terms were, as the renters saw it, lenient. Give him two bales of cotton for the acreage you worked, and the rest of what you raised was yours. The explanation for his largesse was that he was a man of capacious wealth.[9] He owned or managed thousands of acres from Demopolis in adjacent Marengo County to southern Hale County. He lived twenty miles away at his Cottonwood Estate. Admittedly he acquired some of that land by legal maneuver. When black landowners got behind on their taxes, he started paying taxes for them. If they couldn't repay him, or pay the county, he claimed the land and added it to his holdings.[10] For most tenants on the Browder place, however he came by control, their lot didn't seem onerous. There was one other consequence of working for Mr. Jim: he was known as a man who, for good or for ill, was "the law." That reputation meant that there was no point in challenging him. But it also meant that if you got into a scrape, you could turn to him to help you out—"if you were in the right." Even when in the right, as tenants perceived it, you needed a patron to shield you.[11]

All that changed the last week of July 1931, when James Compton died. Management of the Browder place fell to James Compton's fifty-four-year-old brother Earl Compton. Earl Compton lived within view of the household where Alice Sledge dwelt with her mother, Pinkie Sledge. Temperamentally, at least as people recalled it, Earl Compton was almost the mirror opposite of his brother. Mr. Jim had operated with an open hand, as if money didn't matter that much to him. In contrast, "Mr. Earl" was seen as tight, a man for whom every nickel mattered.[12] More than a difference in temperament was involved. When Earl Compton took over in the 1930s, the panic was on. For the landlord, latitude gave way to constriction. Earl Compton shifted black folks from familiar cabins to different locations and dwellings. He brought in white tenant farmers to add to the workforce. It's not clear whether there was a difference in the land they got—whether white tenants got the best land and the black tenants the hindmost. What is certain is that there was no love lost between black tenants and white tenants. The whites were seen as "snakes" and snitches, especially one who was viewed as the landlord's informant about the doings of black folks.[13] The tightening of landowner control was a widespread response to the Depression. Whether Earl Compton would have conducted himself so in good times can't be known. But the change was traumatic for the black farmers.

So things stood when the programs of the New Deal came to Hale County. The landlord put in charge of the road building for the Cassimore segment of the county? Earl Compton. If you wanted public work, you had to please Mr. Earl.[14]

James Lyles realized by 1934 that farming alone would not let him sustain his family or hold on to his land. He and his wife, Eliza, had two young children, with another on the way. Low as they were, taxes were hard to pay. His father's mortgage on their house seat still required payments. He likened life in 1934 to being a "terrapin with a fire on his back."

You had to get out of your shell or perish—to "get out there scratchin'" or lose it all.[15] Road work was one option, but not for long—not under the supervision of Earl Compton. A man who adamantly refused to say *yessir* to white men, James Lyles knew that was a requirement of working for Mr. Earl. Plus Earl Compton cursed: *"Goddamn* this and *goddamn* that!"* James Lyles tried working on the road for a time, but the *goddamns* drove him away.[16]

Far away. With local roadwork out of the question, James Lyles turned back to the one thing he did know: mining. In 1935, he went back to the mines. On and off, for almost a decade, he would labor in the mines, working by the week and coming home on the weekends. Mining work saved the farm. Traveling to and from the mines by bus, watching the land go by on those long days and nights, gave him a view of what was happening to others. The journeys set the stage for a new vision.[17]

The connections between Alice Sledge and the man she would marry were many. Ned Forrest Hargress II was named after his grandfather Forrest Hargress, who by 1932 had become the religious and moral leader of the Cassimore church that was so central to Alice Sledge's young life. Born in 1913, the younger Ned Forrest Hargress had been taken in by his grandparents after his unmarried birth parents gave their child to Forrest and his wife, Betty Cameron Hargress, to rear. Like many, the grandson early on acquired a nickname, "Hooksie," and was always known by that name in the community. Hooksie's father, Ambrose Hargress, had been the manager of the brass band that Toney Sledge had played in. After the birth of his son, Ambrose Hargress left Cassimore, moved to Montgomery, and looked after young men sent to a reform school and prison farm just outside the city.

Alice Sledge certainly had known the older Forrest Hargress as the Cassimore church leader and community patriarch; she dwelt less than a quarter mile from where he lived with his wife and grandson. Still, age and aura put a distance between them: Forrest Hargress was almost fifty when Alice Sledge was born, and she had heard the legend about him that he was the son of famed Confederate general Nathan Bedford Forrest.

However, church and proximity brought nineteen-year-old Alice Sledge and twenty-year-old Ned Forrest Hargress II together, and when they married in 1933, she became the in-law of the grandparents who had reared him.

Alice Sledge Hargress and her husband moved to a small cabin next to the home of her in-laws, and she and Hooksie farmed down at Eddyfield, the rich bottomland that Forrest Hargress had redeemed from debt and back taxes early in the twentieth century. While it was more productive than land of mixed soils on higher ground, Eddyfield continued to be vulnerable to flooding and had been farmed without replenishment for almost a century. With the price of cotton low and sinking lower, Alice Hargress and her husband were barely making it.

When the New Deal came to Hale County and brought public work to the area in the form of rebuilding the highway, Hooksie found a way to supplement their income. The road work job paid cash and allowed them to scrape by. With an easy temperament, Hooksie didn't let the brusque manner of road supervisor Earl Compton get under his skin; he did what he needed to do to keep the job.

Road work gave out by the middle of the decade. By 1936, the young couple had a daughter and another child on the way. How were they going to make ends meet? Alice Hargress's husband proposed that they try sharecropping for a year. She disliked the idea. She had never, not once, worked on the white man's place. But Hooksie was the man of the house and wanted to try it, to see if they could better themselves. They arranged to work as tenants for a farmer who had land eight miles below Cassimore. She raised chickens, sold eggs, carefully husbanded purchases. When she went to sell or barter eggs at the landlord's store, she found that the black man who managed the store favored the white owner. He would try every egg and take only the perfect ones: "He would sell his soul rather than cross that white man." She thought that her husband, Hooksie, took out only the advances that they needed. Nonetheless, at the end of the year, they just broke even. She didn't know whether Hooskie had taken out more than he'd told her. Her suspicion was that the arrangement was never meant for them to come out ahead. For Alice Hargress, one year of sharecropping was enough. They moved back to family land.[18]

The 1937 experience at sharecropping deepened her hostility to the plantation. Not only were you likely to come out behind, but if you tried to stay with it, you could become a debt slave. Worse was the need to pretend that all was well—to smile as if you didn't care that the boss man was watching over you. As she saw it, sooner or later that pretense was bound to get into your mind. You and your husband and your children would come to think that you couldn't get along without Mr. Boss Man. You would be truly lost.[19]

It's not as if the Hargress family land that the young couple returned to was hermetically sealed or even sufficient. Not at all. The same problems that had bedeviled Paul Cameron plagued his successors on the soil: bad to erratic soil and floods on the rich black land made for unpredictable harvests, and long use brought soil exhaustion. Seventy-year-old Forrest Hargress supplemented the little farming he did, given the age of the soil and the age of the man, with other work. He made and sold fish nets and cotton baskets to white customers in Demopolis; he gathered and brought up moss for the white Sledges, owners of a Greensboro florist shop.[20] Hooksie, again living near the grandfather who had raised him, realized that he wasn't much for farming. He supplemented the family income by working at Earl Compton's dairy barn, milking cows twice a day, with the milk going into the cans that were picked up at the highway and sold in the region as unpasteurized B-grade milk.

Neither Alice Hargress nor her husband nor Forrest Hargress was sealed off from white folks. Nonetheless, they did have their own homes and own land, and so they could not be dispossessed if they crossed those they worked for. When one of the Comptons saw Forrest Hargress leaving the community on his wagon on a weekday and asked him where he was going, he replied, "Goin' to town, just like you are."[21] The land might be a porous sanctuary and an anemic source of livelihood. But, "all black and no white," family land served as a refuge for the soul.

As James Lyles traveled home from the mine on weekends, usually having to stand on the crowded bus that carried him from Bessemer to Greensboro, he could not help but notice that the landscape was changing.

Whereas once the plantations and farms he passed had been " 'luminated with black folks," the black population was beginning to thin out. Where once cotton had been everywhere, the crop was declining.[22] A miner by the week and a farmer on the weekend, James Lyles knew that government programs were part of what was happening. The Agricultural Adjustment Act was seeking to halt the 1920s pattern of overproduction by paying landlords to take land and crops out of production. Landlords in turn were supposed to pay a portion of their crop reduction payment to their tenants. Many often did not, forcing former tenants off the land.[23]

It's possible that James Lyles also learned that in response to the evictions, the federal government had started a program to resettle some dislocated farmers—white farmers—in government-owned agricultural communities.[24] If so, such knowledge may have provided the backdrop for a startling vision that he had in the mid-1930s. At the time, he recalled, he was walking down the refurbished Highway 69, straightened and paved thanks to the Public Works Administration road work in the first half of the decade. The sun was overhead and it was hot. He was on his way to the country store right at the corner of the entrance to Cassimore, where the red clay dirt road began that led into the community and to the AME Zion church at the center of it. That was when the vision came. It wasn't a voice, though he heard it. It wasn't a sighting, though he saw it. His mission had come. He was to convey a message to his people, to those who were living through the thirties wreck and seeking somehow to hold on to a livelihood.[25]

Sharecroppers were trying to stay sharecroppers. Landowners were trying to stay landowners. All were seeking to supplement their atrophying income from farming with outside work, especially—like Hooksie—through the milk trade. As James Lyles saw it, that effort would fall short.

What people needed to do, the vision told him, was to hold on to the land they had and to pool resources for those who were being displaced, or soon would be. What he saw in his vision was a future of massive displacement, a replacement of cotton by cattle, the ousting of black people by white-faced cows. He saw a "country torn to pieces, black folks driven out." What was to be done? Blacks who had resources needed to pool what they had. Depression had brought down the price of land. Black folks should buy land and put their own people on it. No point in waiting for the government to come in and provide a refuge. In Hale County, in the Black Belt, that was never going to happen. Black people needed to create a land cooperative. Paul Cameron—and not the government—had once homesteaded their forebears. Now they needed to homestead themselves.[26]

He had the Bible to back him up, to credential him as a prophet whose intense study and whose Mantle of Christ made him a messenger of God. He took his vision to the burial society to which he and his family belonged—the Piney Grove Burial Society, just north of where he lived, down the road from the Mars Hill Baptist Church, which he attended. At the monthly meeting of the society, where members gathered together to pay their dues, to read from Scripture, and to exchange news, James Lyles asked to speak. The room was small and hot. The chairs were tiny, used on other occasions for Sunday school for the young of the Mars Hill church. He told the society members what he foresaw, what God called on to him to say, what needed to be done. They needed to go beyond collecting for the dead. Unless they acted, unless they bought land that would allow those thrown off plantations to have another place to farm, they'd all be put off, with nowhere to go. They had to pool money to buy land and make a place where their own folks could resettle. They needed to collect and act for the living. He even proposed to set aside some land of his own. The Eaton brothers—cousins—offered to set aside land that they owned. The rest of what must be done required them to act—to buy land while the price was low, for the landless to come.[27]

"My own people fouled it," he recalled. Some seemed interested, thinking he was on the right track. But a fellow society member got up and poured doubt on the idea, arguing that they were doing all right with a little farming and a lot of milking. They would get through. The critic scorned the idea that black folk had enough to meet the white man's price. Didn't black people have debt enough without assuming more, putting themselves at risk of losing everything? The skeptic said that he too trusted the Lord—trusted the Lord to see them through. James Lyles's proposal met defeat.[28]

James Lyles knew from thirty years of studying the Bible that he was not the first prophet to be ignored. More often than not, that was the prophet's lot. Rebuffed, he boarded the bus back to the mines, journeying through land increasingly filled with abandoned tenant cabins and white-faced cows.

In the South of the 1930s, as elsewhere in the nation, landless men were compelled to "tramp" to get by. In quite different ways, the wife of James Lyles and the mother of Alice Sledge Hargress opened their homes as havens to men unmoored by the Depression. When hoboing men came by the Lyles household for food, they were never refused. Eliza Pratcher Lyles always fed her family first, then provided meals for the strangers in need.[29] For Pinkie Cabbil Sledge, someone who was not a stranger but had grown up in the Cassimore community became her ward when his thirties wanderings came abruptly to an end.

Louie Rainey was one of those unmoored by the Depression, though restlessness with settled living came long before that upheaval. What he said of churchgoing he might well have said of farm life and the Cassimore community he grew up in: "What they had, I didn't want, and what I had, they didn't want."[30] A big, bold, strapping man, Louie Rainey—like Cameron Cabbil—loved to live large. He heard and retold stories with gusto. He relished games, starting as a youngster who played a mean game of marbles. He found that he was good at gambling, both when it was on the up and up and when he could win with crooked dice. He was in his element at the barbeques and festivals that marked the summer gatherings of the Black Belt. After the ball games and feasting and performances of the brass bands—and sometimes even during them—men would gather off to the side, beer or moonshine in hand, and the gambling would begin. As often as not, when winners were found using crooked dice, or when accusations flared among men who suspected others of fooling with their wives or girlfriends, fights broke out, knives flashed, and the gamblers scattered as assailants went at it. With his winnings, Louie Rainey scattered, too.[31]

Not always, though. In one of those fights, a man died, and Louie Rainey was charged with killing him. A jury found him guilty, and in 1930 the census listed him as imprisoned in the state penitentiary. It's not clear how he got out—whether he was cleared, whether someone else confessed, whether a lawyer stepped in and found error in the trial.[32] Somehow, by 1933, he was out of prison and back in Cassimore. By that time, his one last link to the community—Louisa Rainey, the mother he had pledged to care for—had died. For a time it looked as if he might stay. The PWA road project was under way in 1934, and Louie Rainey—like Alice Sledge Hargress's husband, Hooksie—had signed up for it. But for Louie Rainey, as for James Lyles, the man in charge was the stumbling block. James Lyles had known in advance that he could never work for gruff, demanding, peremptory Earl Compton. Louie Rainey doubted that Earl Compton would abide having him as a worker—at twenty-eight years old, he was too much his own man, too talkative, too loud, too fun-loving. And indeed, while Earl Compton felt compelled to hire him, within weeks the planter sent him packing.[33]

As had James Lyles, Louie Rainey hit the road. Without any special skills, with neither experience nor interest in working in the mines, Louie Rainey had primarily strength and gumption. He hitched rides, sought casual labor, got himself to Mobile. There he met someone the first day who was from Hale County. Though they'd not known each other back home, his new acquaintance took him in and helped him find work on the docks. The material he found himself unloading was covered in salt that coated his hands and arms. It took a nightly bath and an hour's soaking to soothe his corroded skin. He could have stayed in Mobile as long as he wished; his friend urged him to remain. But he took to the road again and wound up in Uniontown, helping a trucker haul lumber. He thought it would just be a job to put change in his pocket before he returned home, but he stayed for three years.[34]

The gaming spirit and gambling touch never left him, and in Uniontown he found that his luck ran so strong that he didn't need crooked dice. He won and won and won again; his good fortune frightened him. He recalled that after he took everything from a fellow gambler, he took pity on the man and gave back some of the winnings. Feeling luckier than ever, he was persuaded to go out to a country house where the gambling went on into the night. Liquor flowed. Louie Rainey later claimed that he didn't really like to drink, especially the rotgut whiskey served up that night. Drink he nevertheless did. Before he knew it, a fight broke out, a knife flashed, and he was cut. The knife that stabbed him in the back severed nerves in his spine. He was paralyzed.[35]

Family folk from Cassimore got word that Louie Rainey was down and got him back home. He moved into the dwelling of Alice Sledge Hargress's mother, Pinkie Sledge. There everyone lent a hand in trying to help him recover. There was agony, there was pain, there were bedsores. The big vigorous man, full of life and energy, was immobilized. Pinkie Sledge, her daughter Alice, and others in the household made his meals, emptied his bedpan, and sought to lift his sights and spirits. They contacted a brother who had left twenty years before and settled in Charlestown, West Virginia. Elmo Rainey sent money and an offer to bus his paralyzed brother east to live with him—an offer that Louie would take up in the 1940s for a few years. But for the moment, Louie Rainey's Depression-fueled exodus was over. Tramping no more, he came to accept a settled life on the small plot of land that he was heir to, and the care of Pinkie Sledge and her family. One day he made it formal, saying to Pinkie Sledge, "Well, I guess I'll adopt you as my momma." She agreed to adopt him as her son.[36]

For Alice Hargress, James Lyles, and their families, Louie Rainey was a man whose fall proved the difference it made to have land to return to.

During the Depression decade, those who lived as renters on the Browder place seemed to be in an enclave where they were secure. Despite the greater supervision, despite tension with white tenants brought in by Earl Compton, they were able to come up with their obligatory cotton payment and to raise corn and hogs enough to make a living. They couldn't dismiss entirely the signs of change all around: the displacement of other tenants, renters, and sharecroppers by cattle. With cotton prices low, with crop allotments restricting production, with the government itself collaborating in the dislocations, they could hardly miss what was happening to others. But they had lived there so long they thought the place was theirs.[37]

Then came the bombshell. The land was to be sold. Was there an offer by the owner to sell some of it to them—an offer they turned down? Memories conflict. York Banks, the son of renter Ben Banks, said no, that no such offer was made or rejected. Ben Banks's daughter, Arie Banks Sears, said yes, there definitely was an offer. For York Banks, not only didn't it happen, it never could have happened. The price of land was too high; those who had spent their lives trying to stay out or get out of debt would never have risked everything to buy that land.[38] They were poor, but not fools. Ben Banks's daughter—and Alice Sledge Hargress—saw it differently. Indeed, there was a proposal to sell plots to four of the renters. What stopped it was that some feared not debt but favoritism. Three renters thought the landowner would favor the fourth—Ben Banks—in the division of the property. They were, in the daughter's view, jealous that Banks would get the good land and that they'd be stuck on lesser ground. So they turned the offer down.[39]

Whatever the truth, the land was sold, and James Lyles's vision was borne out. A cousin came to visit him while he was at work in the mines in 1939. Calling him by the nickname that his close friends used, the cousin told him, "Jack, your vision has done come true."[40]

The purchaser on October 9, 1939 was a man whom black folks called the "man from Missouri." Twenty-nine-year-old Claude Stillman, referred to as "Clydie" Stillman, bought the land at auction for $9,750. Born in Mississippi, he and his older brother Alton had moved to Missouri in the 1930s and had made good money as cattlemen there.[41] It's not known how they settled on the Black Belt of Alabama and on Hale County as the place to bring their cattle. White editors and local promoters had pushed cattle as the alternative to cotton since the boll weevil infestation of the 1910s, and had organized a cattleman's association and developed a model farm to demonstrate the benefits of a shift. For locals, cattle would prove more stable than cotton; the switch would drastically diminish the number of blacks in their midst.[42]

The Hale County promoters did not anticipate that their marketing would bring in a cattleman who seemed neither to care for nor to abide by local mores. Folks on the Browder place had a pretty good sense of what the new landowner intended to do, though some stayed in denial to the very end, when he gathered them together on Christmas Day, 1939, and said they'd all have to move. He gave them time to find new places, and in the meantime set about having the land cleared so that the cattle he brought in from Missouri could have fields of grass to feed on.[43] He got neighboring men and women to do the clearing, and violated local custom by paying then 75¢ a day, well above the local rate of 50¢ for a day's labor.[44] That won him credit, not just for the pay but for his snub of natives who saw their norm defied. The "man from Missouri" also hired blacks to pick corn and ignored the portion that they openly took home for themselves. Alice Hargress recalled being one of those harvesters. She wore the baggiest pants and clothes she had and stuffed corn inside her garments. Stillman saw what was going on and laughed, asking, "You got all you want?" He bragged that it didn't bother him, as he had more corn back in Missouri: "They can't steal it as fast as I can haul it." When someone said something about the $9,750 he paid for the land, he retorted that he spent more than that on a party back home. For those not going through the pain of eviction, Clydie Stillman's style won admirers. He was not your ordinary white man.[45]

The response of landowners to evictions of the renters reflected their view that the Browder place folks should have left long before—or should have seized the rumored chance they had to make the land their own. To the landowners, expulsion set the stage for them to become "true men and women." That was the view of Forrest Hargress's daughter, Betty Hargress Washington. What she meant by that, reflected James Lyles, was that as long as they worked for the white man, however beneficent their deal, they belonged to him. They had to accept his tally on settlement day, to go to him if sick, to turn to him if in trouble. They "could do nothing without Captain Boss Man."[46]

As Cassimore landowners viewed it, once off the Browder place, the evicted renters discovered that they could make it on their own. A number of them did buy small parcels once owned by Tom Ruffin and built their own homes. Yet even those who became landowners did not break all ties to the planters who ruled the region. For many Browder place people, patronage remained a reality. Nonetheless for those who acquired land, a house seat made a difference—"made a heap." They were no longer tenants. They were not tramps. No longer could they be told by a landlord that they "had to git." Whatever happened, they had a place to go. If you and your employer "had a falling out, you could tell him, 'I'm going home.'"[47]

For Alice Hargress and James Lyles, it was neither the programs of the federal government nor the patronage of white planters that saw them through the Depression decade. What anchored and sustained them through "that thirties wreck" and saved others from tramping was having and holding on to the home land.

Thirteen   ✐ New Foundations

THE OLD CHURCH, when new, was a classic of its kind. The weather-boarded exterior was white with wide slatted blue shutters. The church contained one large rectangular room, twenty by thirty feet. Built of yellow pine throughout, it had twelve stiff benches inside, also yellow pine. "Every splinter was hard yellow pine," chuckled Louie Rainey, brought there as a child by his mother, Louisa. Inside it had an iron chandelier that held kerosene lamps, lit when darkness came. Glass chimes hung from the chandelier.[1] Set on an acre of land given in 1899 by Robert and Kizziah Cabbil, the church served early on as a schoolhouse, and for decades as the Sunday house of worship for the black landowners around it and for folks on the Browder place below it. "Mules, horses, and wagons came from all around," recollected Louie Rainey. "You couldn't hardly get in there on a Sunday!"[2]

By 1954, the toll of five decades was evident. The Cassimore church was leaning. It was kept from caving altogether only by long planks holding up one side. The church needed more than propping, more than repair. It needed replacement. In the fall of 1954, that's what was going on, with the men of the church taking down the roof, then the beams, and finally the walls, until nothing but the foundation remained.

Alice Hargress was there when the dispute erupted. Should they build on the old foundation or tear it out and put in a new one? The community carpenter, Lem Cabbil, said that the old wooden foundation was rotten. It had to go. Anything built on that foundation would founder again. Forrest Hargress, at eighty-eight the oldest man in the community and the de facto head of the church, disagreed; he argued that if they tore up the church foundation, they'd never build it back. Alice Hargress and Lem Cabbil answered that they would put in a new foundation, a cement one that would last. Back and forth they went, each side holding its own. Alice Hargress, the carpenter, and the younger set won. "God almighty!" said Forrest Hargress, and stalked away.

With the new foundation in place, the church went up. Forrest Hargress came around, and went with Alice Hargress to get a building loan from the bank. Finished in 1955, the Cassimore church stands to this day.[3]

It would take far more to build a new foundation for the community the church was part of.

The years since the Browder place evictions in 1939 had seen stupendous changes in the country and small ones in the lives of Alice Hargress and James Lyles. The preparations for war and then entry into World War II had reinvigorated American and southern agriculture. In some places—the southwest, the Mississippi Delta, and elsewhere—the government payments for taking land out of production meant that large white farmers had the capital to invest in machinery and thereby to displace thousands of workers who had plowed the land with mules and picked the cotton crop by hand.[4] The demand for cotton brought by the war made that crop profitable once again, in Hale County as elsewhere. So though herds of cows multiplied, cattle did not displace everyone. If black folks were no longer "so thick you couldn't stir 'em with a stick," they were still there, and again finding work to do. The demand spiked by the war meant that James Lyles could come home from the mines. Farming once more paid. His sons and daughters were old enough to work the land with him. Home he came.

At the mines for almost a decade, he'd deepened his faith in collective action. A member of the United Mine Workers of America, led by John L. Lewis, James Lyles had been part of a union that exemplified aggressive collective bargaining. "White and black, we stuck together," was his emphatic recollection. Collective action had been the gleam in the eye of his father, Andrew Lyles, in the 1890s, and the message underlying James

Lyles's vision that was thwarted in the 1930s. When he came home in the 1940s, cooperation was all the more part of his outlook. But opportunities for doing things together were narrow in Hale County. Black folks resisted collaborative efforts, worried about who might get the most and who wouldn't, feared new debts, or just were resigned to the way things were. James Lyles's instinct for cooperation took a practical form in the 1950s, around the time of the church rebuilding. To replace the old well in front of the church that everyone used, he proposed a common piped-in water system for the Cassimore community. Alice Hargress and one other landowner said yes. Others declined. The pair went ahead with the new well and the shared water line. Only then did others see the benefit and want in. "Reverend Lyles was always doing things like that, wanting us to work together," recalled Alice Hargress. It was an uphill struggle.[5]

Cotton growing and child rearing consumed Alice Hargress during the wartime years, while her husband, Hooksie—after stints at the pipe foundry at Holt and the shipbuilding yard at Mobile—tended cattle and milk cows for the white neighbor nearby. His job was to get up in the morning, gather the cows, and get them to the barn and milk them. As his sons got old enough, he conscripted them to help with the tasks, even if it meant that their schooling came second. The work of the parents, and then the children, allowed them to pay debts and taxes on their land. The land continued, for Alice Hargress, to serve as a buffer from the unavoidable pressures of the plantation world around them. Landowner-ship made possible small-scale acts of resistance. Still averse to the etiquette of saying *ma'am* and *sir*, Alice Hargress found herself called out by a white woman she knew well: "Alice, you never say ma'am to me." Her response was silence. On alert, Alice Hargress found other ways to speak that didn't require *yes ma'am* or *no ma'am*, with both women always aware that she was dodging the expectation.

War changed the verbal cat-and-mouse game she'd been forced to play. When wartime rationing of coffee and sugar was implemented, Alice Hargress's family got the coupons but drank little coffee and consumed little sugar, both expensive in wartime. Her white acquaintance asked, "Alice, do you have coupons to spare?"

"Yes."

Next time they met, the woman asked, "Alice, did you bring those coupons?"

"Yes," she said, and handed them over. "From then on," she recalled, "we were best buddies."[6]

The huge change brought by the war was away from the farm. Not only were soldiers going off to war, but wartime production required men and women to work in the factories. While many women filled those wartime jobs until peace came, the demand for workers—including black men—intensified after the war, as privation gave way to the boom of the postwar years. Hoboing declined. Migration took its place. By the 1950s, Alice Hargress's children, like those of thousands of other families, planned to leave as soon as they finished school, beckoned by relatives who'd put down roots in California, Michigan, and Ohio. By bus, by car, occasionally by train, they "left on the first thing smokin'."[7]

For the young who looked to leave, what purpose did the land serve? In the South, as they saw it, they had one option only: "go to field." Farm they did until they could go work in factories. Those who left came back with stories and tangible evidence of the promised lands of the North and the West. They returned with a roll of money, even though the twenty on the outside might cloak the ones and fives in the middle. They came back in new cars and fine suits and jewelry and with tales of good wages and better treatment in the North. For the young, the land served a single purpose: as a springboard for departure.[8]

That was not the view of those who stayed. If the land was no longer a refuge for all, it was to them still a fallback place for those who might need it. James Lyles had nothing but good wishes for those of his children who left. Their success anywhere—a home in Birmingham, a good job in Portland, cars in the garage—was a fulfillment. For Alice Hargress, the progress of her children was also a welcome thing. They got work. They sent back money. Grandchildren in Los Angeles and Detroit were in school. But the longtime residents in Cassimore were also wary. As they saw it, in the city high expenses went with high wages. Those who started the month with cash had to spend it on rent and food and cars and more. Those who came home in flashy cars and garb had bought them on credit, and had to pay off what they owed. What if they fell short? What if they lost their jobs? What if they accumulated debt beyond their means and lost everything? Where could they go? That's where the land came in. The hoboing of the 1930s was gone. But if debt or disaster forced family folks onto the street in a distant city, they would not have to become midcentury tramps. They would have a place to come back to. For Alice Hargress, the land remained redemptive: "They will always have somewhere to stay."[9]

But would they? They might have a physical home to come back to. But to do what, to work where, to be treated how?

One answer could be found through a look at those ousted from the Browder place. Forced to "git," had they "become true men and women"?

Liberation was slow and incremental for Alice Hargress's evicted cousins, Lem and Robert Cabbil. Lem Cabbil became a full-time carpenter, operating out of his own home place on land bought from the daughter of Tom Ruffin. Lem Cabbil could neither read nor write, but he knew his carpentry. He'd apprenticed under Forrest Hargress for the cabin building the older man had done, and he could draw. Now Lem Cabbil drew plans for dwellings made to order, and built on what he'd learned from Old Man Forrest. He built Alice Hargress's home. He built York Banks's home. He said that he built many if not most of the homes in the Cassimore community. He built the church. He built for white folks, too—cabins for sharecroppers of Judge Robert Green, the longtime probate judge of Hale County. He even built the home of Compton descendants. His exile from the Browder place plantation was clearly a release.[10]

Alice Hargress's other cousin, Robert Cabbil, was also put off the Browder place. He went to work for Earl Compton's son, Ben Compton, and did farming and hay baling for him. He didn't mind the work—he wanted the work. Ben Compton let him have a cabin from the plantation. That's when Robert Cabbil turned to a relative, who sold him twenty acres for a house seat, also once part of the Tom Ruffin holding. Robert Cabbil moved the cabin onto his own place, and for him, that move made a world of difference. He continued to work for Ben Compton. He continued to benefit from "considerations"—his ill wife got medical care through "Mr. Ben." Still, his own place made Robert Cabbil his own man: "If I wanted to come home—even to sit—I could."[11]

Doubtless those who admired the get-up-and-go of Tom Ruffin in the nineteenth century—and saw him as the model of what emancipation could do for an ex-slave—would have seen York Banks as the twentieth-century model of how eviction freed the displaced. York Banks's father, Ben Banks, hated having to leave the Browder place and to move up to poorer land in Cassimore that belonged to his wife. Their son York, on the other hand, made the most of the expulsion. York Banks sub-rented other, better land. He sought loans to buy machinery. When bankers wouldn't lend him money—despite his possession of mules, tools, and collateral sufficient to gain loans for whites—he turned to the Federal Land Bank and got a low-interest loan. He hired people to pick cotton for him at harvest time, including Alice Hargress, paying them by the pound. To them his story was less than a triumph, since he paid no better and was no less demanding than the white man. But York Banks had become his own boss.[12]

For each of those Browder place expatriates, farming remained the way of life, either to pursue directly or to benefit from indirectly as builders and carpenters. But for those who went forth to cities of the North and the West and tasted of the fruits of freedom there, farming was something they would never return to, no matter how iffy things got in the city. Nor was that all they refused to come back to. There was the whole social system they had left, the system embodied by the term *Jim Crow*. It was not that they encountered nothing of the sort outside the South. On the contrary. In the West the system was called "James Crow." In the North, discrimination was rampant in housing covenants and redlined neighborhoods, in job caps and de facto segregation.[13] Still, back home, Jim Crow was absolute. That was the rot at the foundation of the South they chose to leave.

Alice Hargress and James Lyles knew the system all too well. They encountered it every time they stepped out of their enclaves. Jim Crow was especially galling in Greensboro. If they went to town on a weekday, it was understood that if they and a white person met on the sidewalk, the black person would give way.[14] That was one reason to go to town on the weekend, when their sheer numbers and local custom meant that the sidewalk was shared without confrontations. Not so when they got to the stores. There, in recollection after recollection, they spoke of themselves as confronted in a different way. They were treated with indifference or suspicion, as unwelcome customers or potential thieves.

For those who had seen Los Angeles or Detroit, what kind of town, what kind of treatment, was that to come back to? In a word, it wasn't.

Those who left had some good memories of the place in which they grew up, memories that softened its limits for their parents and themselves. There was more to life there than getting up in the morning and going to farmwork. When it rained, work stopped, and when the clouds cleared and sun returned, work gave way to play. All gathered at the makeshift ball field by the corner where Peggy and Tommy Benison had their small country store. Young men took to the field, while others gathered their chairs around to watch. The black storekeepers encouraged the ball games, selling pop and sweets for the fans as they watched the game unfold. Those weather-begotten days sifted out the good ballplayers from the bad, trained them up, and identified those who would start for the Cassimore team that took its best players to neighboring communities or challenged other teams to come to Cassimore.[15] Alice Hargress's son Ned, named after her husband and after his great-grandfather, caught the dream from those games that he might play professional ball one day. He pursued that dream to Los Angeles, where it fizzled, but the ambition and confidence that brought him there got channeled into well nigh everything else after he moved to Detroit, where he became a versatile businessman and a gifted minister.[16]

For others of Alice Hargress's children, the nights were what made the memories. Right in the community there was another store, this one run by one of the descendants of Cameron Cabbil. He sold pop and groceries by day, and made available harder stuff by night, even though local prohibition made it illegal to sell or possess drink in Hale County. More than liquor drew folks in. On Saturday night he converted his place into a small dance hall, turned up the jukebox, and set the records in the Rock-Ola spinning with music that pulsed through the community. Fifteen miles from the town of Greensboro, set well back from Highway 69, it proved to be a safe haven from sheriff's deputies who might have been tempted to raid the place and disrupt the good times.

Then there were the characters who were the endless sources of stories, both the stories they generated on their own and the tales they told of those who came before them.

There was the patriarch of the community, Forrest Hargress. Even as he aged into his eighties and nineties, he carried on with a restless energy that put others to shame, often calling on the young for his projects, receiving aid from some and prompting a quick disappearance by others. A mule-tender when younger, he went about the community with his one-eyed mule Henry, who walked when and where he walked, stopped when and where he stopped, always a step behind the shoulder of Forrest Hargress. He loved to tease the young, telling them, "Call Henry." They would, but nothing happened. *"Call him!"* he insisted. Not until Forrest Hargress himself made the call would Henry budge.[17]

Then there were the tales *about* Forrest Hargress. How when he went to town, he paid no mind to the new lights installed at intersections in Greensboro, expecting cars to stop for him, not vice versa—and they did. How the man who grew up with mules insisted on top speed when taken in a car, saying, "If I'd'a known you was a-gonna go this slow, I'd'a walked."[18] How, as legend had it, he even got into cars of strangers—of white strangers—and expected to be driven home. Playing the eccentric? Acting as if he was truly the son of General Forrest? He never forgot to say *Mr.* or *sir.* But he veered to the edge of etiquette expected by white people. Chortled his daughters, "He was a mixed-up man."[19]

Forrest Hargress's oldest daughter lived next door to her father. Born in 1900, Angeline Hargress Banks had married Elijah Banks in 1918, and the couple stayed close to Forrest Hargress all of their days and his. No one in the community was more buoyant than 'Lijah, as he was called by his wife. Like most who grew up and stayed in Cassimore, they were known by their nicknames. Elijah Banks was "Buck," Angeline Banks was "Fang." Disposed to fuss playfully at each other, both spoke their minds. After their farming years, they turned their home into a small soda and candy store, where for nickels and dimes they sold pop and sweets to the children and grandchildren of the community. Every two weeks, a van came to their house to restock their goods, driven by a white supplier whom they affectionately called their "candy man."

Above all, there was Louie Rainey, who, though wheelchair-bound by virtue of the knife fight in 1937 that left him paralyzed from the waist down, was larger than life, a storyteller whose booming voice, prodigious memory, tales, and commentary made him a man whom all visited every time they came home. After Louie Rainey's knife wound had healed, family members had gotten him a wheelchair. During the 1940s, he moved for a time to Charlestown, West Virginia, to live with his brother Elmo Rainey, who'd gone there more than two decades earlier. By the fifties, though, he was back in Alabama, where he went to vocational school in Talladega to learn a trade.[20]

Louie Rainey became skilled at reweaving the cane bottoms of old-fashioned chairs and rockers that every southern family, white and black, had on porches and in their houses. He learned to take long thin strips of cane and soak them in water to make them pliable. Then, patiently, he'd weave new chair bottoms or backs to replace those torn or worn out by years of use. It was work he could do in a wheelchair; his skill brought him customers from all over the county. He built enough trade that his adoptive mother, Pinkie Cabbil Sledge, got him his own house and shop on family property, a three-room place a hundred yards below her home and alongside the red dirt road into the Cassimore settlement. Whether working in the shop or on the front porch, he always had visitors, and talked and listened while he wove.[21]

During the course of a week, most everyone in the community made it a point to stop by to talk with Louie Rainey. Older folks came by to swap stories. Younger ones, whether from the settlement or visitors from afar, came to hear his telling of what he knew. He read books and magazines that people brought to him. He listened to the radio or watched a black-and-white television that was almost always playing, albeit with patchy reception. He didn't just recite what others said. He "put together bits and pieces" of what he heard and learned. He interpreted, questioned, and arrived at his own understanding of past and present, whether talking about why Robert E. Lee went with the South in 1861—reluctantly, as Louie Rainey saw it—or telling his grandmother's tale of the day freedom came to blacks in the county in 1865.[22]

The story Louie Rainey most loved to share was the account of Paul Hargress and Paul Cameron. How Old Man Paul Hargress and Old Man Paul Cameron came out on a coach together, across the Blue Ridge Mountains. How before Paul Cameron left, he gave Paul Hargress a bag of gold. He speculated about what Paul Hargress had done with that bag of gold. Had he used it to buy land from the planter? Had he buried it under the cherry tree in front of his house? Supposedly, after Paul Hargress died, people who thought it was there dug at night, on the sly, never finding the gold but undermining the cherry tree so much that it collapsed into the hole. Like other porch tales, it was an account that might vary with each telling. But the message was the same: the special relationship between the two men—the high standing that the bondsman had with the planter—got Paul Hargress a seat on the coach, the reward of gold, and perhaps an acknowledgment of parity, if not partnership, with Paul Cameron.

The ball fields, the times off, the Rock-Ola, the characters, and the lore of the community—these formed the good times. As long as Cassimore's residents stayed within the bounds of the settlement, that was their world.

But for the young, good times in the community were not enough. Leave the bounds of the settlement, and what might happen? Though the heyday of the chain gang and prison labor in the mines had gone, peaking in the early twentieth century and declining in the 1920s, neither had entirely disappeared.[23] Nor had the apprehension that if found ambling on the road, a man might be deemed a vagrant—or if caught in a dispute with a white, a black man might be judged an upstart—with arrest and jail the outcome. There were tales of those in the community who had been sent to mines, never to return.[24] That worry was enough for young Ned Hargress to abide by the rule of not being found on the highway after dark. A fortress without walls by day, the settlement for some was a prison without walls by night.

For the young, the town of Greensboro was not enough. Leave the community by day, go up to Greensboro to shop, and what did black shoppers face in the forties and fifties and into the sixties? They encountered white clerks who served whites first and foremost. They dealt with store-keepers who sold wares that blacks couldn't touch or try on. "They pretended you weren't there," testified Alice Hargress. The only blacks who worked in the stores were janitors and cleaning women. Alice Hargress and her children chose to shop in Demopolis, fifteen miles away to the south and west. "Greensboro was supposed to be our town, but it wasn't."[25]

For the young, Hale County was not enough. There were low-end jobs that came and eventually went. There was a chicken plant in town, with deadening work of pulling the heads and feet off of chickens in a freezing-cold factory. Anything more by way of industry or development seemed to be of little interest to town leaders, who would have to provide approval and incentives for such to come. There were paved highways going in and out of town, but rutted gravel or red clay roads leading into the black rural settlements. It was not enough.

So when relatives came back with word and proof that there were worlds away from Greensboro and Hale County that offered livelihoods and respect, folks left with little notion that they would ever return, except to visit.

Elders wished the young well but nonetheless kept the land in safekeeping for any who fell between the cracks. For Alice Hargress, safekeeping began with being clear about how they had come by the land and why she and her children must keep it intact for generations to come.

Alice Hargress had, of course, heard Louie Rainey time and again tell the story of Paul Hargress and Paul Cameron and the bag of gold. It was not a story she cared for. It put a premium on being a favorite of the planter. It made Paul Hargress out to be Paul Cameron's "pet." Recoiling at the salute to planter favoritism, Alice Hargress had a different understanding of what Paul Cameron did. He sold "to all black, no white." Her vision was that when Cameron sold, he meant for blacks and blacks exclusively to have the plantation. Black owners not only gained land. They gained an enclave.[26]

That enclave had to be sustained as the undivided possession of all. It was not to be broken up or sold off, making it property or profit for some and excluding others. Alice Hargress viewed the home place she lived on, and which her children would inherit, as "heir land." It was "land for all the heirs." Forebears left land so our "seed would have somewhere to stay—so we wouldn't have to trample up and down the road."[27] She shared a view of land that was—and remains—widespread in rural black communities across the South. It paralleled an understanding of shared possession of land that existed in Africa as well.[28] For her, when blacks bequeathed their land to selected heirs or sold it to outsiders, they cut out other family members who had a right to live on it. "Shut slam out—ain't got a speck of a place to stay" is the way she put it. As to those who sold black land to whites, breaking up the protective enclaves, they were traitors beyond redemption.[29]

James Lyles had a different view of the past and the land's place for the next generation. To be sure, blacks needed to hold family land together. But they needed to have standing in the outside world as well. As James Lyles saw it, what Paul Cameron did, in result if not intention, was to *"homestead"* the black people who acquired his plantation in the 1870s. Their benefactor was not Abraham Lincoln, nor was it the 1862 Congress that passed the Homestead Law. It was the white planter Paul Cameron, "who caused them to be homesteaders." There was a reason James Lyles chose that term. He understood what a homestead meant. In the nineteenth century and beyond, a homestead was a place to claim and perfect through improvement—to achieve "betterment" of the place and the family on it.[30] For whites, the homestead was more. It was the underpinning of citizenship. Standing in the community came with and was confirmed by owning a homestead. No one knew better than the man born in 1896 how incomplete citizenship remained for black southerners. James Lyles knew that only with the fulfillment of "homesteading"—with citizenship—would the young choose to stay in the South.

And that was the question. Could anything—anything in the world— make their small patch of the rural South a place where the next generation might wish to remain? Could anything or anyone make the community a place to which expatriates might return? It would take more than holding on to land for all the heirs, or rebuilding churches from the bottom up. It would take a new foundation for the larger world they were a part of. No one saw that better than the music man.

Lewis Black was the music man, and a good deal more. He taught music in the high schools of Hale County. He came to Hale County in 1951, having grown up just over ninety miles to the south, in Beatrice, Alabama, a small community in Monroe County, the home of author Harper Lee.[31] Born in 1926, he was one of fifteen children. The names given the other children suggested something of the learning and aspirations of their father. Napoleon Black named his daughters Mikado, Ophelia, and Caldonia, and named Lewis Black's twin brother Lucius.[32] Napoleon Black was a landowning farmer, cultured and prosperous enough in the twenties to own a piano and provide music lessons for his children. When the bottom dropped out in the thirties, he had to cut back. His son Lewis continued with the lessons, and watched as his father looked out for others as best he could. Tramps in the neighborhood got food and sustenance; his father trucked near and far for things for his family and strangers.[33] Though he could sustain his son's aptitude for music and help some of the poor, Black's father could not protect his brother when the brother crossed the county sheriff. Father and son watched as Lewis Black's uncle was mercilessly beaten by the lawman he'd riled. It was Christmas Day, 1935; Lewis Black was nine years old. Helpless at the time, forced to stifle anger and shame, he thought, "If the time ever comes . . ."—by which he meant that if the time ever came when he could put a stop to that, he would.[34]

The time to do something seemed remote through the 1940s. Lewis Black served in the Navy, where segregation prevailed, as it did in other branches of the service. He went to Alabama State College and was a classmate of Ralph David Abernathy, the man who in the mid-1950s would become a minister and the right-hand man of Martin Luther King Jr. Neither Lewis Black nor Ralph Abernathy, while in college, was the leader he would later become. Adept at math and music, Lewis Black chose to teach, with music as his first love. His first post was in Coosa County, where he worked with a high school principal who encouraged him and introduced him to the covert work of the NAACP. When an offer came to move, with incentives and a pay raise and promises for what he could do elsewhere, his friend the principal urged him to stay. Black was ambitious, the pay was better, the promise of latitude great, so he took the job.[35]

The move to the new high school—not the navy, not college—brought out the rebel in him. He and the new principal clashed. Lewis Black took music seriously and wanted his students to do the same. He wasn't going to give a pat on the back to those who could merely sing loudly. They needed to read music, to practice, to reach higher. He wasn't going to applaud students who could simply play an instrument, as if that were the final goal. They had to play well. Nor was he going to indulge the principal, who saw the student band as a moneymaker for the school and for himself. He told the music teacher to collect extra for instruments and band uniforms; they'd split the profits. Lewis Black bridled at the proposition. His principal saw that this was a teacher who wouldn't go along. So when Lewis Black arranged a Christmas program in which his students would showcase their talent and demonstrate their skill, the principal undermined it. He told parents not to come, and discouraged the student musicians from participating. On the day of the program, the stage was filled with instruments, a single student, and Lewis Black. The two went on with the show, and between them they performed the scheduled music. To the delight of a tiny audience, they played every instrument. But Black knew he'd lost his job.[36]

So when he got a call from principal C. A. Fredd to come teach in Hale County, Lewis Black was glad to go. There again he sought to raise the bar, and not just to glorify the raw talent his students brought to their music classes. His ambition went further. He had seen and heard professional symphonies. Why not have a symphony close to home—a rural orchestra that would encourage the young to stretch and to win recognition for the talent that went a-wasting for lack of striving or support? He wrote to the Ford Foundation and even corresponded with Eleanor Roosevelt to promote the idea, receiving polite replies but no backing. His aspiration was to make Hale County and the rural world a place where others could remain—a place to flourish, rather than endure until they fled.

Perhaps inevitably, his striving and ambition again led to clashes with the principal who hired him: "Me and him didn't get along. We had to split." The principal moved north of Greensboro, Black moved south to Sunshine High School in the deeply rural part of Hale County. By then his defiance took a broader form. He had a dual message that he conveyed to all students. In his music classes, in the lunchroom, and in the hallways, he exhorted them in his gravelly voice, telling them to do more than just get a diploma and get away. Here and now, he told them, "get that *ed-u-ca-tion.*" There was a second maxim, too: as long as they did remain in the place where they grew up, they should challenge the customs that humiliated their parents and themselves. "Don't buy where you can't work," he'd tell them, moving from music to money. "Boycott!" And he urged them to let those merchants who didn't have blacks working up front, and not just in the back, know what they were doing, and why.[37]

James Lyles learned about Lewis Black from his sons, some of whom took his music classes, all of whom reported on his larger lessons. The man born in 1896 and the teacher born in 1926 couldn't have been more different in their temperaments. But James Lyles recognized they were aligned by a shared wish to bring about change.

James Lyles's guide was always "the Master Book." When discussion came up about choices to make, whether at home or at his home church or as a speaker at Alice Hargress's Cassimore church, he inevitably would say, "Get me the Book." He knew the Bible by heart, knew precisely where to turn to find the right passage, and knew that answers would be in it.[38] Backed by lessons in the Book, his voice deep and insistent, he was fearless.

Lewis Black was a secular man. He liked fine suits. He attended symphonies. He flew his own airplane. He made money and spent it. He broke the bounds of what it was proper for a black man to do. There was not an ounce of humble in him. Was he uppity, even ornery? He'd be the first to agree. Did he look out for himself? Without a doubt. But he looked out for others in equal measure. He respected religion and those who were religious. But the redemption and salvation that he sought, for himself and for others, was in this world. Whites and more cautious blacks found him pugnacious and confrontational. But what Lewis Black wanted was to get to the point where white people would negotiate with black folks. He was ready to work with those who were ready to deal.[39]

"If the time ever comes . . ." Both James Lyles and Lewis Black understood that their lonely battles would remain just that—quests that were solitary and disparaged—until a time came when they might be seen as men of vision. In the mid-1950s, in the nation and in Alabama, the times began to turn. First came the Supreme Court decision of 1954, *Brown v. Board of Education*, which unanimously overturned the Court ruling of 1896 that had sanctioned segregation. The 1954 Court ruled that "separate but equal" was inherently unequal and therefore unconstitutional. The next year, in Montgomery, Alabama, blacks began a thirteen-month protest against segregation on the busses of the city, winning victory in the courts in December 1956. In those two events, James Lyles and Lewis Black saw evidence that their time was coming.

Folks in Hale did more than passively watch and wait for the outcome of the Montgomery struggle. Montgomery was east of Hale County, 120 miles across some of the most change-resistant places in Alabama— Lowndes County, Dallas County, Selma. During the week, women of Hale County made food, and on weekends they drove through the bastions of segregation to Montgomery, where they distributed meals to the boycotting protesters. In the 1960s, Lewis Black and his wife, Mildred Black, got themselves to evening meetings in Selma, where they observed the efforts to organize resistance there. James Lyles remained at home but witnessed the rise to prominence of a young leader who drew on "the Master Book" to preach and practice collective action. In Martin Luther King Jr., James Lyles saw a prophet respected and followed by his own people.[40]

Lewis Black grasped a way to translate the stirrings of the time into a concrete project that went beyond exhortations to the young. As farming became mechanized, as land grew more expensive, as technology cost more and more, as fertilizer became needed, Black saw that farmers who wanted to stay would need money to do so. Some, such as York Banks, had learned that despite land and laborers and equipment to put up as collateral, they still couldn't get loans from private banks. Turned down there, York Banks had borrowed from the Federal Land Bank instead and gotten credit to expand his farming operations. But what of others who had less to put up but wanted to stay and farm the land? Lewis and Mildred Black and six others founded a rural credit union. Black folks would pay in a certain amount. As members of the credit union, they could borrow at low interest. Collectively they could do for themselves what white bankers refused to do.

James Lyles liked what he saw. Whether Lewis Black knew it or not, he was trying to do in 1961 what Lyles's father had attempted seven decades before. Lewis Black was too secular, too much of this world, for James Lyles to consider him a "soul mate." But a brother-in-arms he was.

⁓

Anyone who had a television or radio in the 1960s knew that change was coming: the 1960 sit-ins, starting on February 1 in the "other Greensboro"— Greensboro, North Carolina; the Freedom Riders whose bus was burned outside Anniston, Alabama, on May 14, 1961; the attack dogs and fire hoses used against young protesters in Birmingham in May 1963; the March on Washington in August 1963. Alice Hargress knew the movement was gaining. She didn't have to rely on radio or television to know that the struggle was headed for the Black Belt. Rev. James Lyles led meetings to tell people that the time had come and to enlist them to be part of it. It was their own rights they were demanding, he told them—not favors, not "considerations," but their *rights*. How many of them had voted? Been on a jury? Seen a black sheriff? Up to that point, Alice Hargress and others were with him. But she wondered, "How could we *do* it?"[41]

In March 1965, she viewed on television the extraordinary events that started that month in Selma, sixty miles to the east of Hale County. She watched the attempted march over Pettus Bridge, the attack on the marchers—Bloody Sunday. At home on her television, she saw the speech of President Lyndon Johnson and then federal troops protecting the victorious march from Selma to Montgomery, the triumphant arrival of Dr. King and thousands of others to the state capital—the first capital of the Confederacy.

To get their rights, to build that new foundation in Hale County, did they, too, need to march?

Fourteen ✐ "Unless It's a Must"

ALICE HARGRESS HAD FOLLOWED the movement since its Alabama be-ginnings in Montgomery in 1955. A decade later, in the spring of 1965, the epicenter of the struggle was just sixty miles to the east of Greensboro and Hale County. By television and telephone, she and her friends in the Cassimore community kept up with it. "We knew it was coming."[1]

The meetings in Greensboro and in rural Hale County began in Feb-ruary 1965. It was in that month that Lewis Black and a minister who had come from Mobile the year before, Reverend Arthur T. Days, had con-tacted the Southern Christian Leadership Conference and proposed that they make Hale one of the Black Belt counties targeted for the voter reg-istration drive that the SCLC had decided to undertake in Alabama. The SCLC agreed, urged the two men to identify local leaders, and contrib-uted volunteers and $900 to support the Hale County effort.[2]

Lewis Black and Rev. A.T. Days had no difficulty in locating a leader in the area around Cassimore. This was the moment—the summons—that Reverend James Lyles had been waiting for. At the age of twelve he'd received the call to preach, only to be denied approval by the deacons of his Baptist church. The call had come again in 1925, when he was twenty-nine: a vision had come that the Mantle of Christ—the prophet's role—had fallen on him, and that his destiny would be to receive visions from on high and share them with those who would listen. From his lifelong study of the Bible, he knew that the fate of "God-sent" men—Jonah, Eze-kiel, Elijah—was to be ignored, and his fate was no different. Not so for Martin Luther King Jr., the God-sent man of the movement, who since

1955 had drawn on the Bible, his Christian faith, and a sense of mission to lead blacks and whites out of the wilderness of segregation. Rev. James Lyles, asked to lead in Cassimore and the surrounding church-centered communities, seized the chance: "Doubt or die!"[3]

Lewis Black and Rev. A. T. Days prepared systematically for the voter registration drive in the county. Lewis Black and his wife, Mildred, traveled by night to Selma in the spring of 1965, listening in on the meetings there as leaders from the Southern Christian Leadership Conference and the Student Non-Violent Coordinating Committee prepared their strategy for the Selma campaign.[4] In mid-June 1965, Rev. A. T. Days went to Atlanta, where he attended SCLC training sessions in nonviolence and met the all-star cast of leaders and lecturers assembled for the week, as well as student volunteers from across the country recruited to help with voter registration and to bring outside attention to the Alabama drive.[5]

James Lyles, as he saw it, had been preparing for decades through study of the Bible, the Master Book. From his Hale County comrades, he absorbed the importance of restraint, especially on the part of young people they hoped to recruit. But he knew that at least for his part of the county, restraint was for later, after they had roused people for the rallies and demonstrations to come. The first thing—the prophet's role—was to wake people up.[6]

The call to act took place at meetings, dozens of meetings, many at the Cassimore church. Initially, the efforts of movement leaders to have meetings in town were stifled by opposition from whites, who put pressure on established black church leaders to keep their sanctuaries closed, both to activists from Hale and to "agitators" from outside the county.[7] Ministers, deacons, and church members rightly worried that the price for hosting meetings could be arson—black churches had burned all over Mississippi in 1964. Alice Hargress, church secretary at Cassimore, conferred with the presiding bishop of the Cahaba AME Zion Conference about meetings at Cassimore. He pledged that if the church burned, the district conference would rebuild it. That assurance was enough for her and the deacon board, and Cassimore opened its doors. On Tuesday nights, James Lyles led weekly meetings at Cassimore. Larger rallies moved to A. T. Days' St. Matthews Church in Greensboro.[8]

Listening to James Lyles preach was one thing; concluding that this was a moment to act was quite another. For much of her life, Alice Hargress had pursued an opposite strategy. At home and as supervisor of the Cassimore Sunday School, Alice Hargress had urged the young to cultivate character as the as the way to cope with the forces arrayed against them. "White folks have the money. Whites have the power," she would say, telling black youngsters that the answer was "no big mouth," to keep their distance, and in the meantime, "to be better than them."[9] If they tried to go head-to-head against white folks, they'd get hurt, even crushed.

In the face of the overwhelming power that whites held, Alice Hargress's strategy was neither acceptance nor resistance. She taught instead that "you got to be above the white folks if you want anything. You got to know more than them white children if you want to get anything." Because "we knew whites had the upper hand, whether right or wrong," her advice was, "Don't confront them—unless it's a must."[10] James Lyles's task was to persuade Alice Hargress and those who came to his meetings that confrontation was "a must."

"At first I didn't exactly understand what he was saying," Alice Hargress recalled.

When Rev. Lyles declared that "we weren't getting our equal rights," that she understood. And when he insisted that "white folks didn't care nothing for them," she reserved judgment on that one—some did, some didn't—but she saw what he was saying.[11]

White people tried to persuade selected blacks that they were best friends, paid them a little more, made them butlers instead of field hands. Whites "sweet-talked them, be nice and make them a big shot in the midst of lower-class folks," all to make them feel superior. In return, they expected information, especially after Montgomery, about what other blacks were doing, and particularly whether any were involved in "that mess." "Anything you see going on, you tell me," they'd say. Too often friendship was a white way to make blacks "flunkeys" who held others down.[12] That, too, Alice Hargress understood.

Then what didn't she understand? "We really didn't see where to tackle it," exactly *how* they were to get their equal rights. Some of the uncertainty may have come from James Lyles' way of making his case. To James Lyles, the prophecy was "no secret. It was three thousand years old. It ain't been hid." Women who were the backbone of the church, who attended regularly and duly prepared for Sunday lessons, usually met Rev. Lyles halfway.[13] When he quoted passages from the Bible that foretold that God would bring forth a man and a moment, the women could allow that this might be the moment and King the man. But men, chary about "rulings" from their peers, had long since proved more skeptical of James Lyles's claims to be a messenger of God's truths and visions. "God fixed me up for a leader. But the folks didn't want me," he acknowledged.[14] They might accept the truths of the Bible as timeless. That didn't establish that *this* was the time to confront their enemies, or offer reassurance that faith would see them through. For Alice Hargress, what may have moved her to the brink of action was James Lyles's tone as much as his message. His fiery preaching was that of a prophet long denied whose moment had come. When James Lyles spoke, "he was *mean!*"[15]

It was not, however, the quest for civil rights or equal rights that moved Alice Hargress finally to join the struggle in mid-1965. Nor was it the goal of gaining her personal right to vote. She had already registered to vote in Hale County, though not without an ordeal. The year before, she had gone down to the courthouse, studied up on questions they usually asked, and found herself in the thick of animosity. In the registrar's office, there was loud cursing of Robert Kennedy, no permission to talk to anyone (though the white registrar seemed to help whites), and claims that in Alabama white women didn't have the vote, either. She saw the answers of some thrown into the trash, watched others told dismissively, "You didn't pass." If you "weren't used to curse words, you got so nervous and upset your mind wouldn't function right." Questions ranged from the mundane to the preposterous. Alabama registrars had wide discretion, mostly employed to keep people from passing, occasionally used to allow a few through. And she had passed, or been passed. She was one of the 236 blacks in the county—including James Lyles—to be on the voter lists at the beginning of 1965.[16] It was the other 4,000 adult blacks in Hale County, many illiterate and unable even to take a test, who couldn't vote.

Nonetheless, she decided that "I had to go." As it became clear from the meetings she attended at St. Matthews in town and at her own church at Cassimore that the voter rights movement would come to Hale County, she wondered whether her mother or Forrest Hargress had ever voted. She knew about the poll tax. Had either ever paid it and voted in back times? No, she discovered after asking them. She knew that Forrest Hargress was a landowner, and assumed that for him, as for whites, landownership and voting at some point had gone hand in hand. Again, she found out that the answer was no. Well, had Forrest Hargress ever *wanted* to vote, or thought that he should have the vote? "He didn't know what I was talking about. You know, people, they was brought up inferior, they don't deserve what the next man have."[17]

That's what got her, Alice Hargress asserted. Forrest Hargress, whom she and others called "Poppa"—conceived in 1865, when Lincoln was president; born in 1866, when Andrew Johnson was president; ninety-nine and a half years old in 1965, when Lyndon Johnson was president—"lived here all his life and never voted." The same was true for her mother, Pinkie, born in 1890 and seventy-five years old in 1965: "she just *lived* here—never a citizen." When it came to what being "never a citizen" meant to her, Alice Hargress didn't detail legal consequences—no right to serve on a jury, no right to be judged by a jury with black folks on it, no say in elected officials from sheriff to mayor to governor to president. She put it differently: if you got into difficulty, it meant that you needed "influence"—a white man—to help you out. Whether he did so out of kindness or interest, it didn't much matter. You'd be beholden, "body and soul," she said, and "I thought that was a big handicap." It was to get the vote and citizenship for her mother and for Poppa that "I had to go."[18]

Before it was all over, all of them—Alice Hargress, James Lyles, and Lewis Black—would learn the cumulative toll of decades of citizenship denied. In jeopardy was the very land they lived on—land for their livelihood, land for their heirs.

The voter rights drive in Greensboro started indirectly, with a boycott of stores that discriminated against blacks—cafés that didn't serve them, stores that didn't hire blacks above the level of custodians or cooks. The goal, Lewis Black noted, was more than service and employment. The goal was to put pressure on merchants so they would spur town leaders to register black voters. The refusal of merchants and officials to budge would confirm to blacks the need for more direct action.[19] Direct action intensified in early July, when 500 people marched to the county court-house to protest the dragged-out pace of registrations. Standoffs drew black youth and white youths to either side of the street in front of the courthouse. Tensions ran high. On July 16, a gang of whites attacked black demonstrators. Seventeen protestors were taken to a hospital in Selma. Organizers called for more demonstrations, and for reinforcements from Hale County and beyond. Klan leaders in Tuscaloosa, thirty miles to the north of Greensboro, called for backups as well. As both sides mobilized, it looked as if Greensboro would be the next Selma. On July 17, the country church of Rev. A. T. Days, where he was also minister in addition to town-based St. Matthews, was burned to the ground. On the same day, arson destroyed a second black church in a township outside of Greensboro.[20] The call went out to marshal forces in Hale County.

Alice Hargress and James Lyles showed up for the July 26 protest march from St. Matthews Church down Main Street to the courthouse. The demonstrators were stopped and told they could only march away from downtown. Barricades halted their advance onto Main Street. Reinforce-ments for the limited Hale County contingent had come "by the truck-load" from neighboring Perry County, to the east, and Greene County, just to the west. Perry County SCLC and local leader Albert Turner urged the demonstrators to "love that barrier down." Young people began to shout at the police, "Arrest us, arrest us!"[21] Arrests began; tear gas was sprayed into the crowd. Demonstrators scattered. Alice Hargress found a towel and took refuge in a nearby black funeral parlor. Others headed for Rev. Days's parsonage, near St. Matthews Church. Tear gas followed them, and one canister—with a loud pop—landed on the porch of the parsonage, where the minister's baby daughter lay. It scalded her. The barricade, the attack, the tear gas, and the baby's scalding all deepened the resolve of the demonstrators.[22] Their leaders vowed to return.

Alice Hargress, her neighbor and friend Bertha Wallace, and three Wal-lace youngsters readied themselves on the morning of July 28 to demonstrate again. Bertha Wallace's husband was warned not to go to Greensboro that day, or to permit his family to go. Joel Wallace complied, but reported back that "I can't do nothing with them children" or his wife. Expecting a long but more peaceful day, the two women prepared chicken lunches and took portable chairs so they when they got a break from standing in protest, they could sit for lunch. They left the chicken and chairs in Bertha Wallace's car.[23]

When the two women arrived for the demonstration, what greeted them was not at all what they expected. They saw four busses. They saw armed men—not just the state patrols and the Hale County sheriff's men but civilians deputized for the day, shotguns in hand. Alice Hargress, Bertha Wallace, and the children were given a choice: they could turn around and go home, or they could get on a bus and be taken to jail—somewhere out of town, because the tiny jail in back of the courthouse could hold just a handful of inmates. They had not expected the busses or the ultimatum, but they'd been prepared how to respond. They got on the busses. Alice Hargress knew one of the deputized men—he was a white neighbor. He pretended not to recognize her. On the bus, two male black neighbors found each other in the back and talked about disarming the deputy at the front. Alice Hargress called them out. They had been told to be humble, to be obedient, she reminded them. It was the "only way you gonna beat this thing." If the men went for the weapon, they would mess everything up.[24]

In the bus filled with protestors, some Alice Hargress's age and many much younger, demonstrators kept their spirits up with songs as they were taken almost to Selma, where the driver halted at the county jail. Outside the windows were cars and spectators, black and white. Cars belonging to the white spectators had KKK bumper stickers. "I told them children, who'd been playing and singing, 'Look like we got to pray now!'"[25] The county jail, as it turned out, was already full, so the bus got back onto Highway 80 and found its way to a men's prison camp on the outskirts of Selma. While the bus and its passengers sat in the sun, the prisoners were herded out of the building. State police took photos of each marcher holding a sign with their name and date of birth. Then women and men from the march were brought into the small prison house. A partition was erected to separate the sexes. There was room to stand but not to sit or lie down. The jailors brought in a #2 tub, filled it with water, and put a "skillet with a long handle" into the tub. The makeshift dipper fell into the tub after each use. Then jailors brought in a single toilet and deposited it in the middle of the cell. That was the unshielded commode for one and all. Partly as defiance, the men jailed on the other side of the partition sang loudly all night and slept by day. The women took turns standing and lying down, Alice Hargress recalled; "I don't know what we did for sleep." Alice Hargress languished there from Wednesday to Saturday until James Lyles and her cousin put up a property bond to gain her release.[26]

On July 31, 1965, Alice Hargress finally returned home to her mother, Pinkie, who'd been looking after two grandchildren, and to her twenty-five-year-old sons, twins who'd come for a visit from the North only to learn when they arrived that "your momma's in jail!"[27]

"We won, we sure did," Alice Hargress reflected a dozen years after her arrest. The demonstrations in Greensboro and Hale County and in other counties in the Black Belt helped bring decisive pressure on the Congress to pass the Voter Rights Bill of August 4, 1965. Ever since Selma, President Lyndon Johnson had pressed for the bill. It took all of his unsurpassed legislative skill to get it over the hurdles and obstructions of opposed southern Democratic congressmen and their conservative Republican allies. Demonstrations in the Black Belt kept up the pressure. When the bill passed, it ended tests to register, and provided that federal registrars could be sent in to oversee voter registration in counties with an undeniable record of voter obstruction. The protests in Hale County, the history of hindrance, and the arrests and jailing of demonstrators placed Hale among the first Alabama counties to which federal registrars went by the end of August 1965. Further delays, foot-dragging, lawsuits, and subterfuge greeted them. But registration was under way. By the end of the next year, more than 4,000 black voters were registered in Hale County.[28]

For Lewis Black, the federal law and the federal registrars constituted not the culmination of the struggle but the start of a new stage. "The whites [were] already spreading the word among Negroes that the civil rights movement [was] run by communists," that they would evict or deny credit to those who use the vote. Things would be different but no easier than before.[29] Alice Hargress would discover that he was right. For her, however, the immediate personal victory was that her mother got to vote. Pinkie Cabbil Sledge was spared the humiliation of a test, which her daughter was sure she could never pass, literate though she was. She would encounter no cursing or shouting. She would just go to Greensboro and vote, without harassment. Or so they thought.

Alice Hargress drove her mother to the Greensboro post office, where voting took place, parked her car, and began to walk her mother in. "Get off the grass," an official shouted. Her mother was directed to the side and downstairs. Officials barred Alice Hargress from going down with her. The daughter could only hope her mother "voted the right way!" Pinkie Sledge voted two more times before she died in 1969. Alice Hargress had dreamt that she might be able to take Forrest Hargress to vote as well, making him the oldest black in Hale County to cast a ballot. But he had died on June 7, 1965, at the age of ninety-nine and a half—two months before President Lyndon Johnson signed the Voting Rights Act on August 6.[30]

In time, Alice Hargress came to recognize that gaining the vote, as Lewis Black insisted, was just the beginning. Getting black folks to "vote the right way"—to trust each other rather than to follow ingratiating or bullying white folks—would prove to be a battle that would go on for decades.

As James Lyles saw it, the voting rights struggle brought more fulfillment than setbacks. The "vote was nothing to the other fellow, what had always been free. It was nothing to him. To a man without freedom, it was a great asset." To be sure, in years to come, two of his sons ran for office in Hale County and lost; Mildred Black ran and lost; Lewis Black ran and lost. But James Lyles placed three of his sons in Hale County High School, despite the opposition of white officials high and low. Sons stayed in Greensboro and established businesses there. Gradually if grudgingly, blacks from home or out of town were allowed to eat or go where they wanted. So could visiting whites. Things for which trespassers against custom had been killed in the sixties—civil rights workers and ministers from the North, black youths from nearby counties—one could do by the late 1970s. "We broke all that down," James Lyles declared.[31]

For James Lyles, perhaps the greatest legacy of the struggle was the realization of his dream of black cooperation to hold on to the land. In the 1960s, even more than in the 1930s, small black farmers were losing land and livelihoods, intensified by the denial of federal benefits granted to large white farmers and "agribusiness" by the Department of Agriculture.[32] Unable to get credit, government assistance, or affordable equipment for cash crops, black landowners were folding at a startling rate. Replaced by machines, livestock, or fish farms that required little labor, black tenants on white-owned land faced evictions, accelerated by anger at the Movement.[33] The editor of the *Greensboro Watchman*, the leading newspaper of the county, told a federal examiner, "We like our Nigras, but we can't afford to keep 'em around. The county's economy can't take it."[34] For James Lyles, who in the 1930s had foreseen the massive uprooting, the answer remained the same: blacks had to work together if they wanted to remain on the land.

Led by his ally and friend Lewis Black, the cooperative effort took many forms, each of which targeted areas where black farmers were most vulnerable. The first step was a credit union, which Lewis Black and his wife, Mildred, initiated in 1961. Rather than be dependent on white bankers or government agencies, which either denied or constricted credit, blacks paid into the Greenala Citizens Federal Credit Union, which then disbursed loans to farmers. What began with eight backers and deposits of $42.50 grew to a thousand members and assets of $80,000 by mid-1966.[35] Another was the drive, begun in 1965, to get blacks on the all-white agricultural committees that decided who got loans and payments from the federal price support and soil bank programs. A third mission, and for James Lyles the most compelling, was the creation of the Federation of Southern Cooperatives and the acquisition of just under 1,100 acres of land in nearby Sumter County as a rural training center to help black farmers retain their land. At the training center, blacks could learn about improved farming techniques and better crops to grow. Supremely importantly to James Lyles was that the cooperative provided an option for both landowning and displaced black farmers. Those who wanted to stay—and "to save, protect, and expand the landholdings of Black family farmers in the South"—gained a means to do so.[36]

Even in the thick of the struggle for voting rights, Lewis Black believed that the real issue was whether blacks could achieve "an economic base" to allow them to stay in the South and freely exercise the vote. He "was big on economics," confirmed fellow Hale County leader Rev. A. T. Days. A man with a "bulldog spirit, that Lewis Black was ahead of his time."[37] At every point, Black confronted entrenched white leaders who obstructed black voting and undermined black economic aspirations. What gave him hope, and what he resourcefully utilized as the means to black cooperation and economic salvation, was the pivotal federal program at the heart of President Lyndon Johnson's goal of a Great Society. In August 1964, Johnson wrested congressional backing to fund his signature initiative, the War on Poverty. The legislation created a cabinet-level Office of Economic Opportunity. The OEO was to receive proposals and oversee plans from local "community action committees." It had $400 million to allocate in antipoverty funds.[38]

Lewis Black became a tenacious leader in what turned out to be a grueling six-year struggle to gain antipoverty money for cooperative efforts by Black Belt farmers. Historian Susan Youngblood Ashmore has powerfully chronicled Lewis Black's relentless quest. In August 1965, he formed an association to sponsor an antipoverty program in Hale County. He teamed with fellow activist Albert Turner of Perry County to call for a cooperative program for their adjacent Black Belt counties. In 1966, he won support in two additional counties for a proposal to create a black-run cooperative that would grow and market vegetables on small plots of land. Commercial truck farming would require less acreage and require less investment and equipment than cotton—and enable black farmers to stay on the land. In the fall of 1966, black farmers in all ten counties of the Black Belt joined the effort, forming the Southwest Alabama Farmers' Cooperative Association (SWFCA). Despite unceasing opposition, harassment, and delays at the behest of white mayors, congressmen, bureaucrats, and the governor of Alabama—and calls for FBI investigation of "these professional troublemakers"—SWFCA received an initial grant of $400,000 and a subsequent grant of $600,000 from the OEO. In 1967, further support from the OEO and from private foundations bolstered the Cooperative and its promise for a "rebirth of the Alabama Black Belt."[39]

To James Lyles, it was the cooperative effort, especially the acreage set aside in Sumter County, that realized his "dream for people to get some land, to have somewhere to stay, not to be driven out." Even for those Alabama "people out of state," who had never farmed or never intended to farm again, black-owned land would allow them to say, "I'm going home—I've got a home out there." As James Lyles put it, "Plenty people in the North wished they had somewhere right now!"[40]

For James Lyles and Alice Hargress, the great achievement of the mid-1960s was to "lift the burden off many people," old and young. For Lewis Black and the generation to follow, the burden became to "carry it on."[41]

Epilogue

"A Heavy Load to Lift"

BY THE FALL OF 2008, Alice Hargress and I had known each other for thirty years.

I had first phoned Alice Hargress in July 1978 to ask if she knew anything of Paul Cameron and the black people he'd sent out from North Carolina in 1844 to work an Alabama cotton plantation. "That's right," she'd replied. That answer, and many conversations that followed, opened up a world of black striving to me. When I called in October 2008, she was ninety-four years old and still going strong.

It was just a month before the presidential election. I felt anxiety and yet also a sense of impending fulfillment. The nation's economy was in free fall, with no end in sight. At the same time, something that had been impossible to foresee in 1865, 1965, or 1978 seemed on the verge of happening—the election of a black president. I had expected Alice Hargress, the family matriarch, to be as hopeful and excited as I was. Instead, I found her subdued and guarded: "Whoever gets that job will have a heavy load to lift."

Alice Hargress had lived through the Great Depression. But it was more than the possibility of another 1930s calamity that prompted her unease. It was all that had happened—and not happened—since the civil rights movement days of 1965. She, James Lyles, and others had thought that a great turnaround would come in the wake of their demonstrations in July 1965 and the Voter Rights Act signed on August 6 of that year. For sure, immense changes had come. Yet there was no denying the setbacks and disappointments. Overcoming the legacy of the plantation past had proved to be a vastly more strenuous task than anyone had imagined. So even with a historic breakthrough on the horizon, she kept her expectations in check. The years since 1965 had taught her to be wary about declaring victory.

Alice Hargress had to do no more than follow the struggles of Lewis Black to see what they were up against. Lewis Black had said from the start that getting the vote was just a first step, and he was right. He predicted that whites would try to deter black voters, as they had during Reconstruction, and when blacks did cast ballots, they would attempt to manipulate the process. He was right. Names of black candidates got left off the ballot. Ballot boxes suspiciously burned. When Reverend James Lyles's son Eugene ran for mayor, he sought votes of whites as well as blacks. A white man he canvassed said he wasn't going to vote for him, but he hoped that if he won, "you won't do the same to us as we've done to you." Lyles lost when absentee ballots came in. When Lewis Black ran for probate judge, he found himself demonized as too controversial, not to be trusted with power or purse. Even after black voters became a numerical majority, many didn't vote for black candidates. "We didn't trust one another," Alice Hargress lamented. As Lewis Black saw it, the plantation legacy was still at work. There remained "a tendency in us to satisfy the master."

Even the Voting Rights Act of 1965, Lewis Black noted presciently, only "gave black people the temporary right to vote." Every "three or four years, we've got to go back to Congress," where "white folks got to decide to extend our voting rights." Blacks were only "temporary voting citizens."

Beyond securing citizenship, Lewis Black's foremost goal was keeping blacks on the land. By 1966, he focused his efforts on winning funds to create black rural cooperatives. He got federal grants totaling almost a million dollars, and gained foundation support as well. But the federal money had to come through the Community Action Program of the War on Poverty, and required governing boards made up of whites and blacks. White officials, from mayors and county commissioners to Governor George Wallace, first opposed the grants altogether, then demanded control of the funds and handpicked for the boards blacks who they thought would be cooperative. Ready to participate, Lewis Black and other movement organizers were left out in the cold. Their leadership had made them "militants." Notwithstanding white resistance, the Southwest Alabama Rural Cooperative Association received $865,000. The association trained small black farmers to raise vegetables rather than cotton, and won contracts for the sale of cucumbers and other truck farm produce. By 1967, co-op farmers began to market their crops. But obstructions never ended. The state highway patrol joined the sabotage. One day it stopped a refrigerated truck on the highway, kept it idling until its fuel ran low and its Freon ran out, and released it only after its cargo of cucumbers spoiled.

In the quest to keep blacks on the land, Lewis Black had expected harassment from local and state officials and bureaucrats, and so he looked to the federal government. In 1967, he urged rural blacks to "utilize federal agencies" to bolster "their economic base." But he had miscalculated. The most determined opposition to helping black farmers came from a branch of the federal government—from the United States Department of Agriculture.

Federal farm policy from the 1930s on was designed to favor large-scale agricultural farmers, to supply them with payments to take land out of production, to fund their acquisition of up-to-date machinery, to give them advice on best farming practices, and to offer them loans for equipment and fertilizer. The goal was farm efficiency and the withering away of tenants, sharecroppers, and "useless non-commercial farmers." Intensifying after 1945, the policy of the department and its agents was to provide technical assistance, loans for mechanization, and membership on crop allotment committees to farmers with 5,000 acres or more. Large farmers were overwhelmingly white. In historian Pete Daniel's words, agri-government aided agribusiness. New technology, the cost of machinery, and federal favor of large farmers accelerated the exodus of blacks from the land. Between 1965 and 1982, 150,000 black farmers left the land, leaving behind only 33,000 in the rural South.

By 1981, Lewis Black realized that his faith in federal help was misplaced. "When I came to Hale County" in 1951, he recalled, "we had about 350 farmers, and 75 of them were black farmers." By the early 1980s, there were "less than ten black farmers in the whole county." The cooperative association, founded in 1967, ceased operations in January 1981. The "government helped in the revolution, but it wasn't the kind of revolution that we were working for," he reflected. "Every dirty thing that we accuse these local whites of, the Federal government was a part of it." Profoundly disillusioned, he came to believe that all federal programs—and especially the War on Poverty—were a sham. The promise of funds deceived him and others, got blacks to join with whites to get grants, and then funneled money, jobs, and power back to white folks. To Lewis Black, the War on Poverty "stole the movement." It "made a fool out of all of us."

The saddest consequence of black land loss, as Lewis Black saw it, was that "when young people grow up, like my children, they don't see the necessity of owning land. . . . My parents, my grandparents, suffered all their lives to buy eleven hundred acres of land." For the older generations, the land "had a sentimental value to it, 'cause we had to get a livelihood from that land, we had to get our bread from that land. . . . Now children think that milk comes out of the store. . . . They don't see the relevance of land." They "have no idea what it took for black folks to own land."

Even if you "take one of us and make us president of the United States, it really doesn't change things," Lewis Black contended in 1981. Even "if you elect us to the office, it really ties us more than it would if we wasn't in there." As he put it, "We're a long way from being free."

As the nation verged on the election of a black president in October 2008, Alice Hargress's outlook was cautious but not bleak. She knew what disappointments had driven Lewis Black to despair. Still, she could hope that his prediction wouldn't come true—that the election of a black president would indeed change things. Neither Lewis Black nor Alice Hargress could have anticipated that the man elected in 2008, and reelected in 2012, would himself come to temper his understanding of how much change a president could achieve.

In an interview in mid-2015, Barack Obama reflected, "When I ran in 2008 there were those posters out there: 'Hope' and 'Change.' And those are capturing aspirations about where we should be going." But "as soon as you start talking about specifics," there are "choices you have to make. . . . You've got these big legacy systems that you have to wrestle with and you have to balance what you want and where you're going with what is and what has been." Noted Obama, "Sometimes the task of government is to make incremental improvements," improvements by degrees, so "that ten years from now suddenly we're in a very different place than we were."

My last visit to Alice Hargress came in December 2013. She was ninety-nine years old. By that time she spent most of her day in the television room of her home, keeping up with the news and receiving check-in calls from her children and grandchildren. In the years since we first met in 1978, four of her grown children had come back to Alabama, three to live on family land, one to a home bought in Demopolis, twenty-five minutes away. Elsewhere in the community, others had come back as well, some from California, as had her adult children, some from cities in Michigan and Ohio. For them, the commitment to heir land remained in force, enforced not by law—where the practice and concept was vulnerable—but by shared understanding. Heir land was a precept that Alice Hargress had abided by for the length of her life. She pressed the next generation to do the same. Her wish was that Cameron Place remain in family hands, as it had been since Paul Hargis and other forebears had bought it and descendants had kept it for a hundred and forty years. The land should stay undivided, open to and for "all the heirs."

Though Alice Hargress's house was the same as it had been for many years, photographs and a wall hanging revealed that in 2013 she and the country were in a different place. On the wall hanging, placed on a side wall in the television room, was the seal of Camp David, the Maryland retreat of presidents going back a half century to Dwight Eisenhower and up to the current president. It was a gift from her grandson, David Hargress. David was the son of Ted Hargress, one of her eight children, who had become a career Navy man. David had followed in his father's footsteps and carved out a niche as a navy cook. His skills, honed at sea, had won admiration, and when he rotated back to land those skills had gotten him a plum assignment: cooking for the president and the president's family at Camp David. In Alice Hargress's TV room, on a table across from the wall hanging, was a framed photograph of David Hargress and his wife, Annalisa, with Michelle and Barack Obama.

The demonstrator arrested in 1965 and her grandson, descendant of the Ned Forrest Hargress born in 1866, were in a very different place.

At the end of my visit in December 2013 there was a gathering of young people and community residents at a small museum honoring the civil rights struggle of the 1960s in Greensboro.

The Safe House Museum commemorated in particular one of the visits of Martin Luther King Jr. to the area. After his appearance in late March 1968, local leaders got word that night riders were roaming the road back to Montgomery, and so decided he should spend the night at a dwelling in town, well protected by armed neighbors. Years later, after a determined campaign by Theresa Burroughs—a leader of the demonstrations of July 1965, and whose home gave sanctuary to Dr. King that night in 1968—the dwelling became the Safe House Museum and a state historic site. In the museum were photos of those arrested that July, photos taken by the Alabama Department of Public Safety. They were glorified mug shots. Each person arrested held a foot-long rectangular card with his or her name and date of birth inked on it in large print. The protesters were first photographed, then jailed. Theresa Burroughs had obtained copies of the photographs, framed them, and hung them on the interior walls of the museum. Alice Hargress and James Lyles were among those honored with their prisoner photographs on the Safe House wall.

I took Alice Hargress to the gathering. Theresa Burroughs was speaking to fifteen young people from area schools when we walked in. The moment she saw us, she concluded her talk, waved Alice Hargress over, and introduced her: "This is Mrs. Alice Hargress, the oldest living person of those who marched in July 1965 and won your right to vote." Spontaneously, the young people applauded. Theresa Burroughs asked for a few words, and Alice Hargress obliged, talking about the struggle of that day and since. Then she gave them a look I'd come to recognize as signaling a message. She peered down over her glasses and paused, her eyebrows arched. Then she extended her hand toward the young people and said, "I'm moving on. *It's your turn now.*"

Theresa Burroughs then asked Alice Hargress to lead the group in song as they walked to the meeting room where the program would start. Without hesitation, in that rich melodious voice of hers, she led the way.

> Ain't no body gonna turn me 'round,
> Turn me around, turn me around;
> Ain't no body gonna turn me 'round,
> Keep on a-talking, keep on a-walking,
> Marching up to Freedom Land.

Alice Hargress passed away on August 2, 2014, eighteen days shy of her hundredth birthday. She had spent most of her life on land made free by the striving of ancestors. She had kept the land free for herself and heirs by her labor and dedication. Nobody ever turned her around.

Appendix

The People of A Mind to Stay

Antebellum

NORTH CAROLINA

Duncan Cameron The most successful lawyer and planter in Piedmont North Carolina, he bought and kept enslaved families together.

Lawrence Hargis In 1814, he ran a country store. Indebted to Cameron in 1829, he settled by transferring the enslaved family of George Hargis to the planter.

George Hargis Conveyed to Duncan Cameron, George Hargis became a courier and later a plantation foreman.

Paul Cameron Son of Duncan Cameron, he took charge of the Piedmont plantation in 1837. He used his father's wealth to buy land and send workers to Alabama in 1844 and to Mississippi in 1856.

Paul Hargis Two years old when Duncan Cameron acquired his parents in 1829, he grew up at the planter's home quarter. In 1844, Paul Cameron moved him to Alabama.

ALABAMA

James Ruffin A relative, he advised Paul Cameron to purchase a secondhand cotton plantation in Alabama. Cameron subsequently felt he had been duped into buying poor land.

Charles Lewellyn Cameron's first overseer in Alabama, he imposed rigid discipline on Cameron's enslaved workers, prompting flight and sabotage.

Milton and Toney Both men resisted subjection in Alabama. Toney escaped, then burnt his foot; Milton fled 150 miles before recapture.

Sandy Cameron An enslaved carpenter, he was the most valued of the 114 workers sent to Alabama in 1844. He remained on Cameron land after emancipation.

Hargis siblings Paul Hargis was taken to Alabama with his brother Jim and his sisters Sally and Nancy, leaving behind their aged parents and their brother Squire.

John Webster Alabama overseer who came to understand the limits of the plantation's soil and the futility of hard driving. He quit in late 1856, after taking thirty-five Alabama workers to a new Cameron plantation in Mississippi.

MISSISSIPPI

Samuel Jeter The first overseer of Cameron's uncleared 1,811 acres in northern Mississippi. Urged by Cameron to pursue both patience and profit, he vacillated between laxness and the lash.

William Lamb Cameron's second Mississippi overseer. He used quotas and punishments to maximize cotton production and profits.

Len The most defiant man on the Mississippi plantation, he ran away four times. Scars from lacerations inflicted by overseers marked him as ungovernable.

Zack and Ned Workers from North Carolina, they were brought to Mississippi in 1860. Bullied, Zack attacked the overseer with an axe, and Ned intervened. Subdued and tried, Zack was hung and Ned sold.

Squire Hargis Older brother of Paul Hargis, he was left in North Carolina in 1844 but in 1860 was sent to Mississippi. In 1862, he was evacuated to Alabama, where he disclosed what had happened in the Delta.

Postwar

Paul and Dicey Hargis Became a couple in Alabama. In 1864, they were taken back to North Carolina. Two years after emancipation, they returned to Alabama.

Wilson Oberry Alabama overseer after the war, he made Paul Hargis the "head of the hoes." In 1872, he urged Cameron to sell blacks land for a church and a school.

Sandy Cameron Formerly the carpenter on the Cameron place, he remained after 1865. In 1873, he became the first freedman to acquire Cameron land.

Brister Reese He moved onto the Cameron place in 1867, where he became a Union League organizer, exhorting freedmen to demand their rights.

Paul Cameron Wanted desperately to sell his Alabama plantation, but held out until the end of 1872, when he gave up hope of getting a good price from a white buyer.

Thomas Roulhac Nephew of Paul Cameron, he became Cameron's land agent in 1873. He sold almost all of the 1,600-acre plantation to black purchasers.

Robert and Kizziah Cabbil They bought 120 acres of Cameron's land in 1874, and in 1899 donated an acre for what became the Cassimore AME Zion Church.

Tom Ruffin Formerly enslaved to Alabama planter James Ruffin, after emancipation he moved just north of Cameron's place. By 1900 he was the largest black landowner in the county.

Ned Forrest Hargress Believed by family members to be the son of Confederate general Nathan Bedford Forrest, the result of a forced union with his enslaved mother, Dorothy, in April 1865. Squire Hargis married his mother in 1867. His service to aging Paul Hargis earned him a bequest of land in 1912, by which time the family had changed its name to Hargress.

Twentieth Century

Louie Rainey Born in 1906. His prodigious memory and vivid storytelling made him the oral historian of the Cassimore community in the twentieth century.

Alice Sledge Hargress Born in 1914, she viewed family land as a sanctuary from the submission expected by white planters and neighbors, and committed herself to keeping the land inviolate for heirs. She marched for voter rights in 1965.

James Lyles Born in 1896, he grew up on Cameron land purchased by his grandparents. A man of prophetic visions, he foresaw mass expulsions of black farmers in the 1930s. He summoned blacks to march for full citizenship in the 1960s.

Lewis and Mildred Black They founded a credit union for black farmers. In the 1960s, they organized for voter rights. After 1965, Lewis Black pursued support for marketing cooperatives to keep black farmers on the land.

Notes

1. Spared

1. Jean Bradley Anderson, *Piedmont Plantation: The Bennehan-Cameron Family and Lands in North Carolina* (Durham, NC: Historic Preservation Society of Durham, 1985), chapters 2–3.

2. In the 1910 Federal Census, Paul Hargress gave Virginia as the birthplace of his parents. See the 1910 U.S. Federal Census for Cedarville, Hale County, Alabama, Roll T624_15, page 24, Enumeration District 0048, Microfilm #1374028, accessed through Ancestry.com. In earlier census listings, with his name spelled differently, Paul Hargress gave North Carolina as his parents' birthplace.

3. Deed of February 27, 1829, Lawrence Hargis to Duncan Cameron, found in Cameron Family Papers, Southern Historical Collection, Wilson Library, University of North Carolina at Chapel Hill (hereafter abbreviated as CFP). The 1829 deed gave the names and ages of each member of the enslaved Hargis family.

4. The Hargis-Cameron partnership began in 1808, when Lawrence Hargis operated Cameron Mills, a mill and mill store in Person County. See Anderson, *Piedmont Plantation*, 35–36, and L. V. Hargis to Duncan Cameron, September 25, 1813, CFP. The stipulation regarding Cameron's third of the profits is in Article 8 of the memorandum from Duncan Cameron to Mrs. Rebecca Cameron, February 16, 1816, CFP.

5. When Lawrence Hargis later defaulted, his country store came into the hands of Moses Chambers; Isham Malone to Duncan Cameron, August 14, 1830, CFP. A subsequent account by one of Moses Chambers's enslaved workers, which details the caprice and cruelty of bondage under Chambers, notes the role of one of Chambers's workers as the operator of a shop where he made hats. I speculate that George Hargis had a parallel role while enslaved by the previous storekeeper, Lawrence Hargis. See "Narrative of James Curry," in John Blassingame, ed., *Slave*

Testimony: Two Centuries of Letters, Speeches, Interviews, and Autobiographies (Baton Rouge: Louisiana State University Press, 1977), 129–130.

6. The first report of Lawrence Hargis's poor health came from Rebecca Cameron to Duncan Cameron, October 16, 1816, CFP.

7. Letters to Duncan Cameron starting in the spring of 1828 confirm the onset of hard times. See incoming correspondence to Cameron, January 28, February 28, and April 9, 1828, CFP.

8. Thomas V. Hargis to Duncan Cameron, July 21, 1821, August 11, 1824, CFP. In 1824, Thomas V. Hargis offered to sell blacks for Duncan Cameron, who had indicated that he wished to sell six people. "I am now on my way to South Carolina with a parcel of negroes & if you wish to send yours by me, I will take them and make the best sales I can, on usual commissions which is 10%."

9. Lawrence Hargis, sale of seven Negro slaves to Duncan Cameron, in settlement of indebtedness to Cameron, February 15, 1829, CFP. Hargis had given his note of indebtedness two years earlier, on February 15, 1827. The seven persons sold by Hargis were George and Agga and their five children, Jim, Squire, Sally, Paul, and infant daughter Nancy. Paul, the youngest son, was two years old. Cameron accepted the payment of the seven enslaved people but later sued, successfully, for further compensation. J. W. Norwood to Duncan Cameron, June 24, 1830, CFP. In 1830, both Hargis brothers were virtually bankrupt. See John Burwell to Duncan Cameron, January 9, 1830, CFP. Lawrence Hargis died in 1830.

10. John A. Cameron to Duncan Cameron, March 21, 1816; Fabius Haywood to Cameron, February 4 and February 5, 1828; J. G. Stanley to George Badger, March 10, 1831, all in CFP. See also John D. Hawkins to Cameron, March 15, 1828; S. E. Kollock to Cameron, November 5, 1828, CFP. But note that in 1824, Cameron did sell six slaves, and likely did so at other times. By timely sale of stock in 1827, he had cash to buy, whereas others in hard times faced heavy debts or bankruptcy, and were compelled to sell enslaved property. On the timely stock sale, see George Anderson to Duncan Cameron, January 24, 1827, CFP.

11. Sydney Nathans, *To Free a Family: The Journey of Mary Walker* (Cambridge, MA: Harvard University Press, 2012), 19. The statement came in an interview with descendants of Cameron's enslaved workers, conducted in the 1990s by Alice Eley Jones, and on file at the Stagville Center for Historic Preservation, Durham, North Carolina. For the patterns of purchase, see Anderson, *Piedmont Plantation*, appendix B.

12. See the ledger of credits and purchases by blacks at the Richard Bennehan store in his account book for 1810–1812, CFP, and also Nathans, *To Free a Family*, 15–16, and 266 n. 17. Michael Tadman develops the concept of what he terms "Key Slaves" in his new introduction to the paperback edition of Tadman, *Speculators*

and Slaves: Masters, Traders, and Slaves in the Old South (Madison: University of Wisconsin Press, 1996), xxxi–xxxvii.

13. See the 1834 list of enslaved workers for Fairntosh—identified as the "Home" quarter.

14. Anderson, *Piedmont Plantation*, 28–29.

15. Most enslaved persons were listed only by first names. There were numerous men named George on the Cameron plantation, and several of them were men who had important roles on the place. One George was a courier in the 1810s and 1820s; he was an older man by 1834. The George who was placed second on the 1834 list was unambiguously George Hargis: he was listed by both his first and last name. Later letters identify this George as a courier among quarters and between Fairntosh and nearby towns.

16. Anderson, *Piedmont Plantation*, 99–100; Nathans, *To Free a Family*, 17; Duncan Cameron to Paul Cameron, May 2, 1838, CFP.

17. See the 1830s slave registers and then the 1840s listings for the shift from carter Joe to "Rascal Joe." Pompey was exonerated of the charges but ultimately removed from the wagoner's role.

18. Anderson, *Piedmont Plantation*, 41–43.

19. The contrast in the two brothers' aptitude and quickness was spelled out in W. P. Mangum to Duncan Cameron, October 5, 1814, CFP. Thomas D. Bennehan to Mary [Cameron], February 5, 1821; William H. Haywood to Duncan Cameron, March 19, April 20, 1821, CFP. See also Rebecca Cameron to Duncan Cameron, December 13, 1822, CFP.

20. William Haywood to Duncan Cameron, April 20, 1821; Rebecca Cameron to Duncan Cameron, December 13, 1822, CFP.

21. When Paul Cameron subsequently enrolled in Washington College (later Trinity College) in Hartford, he had to "take up the Greek altogether *de novo*." T. C. Brownell to Duncan Cameron, May 31, 1827, CFP.

22. Samuel Yarbrough to Thomas Bennehan, May 24, 1824, CFP; Anderson, *Piedmont Plantation*, 42.

23. Soon after he arrived, Paul Cameron violated academy rules and was dismissed. He subsequently promised "in future to be obedient" if reinstated. Paul Cameron to Captain [Alden] Partridge, October 11, 1825, Alden Partridge Records, Norwich University Archives, Kreitzberg Library, Northfield, VT. AP-1825-10-11. Academy principal Alden Partridge reported the episode and reinstatement to Duncan Cameron, who wholeheartedly endorsed the principal's firmness. The father was "well aware of the necessity" of "strict discipline": "It has been my lot to govern others in various capacities" and "I have always practiced discipline and enforced it"; "it is *indispensably* necessary." Cameron lamented the "impetuosity

of his [son's] ill-governed passions" and trusted he would "faithfully keep" the promise "to govern himself." Duncan Cameron to Alden Partridge, November 16, 1825, Alden Partridge Records, Norwich University Archives, Kreitzberg Library, Northfield, VT. AP-1825-11-16_03.

24. Paul Cameron to [Mary Anne Cameron], August 12, 1825; January 5, February 14, June 24, 1826, CFP; W. E. Anderson to Duncan Cameron, December 13, 1825, CFP.

25. Paul Cameron to Mary Anne Cameron, April 11, 1826; Captain Alden Partridge to Duncan Cameron, May 14, October 23, 1826; Paul Cameron to Duncan Cameron, October 24, 1826, CFP.

26. Alden Partridge to Duncan Cameron, April 16, 1827; Paul Cameron to Rebecca Cameron, April 25, 1827, CFP.

27. Paul Cameron to Duncan Cameron, June 21, 1827, CFP.

28. Paul Cameron to Duncan Cameron, [January 30, 1835], CFP. "I need, and must have your sustaining countenance," the son wrote. His father was "both older and wiser than myself," and it "is of the utmost importance to me, to look steadily to you as the friend and counselor whom it is wisdom to obey."

29. Paul Cameron to [Mary Anne Cameron], February 17, 1829, CFP; Anderson, *Piedmont Plantation*, 33–34.

30. William Anderson to Duncan Cameron, December 12, 1828, CFP; Nathans, *To Free a Family*, 18–20.

31. Anderson, *Piedmont Plantation*, 47.

32. Ibid., 44.

33. Nathans, *To Free a Family*, 23–24.

34. Ibid., 24–25.

35. Anderson, *Piedmont Plantation*, 100.

36. Thomas Ruffin to Paul Cameron, January 24, 1834, CFP; Anderson, *Piedmont Plantation*, 49.

37. [Ellen Boylan?] to Catherine Ruffin, January 27, 1832; Catherine Ruffin Roulhac to Joseph G. Roulhac, July 21, 1837, in Ruffin, Roulhac, Hamilton Family Papers, Southern Historical Collection, Wilson Library, University of North Carolina at Chapel Hill; Thomas Bennehan to Paul Cameron, July 20, 1837, CFP.

38. Anderson, *Piedmont Plantation*, 49–50; Anne Ruffin Cameron to Paul Cameron, April 1, 1833, CFP.

39. Senior overseer Samuel Yarbrough reported in 1824 that his fellow overseers "have carried on their work in peace without having to use any rash terms." Samuel Yarbrough to Thomas D. Bennehan, May 17, 1824, CFP.

40. Paul Cameron to Duncan Cameron, April 26, 1835, CFP. Cameron's detailed account of the episode was penned on the back of a more cryptic note from Rebecca Cameron to her husband about the "difference" between Jim and his overseer.

41. Paul Cameron to Duncan Cameron, April 26, 1835, CFP.

42. Paul Cameron to Duncan Cameron, May 20, 1835, CFP.

43. Paul Cameron to Duncan Cameron, June 10, 1836, CFP. The former enslaved worker who reported the hearsay about Paul Cameron was James Curry. Before he escaped bondage, Curry lived in Person County and was the property of Moses Chambers, who had acquired the Hargis country store after Lawrence Hargis died. Paul Cameron owned a small plantation quarter nearby—a bequest from his uncle Thomas Bennehan in 1831. Periodically, Paul Cameron came to the Person plantation to check on the overseer and the work of the enslaved laborers. In a narrative published after his escape, Curry claimed that he had been told that Paul Cameron "used to go out once in two or three weeks, and while there, have one or two slaves tied and whip them unmercifully," merely, "as he said, *to let them know he was their master.*" The hearsay claim is in "Narrative of James Curry," 139.

44. Thomas Bennehan to Rebecca Bennehan Cameron, September 11, 1824, August 17, 1825; Paul Cameron to Mary Anne Cameron, January 5, 1825, CFP.

45. Rebecca Cameron to Duncan Cameron, January 2, 10, 12, 1836, CFP.

46. Paul Cameron to Duncan Cameron, February 8, 1836, CFP.

47. Thomas Bennehan to Mary Anne Cameron, June 30, 1836, CFP. Paul and Anne Cameron moved to Fairntosh in November 1837. Anderson, *Piedmont Plantation*, 50.

2. "Emigrants"

1. Paul Cameron to Rebecca Cameron, June 28, 1838, CFP.

2. Between 1834 and 1841–1842 there is a gap in extant lists of enslaved workers. George was the number two man at Fairntosh in 1834. George was the number one man listed at the Bobbitt quarter in 1842. I speculate that it was Paul Cameron who made the shift after he took control of the plantation in 1837.

3. In 1976, historian John Blassingame proposed that the hierarchy of roles most valued by the planter and the hierarchy of roles most valued by enslaved workers stood in contrast to each other. Owners most highly ranked house servants, drivers, and skilled workers. Enslaved people, Blassingame suggested, put conjurors, black physicians and midwives, black preachers, elders, teachers, and entertainers at the top of their hierarchy. See John W. Blassingame, "Status and Social Structure in the Slave Community: Evidence from New Sources," in Harry P. Owens, ed., *Perspectives and Irony in American Slavery* (Jackson: University Press of Mississippi, 1976), 137–151. It is clear from other studies that slave drivers found themselves in a profoundly ambiguous place—gainers in authority but obliged to use it to press or punish fellow workers. See Randal M. Miller, ed., *"Dear Master": Letters of a Slave Family* (Ithaca, NY: Cornell University Press, 1978), and William Van Deburg, *The*

Slave Drivers: Black Agricultural Labor Supervisors in the Antebellum South (Westport, CT: Greenwood Press, 1979).

4. See the 1842 "Shoe List" for enslaved workers at Fairntosh. For mention of Squire's role as a courier, see Duncan Cameron to Paul Cameron, March 10, 1843, CFP.

5. Paul Cameron to Duncan Cameron, December 19, 1835; Paul Cameron to Thomas Bennehan, January 24, 1844, CFP.

6. Duncan Cameron, letter of introduction for the southwestern visit of Paul Cameron, January 15 [1839], CFP. This letter of introduction is found in the file for January 15, 1836. Given that Paul Cameron embarked on his trip in November 1838, I conjecture that the correct date of the letter is 1839, dated in anticipation of his son's imminent arrival in the southwest. Paul Cameron carried a companion letter of introduction from a Raleigh family friend, addressed to an acquaintance in Canton, Mississippi: "Mr. Cameron visits your State with a view of making an extensive purchase of lands . . ." S. F. Patterson to Col. Wm. F. Jones, November 19, 1838, CFP.

7. Duncan Cameron to Richard Bennehan, April 4, 1818, CFP.

8. Rebecca B. Cameron to Alice Ruffin, February 8, 1834, CFP.

9. Duncan Cameron to Paul Cameron, June 24, July 3, 1836; October 4, 1836; December 4, 1836, CFP.

10. Anne Ruffin Cameron to Paul Cameron, November 24, 1838; Duncan Cameron to Paul Cameron, December 13, 1838, CFP. These and subsequent letters were addressed to Cameron in Greensboro.

11. Paul Cameron to Duncan Cameron, November 19, November 24, December 13, December 28, 1838; January 4, 1839, CFP. Paul Cameron's Hillsborough acquaintance V. M. Murphey had gone to Mississippi in 1836 to be an overseer, and reported back that "the land here is inexhaustible"—a perfect opportunity for young Cameron to add "to your fortune." V. M. Murphey to Paul Cameron, September 14, 1836, CFP.

12. V. M. Murphey to Paul Cameron, January 18, 183[7]; V. M. Murphey to Paul Cameron, September 1, 1839, CFP.

13. Jean Bradley Anderson, *Piedmont Plantation: The Bennehan-Cameron Family and Lands in North Carolina* (Durham, NC: Historic Preservation Society of Durham, 1985), 51; Sydney Nathans, *To Free a Family: The Journey of Mary Walker* (Cambridge, MA: Harvard University Press, 2012), 21–22.

14. Paul Cameron to Duncan Cameron, December 19, 1842, CFP.

15. Duncan Cameron to Paul Cameron, January 30, 1836, CFP.

16. Duncan Cameron to Paul Cameron, January 26, October 28, 1840, March 12, 1841, CFP.

17. The shuffle is evident from the quarter-by-quarter lists of workers and the changes coming in and after 1842.

18. Duncan Cameron to Paul Cameron, March 10, 1843, January 24, 1844, CFP.

19. Duncan Cameron to Paul Cameron, February 5, 8, March 10, 1843; Thomas Hicks to Duncan Cameron, January 4, July 22, 1843; Duncan Cameron to Paul Cameron, August 28, 1843; R. W. Brown to Duncan Cameron, June 24, 1844, all in CFP.

20. Paul Cameron to Duncan Cameron, August 16, September 4, October 12, 1844, CFP.

21. Paul Cameron to Duncan Cameron, September 4, 1844, CFP.

22. Damian Alan Pargas, *Slavery and Forced Migration in the Antebellum South* (New York: Cambridge University Press, 2015), 59–67. Pargas cites multiple sources—from British observer James Buckingham to former bondsman Jacob Stroyer—to argue that "when most slaves envisioned the southern interior . . . they saw a nightmare." Wrote Buckingham: "All the slaves have a great horror of being sent to the south or the west." Pargas, *Slavery and Forced Migration*, 61.

23. Greene County, Alabama, would be divided in two in 1867, with the eastern half renamed Hale County.

24. Hank Trent, ed., *Narrative of James Williams, an American Slave* (Baton Rouge: Louisiana State University Press, 2013).

25. Cameron made a half dozen drafts of workers "to go South" before the final list of 114 people.

26. Paul Cameron to Duncan Cameron, October 25, 1844, CFP.

27. Milton was a trusted Fairntosh courier in the 1830s. See Paul Cameron to Duncan Cameron, October 21, 1834; Rebecca Cameron to Duncan Cameron, January 25, 1836, CFP.

28. Paul Cameron to Duncan Cameron, July 2, 1835, CFP.

29. Paul Cameron to Duncan Cameron, [October 23, 1844], CFP.

30. Paul Cameron to Duncan Cameron, November 5, 1844, CFP.

3. "A Place Perfectly Detested"

1. Paul Cameron to Duncan Cameron, December 2, December 30, 1845, CFP.

2. James H. Ruffin to Thomas Ruffin, February 13, 1834, in J. G. de Roulhac Hamilton, ed., *The Papers of Thomas Ruffin* (Raleigh: North Carolina Historical Commission, 1918–1920), II:111 (hereafter *Ruffin Papers*). Originals of the published *Papers* are found at the Southern Historical Collection (SHC) in the Thomas Ruffin Papers and the Ruffin, Roulhac, and Hamilton Family Papers. Not all of the originals were included in the published *Papers*. Of those included, some letters were

edited or abridged. When I draw on a letter that was omitted or abridged, I cite the manuscript collection at the SHC.

3. Cameron's friend in Mississippi was V. M. Murphey, originally from Hillsborough, who had gone to Macon, Mississippi, to be an overseer. He wrote that "most of the land here is inexhaustible" and that if young Cameron bought there he could readily add "to your fortune. Many planters say an efficient hand can pick from 250 to 300 pounds per day." V. M. Murphey to Paul Cameron, September 14, 1836, CFP.

4. V. M. Murphey to Paul Cameron, September 1, 1839. Murphey had acknowledged in an 1837 letter that though the soil was astoundingly productive, the people were unreliable. Mississippi was "a rascally country to live in; everything commands two prices; a fictitious value is given to every thing by the rise of Cotton and speculation." Murphey to Cameron, January 18, 183[7], CFP. For Paul Cameron's sense of his vacillation between guardedness and gullibility, see Paul Cameron to Duncan Cameron, December 30, 1845, CFP. "God help me," wrote Cameron to his father. "I am sometimes without confidence in my fellow man & then I give it as I would a hungry man bread."

5. Paul Cameron to Duncan Cameron, September 5, 1844, CFP.

6. Memo from Paul Cameron to Duncan Cameron, summarizing the trip of the overseer and his enslaved people from North Carolina to Alabama, November 24, 1844, CFP.

7. Paul Cameron to Duncan Cameron, November 27, 1844, CFP.

8. Paul Cameron to Duncan Cameron, December 2, 1845, CFP.

9. Paul Cameron to Duncan Cameron, January 5, 1845; December 2, 1845. Cameron was made doubly anxious by a last-minute letter from his father—received *after* his agreement to purchase—urging him to rent land rather than buy it. The election of James K. Polk as president in November 1844 guaranteed the annexation of Texas and addition of new lands for slave labor. Duncan Cameron thought the result would be that land prices "in the South & Southwest must decline. . . . I think it would be more prudent to *rent* (if possible) . . . than to purchase it at a disadvantage." The son responded that his father's letter came too late, and furthermore that he would never rent out his workers. Duncan Cameron to Paul Cameron, November 19, 1844, CFP.

10. Paul Cameron to Duncan Cameron, January 5, 1845, CFP.

11. Ibid.; Anne Ruffin Cameron to Paul Cameron, January 9, 1845; Margaret Cameron to Paul Cameron, January 18, 1845, CFP.

12. That Cameron had a collapse in front of his enslaved people is clear from a letter written by James Ruffin, who got word of what transpired. My inference that drink was involved comes from Ruffin's reprimand of Cameron for losing

"control over your mental and bodily powers." Paul Cameron did not give voice to his doubts of January 1845 in letters written that month. It was when he returned to Alabama in mid-November 1845 that he bluntly and repeatedly asserted to his father that the Alabama crop bore out his conviction that he'd been swindled. James Ruffin to Paul Cameron, January 5, 1845; Paul Cameron to Duncan Cameron, November 18, December 2, December 13, 1845, CFP.

13. See James Ruffin to Paul Cameron, January 5, 1845, CFP. Although the overseer, Charles Lewellyn, had been recommended by Alabama neighbor William Beverly, the overseer was on a first-name basis with James Ruffin, who referred to him as "Charlie." The overseer would have witnessed the breakdown, and I speculate that "Charlie" was the person who reported the incident to Ruffin. The apology to Ruffin was made indirectly and obliquely, relayed through a mutual friend. "I was astonished to learn from Mr. Cain that you thought I took offense at something you may have said or done. I was only mortified and grieved," Ruffin wrote to Cameron. Ruffin to Paul Cameron, January 5, 1845, CFP.

14. See James Ruffin to Thomas Ruffin, January 5, 1845, in the Ruffin, Roulhac, and Hamilton Family Papers, SHC.

15. In 1837, Paul Cameron began recording the deaths of workers on his plantation quarters, with the name, age, cause of death, and value of each person who died. The one younger man who died was twenty-four-year-old William. See Paul Cameron's record of deaths after 1837, CFP. The reference to the enfeebled look of the elders can be found in Paul Cameron to Duncan Cameron, November 18, December 2, 1845, CFP. The older man Lewis, ill for a long time, managed to survive.

16. For a recent and provocative account of the distinctive skill required—and escalating speed demanded—for picking cotton in the western lands of the South, see Edward E. Baptist, *The Half Has Never Been Told: Slavery and the Making of American Capitalism* (New York: Basic Books, 2014), 112–117, 138–140.

17. Charles Lewellyn to Paul Cameron, June 1, August 16, September 17, October 8, 1845, CFP.

18. Hank Trent, ed., *Narrative of James Williams, an American Slave* (Baton Rouge: Louisiana State University Press, 2013); Baptist, *Half Has Never Been Told*, 135–136; Damian Alan Pargas, *Slavery and Forced Migration in the Antebellum South* (New York: Cambridge University Press, 2015), 136–148.

19. Paul Cameron to Duncan Cameron, November 18, 1845, CFP.

20. Ibid.

21. Paul Cameron to Duncan Cameron, December 2, 1845, CFP. A subsequent letter refers to the overseer's opinion that Toney burned his foot to stay out of the field. Paul Cameron to Duncan Cameron, December 30, 1845, CFP.

22. Paul Cameron to Duncan Cameron, December 30, 1845, CFP. For the ages of enslaved persons, I rely on the 1850 Alabama slave list. A second list, also with ages given, was made in 1852. On the 1852 list, most persons are listed as several years older—for example, Lewis, whose age was given as sixty in 1850 and as sixty-six in 1852.

23. Paul Cameron to Duncan Cameron, November 18, December 2, December 13, 1845, CFP.

24. Duncan Cameron to Paul Cameron, December 13, 1845, CFP.

25. Paul Cameron to Duncan Cameron, December 30, 1845, CFP.

26. Paul Cameron to Duncan Cameron, November 18, December 2, December 13, December 23, December 30, 1845; Duncan Cameron to Paul Cameron, December 13, 1845, CFP. The excision of "redemption and" was made by Paul Cameron.

27. For naming patterns by the Hargis daughters, see the 1850 Alabama slave list. On none of the Alabama lists in which Paul and Dicey were enumerated together were there any children listed in their household. In the 1900 Census, Dicey Hargis reported having had two children who died. 1900 U.S. Census for Cedarville, Hale, Alabama, Roll 18, page 124, Enumeration District 0056, FHL Microfilm #1240018, accessed through Ancestry.com.

28. Charles Lewellyn to Paul Cameron, August 18, September 10, September 21, October 11, 1846, CFP.

29. Paul Cameron to Duncan Cameron, December 1, 1846, CFP.

30. Paul Cameron to Duncan Cameron, October 21, 1834; Rebecca Cameron to Duncan Cameron, July 25, 1836, CFP.

31. See the overseer's reports of repeated illness that kept Milton in the house and out of the field. Charles Lewellyn to Paul Cameron, August 18, September 10, September 21, November 3, 1846, CFP.

32. Charles Lewellyn to Paul Cameron, January 18, 1846, CFP.

33. Charles Lewellyn to Paul Cameron, January 18, February 9, February 27, 1847, CFP. John M. Chapron was an absentee owner of a plantation and enslaved laborers some miles south of Cameron's place. He sought to use incentives rather than punishment to extract labor from his workers, promising the men new suits and the women new dresses for faithful work. John M. Chapron to James Martin, May 25, 1839, July 22, 1840, April 22, 1841; Chapron to Dr. L. L. Beverly, June 10, 1841, all in John M. Chapron Letterbook, Alabama Department of Archives and History, Montgomery.

34. Tuskegee jailor W. Wade to Charles Lewellyn, February 5, 1847; Allen C. Jones to Paul Cameron, April 8, 1847; Charles Lewellyn to Paul Cameron, March 23, 1847, CFP.

35. Charles Lewellyn to Paul Cameron, May 21, 1845, CFP.

36. Charles Lewellyn to Paul Cameron, June 15, July 31, 1847, CFP.

37. Thomas Bennehan to Paul Cameron, December, 1845; Paul Cameron to Duncan Cameron, December 30, 1845, CFP.

38. Acting as proxy for his son, in 1847 Duncan Cameron sent letters of inquiry to selected planters and cotton brokers about interest in acquiring another western plantation, and received enthusiastic replies from two about large plantations for sale, one in Mississippi and the other in Louisiana.

39. Ogden [New Orleans broker] to Duncan Cameron, December 4, December 28, 1847; Duncan Cameron to Paul Cameron, February 4, 1848, CFP.

40. Jean Bradley Anderson, *Piedmont Plantation: The Bennehan-Cameron Family and Lands in North Carolina* (Durham, NC: Historic Preservation Society of Durham, 1985), 55.

41. Sydney Nathans, *To Free a Family: The Journey of Mary Walker* (Cambridge, MA: Harvard University Press, 2012), 25–28.

42. Charles Lewellyn to Paul Cameron, October 16, October 20, October 31, 1847, CFP.

43. Paul Cameron to Duncan Cameron, December 2, December 30, 1845, CFP.

44. Pargas, *Slavery and Forced Migration*, 148–152.

45. Paul Cameron to Duncan Cameron, July [n.d.] 1848, CFP.

46. Nathans, *To Free a Family*, 27.

47. Historian Walter Johnson explores the reasons behind the spread of the impersonal term *hands* for enslaved workers in the rich cotton-growing region of Mississippi. The particular cotton that grew best there—Petit Gulf cotton—"was adapted to the mechanical capabilities of the human hand. And in the Cotton Kingdom, hands were likewise suited to their labor." Cotton planters began the year by calculating "'to the hand.' By multiplying the number of hands times the number of acres each hand could be expected—would be forced—to tend, they planned their sowing." Walter Johnson, *River of Dark Dreams: Slavery and Empire in the Cotton Kingdom* (Cambridge, MA: Harvard University Press, 2013), 152–154. For enslaved workers in the Delta, the planter's former term—"our black family"—became a relic.

48. Paul Cameron to Duncan Cameron, November 2, 1848, CFP.

4. Held Back

1. Duncan Cameron to Paul Cameron, November 4, 1848, CFP.

2. Paul Cameron to Duncan Cameron, November 6, 1848, CFP.

3. Paul Cameron to Duncan Cameron, November 29, 1848, CFP.

4. Frederick Nash to [Sally Nash], January 2, February 3 [1849], Francis Nash Manuscripts, Box 72.2, North Carolina Department of Archives and History. Duncan Cameron II died on November 16, 1848.

5. Jean Bradley Anderson, *Piedmont Plantation: The Bennehan-Cameron Family and Lands in North Carolina* (Durham, NC: Historic Preservation Society of Durham, 1985), 47, 58, 199 n. 86. For the continued invalidism of Mildred Cameron, see Sydney Nathans, *To Free a Family: The Journey of Mary Walker* (Cambridge, MA: Harvard University Press, 2012), 25–27.

6. Paul Cameron to [William Cain], December 19, 1848; William Cain to Paul Cameron, January 9, January 27, 1849; John Webster to Paul Cameron, June 11, November 18, 1851; Webster to Cameron, June 15, November 29, 1852, CFP.

7. Slave list, with values for each individual, June 4, 1852. Webster enclosed the valuations in his letter from John Webster to Cameron, June 15, 1852, CFP.

8. Colonel Tindall to Paul Cameron, November 3, 1851, CFP.

9. John Webster to Paul Cameron, June 7, June 15, July 24, August 31, September 8, 1852, CFP.

10. Paul Cameron to J. G. Roulhac, March 31 [1854], CFP. In pencil, this letter is misdated as 1855. Joseph G. Roulhac was Cameron's brother-in-law. Cameron wrote that he would set out in a day or two on horseback with a servant to look at the country along the line of the Mobile & Ohio Railroad.

11. Deed of purchase, citation to Tunica, Samuel Tate to Paul Cameron, November 7, 1856, CFP. Cameron paid $27,165 for 1,811 acres, roughly $15 per acre. The indenture was copied by Cameron's fellow planter, A. C. Wright, on July 3, 1857, and referred to on July 14, 1857, CFP. John Webster reported as he traveled west that people repeatedly asked whether he was headed "to the bottom of the Mississippi." John Webster to Paul Cameron, December 6, 1856, CFP. Promoting land in Coahoma County, Mississippi, planter Ben Barbee declared his 1,600 acres as "a making bank." Ben Barbee to Paul Cameron, August 1, 1852, CFP.

12. Webster decided to "leave out Peter and his family." John Webster to Paul Cameron, November 24, 1856, CFP. The final list included Nat and Jake, cited as runaways in John Webster to Paul Cameron, December 27, 1854 (Nat), and December 30, 1855 (Jake), as well as Toney and Juber, who had fled before Webster became overseer. The total included fifteen men, fifteen women, and five children, making thirty-five in all. See the list Property in Tunica, Mississippi, March 23, 1857, made out in Cameron's handwriting.

13. The will of Duncan Cameron, and, before his death, that of Thomas Bennehan, deeded most of their properties directly to Paul Cameron. He was named the guardian for property—land and people—bequeathed to his sisters, Margaret Cameron and Mildred Cameron, and given to his impaired brother, Thomas

Cameron. Soon after Duncan Cameron's death, Margaret Cameron became engaged to George Mordecai, Duncan Cameron's successor as president of the Bank of North Carolina. After a bitter dispute between Paul Cameron and his prospective brother-in-law, George Mordecai and Margaret Cameron signed a prenuptial agreement that kept the property in her hands, rather than becoming the property of her husband, as it otherwise would have. Management of Margaret Cameron Mordecai's land and enslaved people fell to her husband, who in fact sold away a large group of people in 1859. Nathans, *To Free a Family*, 102. For the sale, see George W. Mordecai to Margaret Cameron Mordecai, November 24, 1859, CFP.

14. H. W. Vick to Paul Cameron, January 22, 1849, CFP.

15. A planter who claimed to be a distant relative sought to entice Cameron to buy his plantation in Texas. He asserted that "it is considered small cropping to get less than a bale of 500 lbs per acre." Jno. A. Rogers to Paul Cameron, February 23, 1856, CFP; Jacob Thompson to Paul Cameron, November 4, 1860, CFP.

16. In February 1860, Cameron set out to Mississippi to "devote a month to the purchase of another plantation." Paul Cameron to New Orleans cotton brokers Battle & Noble, February 22, 1860, CFP.

He found none to suit him that spring, but left word that he "wished to purchase a large body of land" in Tunica. William F. Dowd to Paul Cameron, August 10, 1860; Leland Bradley to Cameron, August 10, 1860; cotton broker E. M. Apperson to Cameron, October 5, 1860, CFP.

17. John Webster to Paul Cameron, November 24, 1856, CFP. Samuel Jeter had previously worked for planter John Collins at his place in Prairieville, Alabama, eight miles south of Cameron's land.

18. John Webster to Paul Cameron, December 6, 1856, CFP; Paul Cameron to Thomas Ruffin, December 19, 1856, Thomas Ruffin Papers, SHC.

19. Samuel Tate to Paul Cameron, December 1, 1856; John Webster to Paul Cameron, December 24, 1856, CFP.

20. John Webster to Paul Cameron, December 24, 1856, CFP.

21. Andrew Polk to Paul Cameron, June 8, 1858, CFP.

22. Samuel Tate to Paul Cameron, December 26, 1856, CFP.

23. John Webster to Paul Cameron, December 24, 1856, CFP.

24. James Williamson to Paul Cameron, December 26, 1856, and January 2, 1857; Samuel Tate to Paul Cameron, January 16, 1857, CFP.

25. Paul Cameron to Thomas Ruffin, March 21, 1857, in *Ruffin Papers*, II:549–550. I use and cite not only the *published* edition of the Ruffin Papers but also *original* letters to Ruffin that were not included in the edited volumes, or not included in full. Paul Cameron to Anne Cameron, March 24, 1857; Andrew Polk to Paul Cameron, January 25 [1858], undated correspondence, Box 80, letters P-Q, CFP.

26. Samuel Jeter to Paul Cameron, December 22, 1857; Andrew Polk to Paul Cameron, January 25 [1858], undated postscript [January 1858], undated letters, Box 80, letters P-Q, CFP.

27. Paul Cameron to Thomas Ruffin, February 1, 1858, in *Ruffin Papers*, II:582–583.

28. Paul Cameron to Tartt Stewart & Company (Mobile cotton brokers), March 30, 1852; report of Tartt Stewart to Paul Cameron, June 10, 1854; John Webster to Paul Cameron, December 27, 1854, December 30, 1855, February 24, 1856; CFP. Tartt Stewart to Paul Cameron, February 19, 1857, CFP.

29. John Webster to Paul Cameron, September 28, 1856; Wilson Oberry to Paul Cameron, January 30, 1857, CFP.

30. A[rchibald] C. Wright to Paul Cameron, October 16, November 6, 1858, CFP.

31. Paul Cameron referred to Len as a "hard man" in a January 10, 1860, letter to Lamb. See Lamb's reference and reply, William Lamb to Paul Cameron, January 28, 1860, CFP. For the escalation of coercion and quotas, see Edward E. Baptist, *The Half Has Never Been Told: Slavery and the Making of American Capitalism* (New York: Basic Books, 2014), 115–137.

32. Paul Cameron to [Thomas Ruffin], [January 1859], in Thomas Ruffin Papers, SHC.

33. William Lamb to Paul Cameron, February 20, April 12, May 21, July 29, September 9, October 9, 1859, CFP.

34. William Lamb to Paul Cameron, October 9, 1859, CFP.

35. William Lamb to Paul Cameron, July 11, December 4, December 24, 1859, CFP.

36. William Lamb to Paul Cameron, December 4, 1859; Lamb to Cameron, January 7, February 4, April 14, 1860, CFP.

37. William Lamb to Paul Cameron, September 9, September 16, 1859, CFP.

38. William Lamb to Paul Cameron, September 17, 1860, CFP.

39. William Lamb to Paul Cameron, September 17, September 24, 1860, CFP.

40. William Lamb to Paul Cameron, October 28, November 1, November 4, 1860, CFP.

5. Reversals

1. William Dowd to Paul Cameron, August 1, 1860; Leland Bradley to Cameron, August 10, 1860; E. M. Apperson to Cameron, October 5, 1860, CFP. Born in North Carolina in 1810, Jacob Thompson went to private school in Orange County and graduated from the University of North Carolina in 1831. It is likely that he and Cameron (born in 1808) knew each other before Thompson moved to Pontotoc, Mississippi, in 1835.

2. Battle & Noble [New Orleans cotton brokers] to Paul Cameron, October 9, 1860, CFP.

3. Jacob Thompson to Paul Cameron, November 4, 1860, CFP.

4. William Lamb to Paul Cameron, December 1, December 15, 1860; January 20, 1861, CFP.

5. Memorandum from Paul Cameron to Anne Ruffin Cameron, February 13, 1861, CFP. Having received the telegram, Cameron made arrangements to leave for Tunica, and gave information and instructions to his wife prior to departure. The telegram and report of its contents came in William K. Ruffin to Thomas Ruffin, February 18, 1861, Ruffin, Roulhac, and Hamilton Family Papers, SHC, also published in *Ruffin Papers*, III:127.

6. I have reconstructed the episode, and a view of overseer errors that led up to it, from two letters written by neighboring planter Archibald C. Wright to Cameron, March 18, 1861 and January [11], 1862, CFP.

7. Cameron had befriended A. C. Wright's son when the youth had been a school classmate of Cameron's son, and subsequently a student at the University of North Carolina at Chapel Hill.

8. A. C. Wright to Paul Cameron, March 18, 1861, CFP.

9. The indictment, charges, and outcomes of the separate cases were detailed in the Minute Book of the Circuit Court of Tunica County, 1857–1873, which I located in the attic of the Tunica County Courthouse. The indictment, recorded in *State of Mississippi v. Zack & Ned, Slaves*, Case No. 62, came on April 2, 1861. The details of the two men's cases are in the Minute Book, 161, 167, 170. James Alcorn spirited away "the one acquitted lest if left, the mob might hang him." A. C. Wright to Paul Cameron, April 11, 1862, CFP.

10. William Lamb to Paul Cameron, April 18, 1861, CFP. Byrd Hill was the sometime partner of Nathan Bedford Forrest in his Memphis slave-trading business. Steven Deyle, *Carry Me Back: The Domestic Slave Trade in American Life* (New York: Oxford University Press, 2005), 260.

11. The infant Paul was enumerated with his parents, Squire and Suse, on the Tunica plantation list of March 1, 1861.

12. See Chapter 10, "A Game Rooster."

13. A. C. Wright to Paul Cameron, April 21, 1861, CFP.

14. A. C. Wright to Paul Cameron, August 11, 1862, CFP.

15. On August 2, 1862, Union troops skirmished with Confederate soldiers at Austin, Mississippi, about ten miles from Cameron's Tunica County plantation. See Bud Hannings, ed., *Every Day of the Civil War: A Chronological Encyclopedia* (Jefferson, NC: McFarland, 2010), 210. For Union raids and skirmishes in nearby Delta counties during the summer of 1862, see Hannings, 204–214.

16. A. C. Wright to Paul Cameron, August 11, 1862, CFP.

17. A. C. Wright to Paul Cameron, September 5, October 26, 1862, CFP.

18. In August 1863, Cameron reported a false alarm that Union troops might be threatening to invade the Alabama Black Belt, in which case he might have to "run 180 people" from Alabama to North Carolina. Paul Cameron to George Mordecai, August 11, 1863, George W. Mordecai Papers, SHC.

19. Wilson Oberry to Paul Cameron, January 2, 1861, CFP. Wilson Oberry was a phonetic speller; in most instances, but not all, I have corrected his spelling.

20. Wilson Oberry to Paul Cameron, April 13, May 23, July 27, 1862, CFP.

21. Wilson Oberry to Paul Cameron, March 29, October 2, 1863, CFP.

22. Fannie J. Erwin to brother, March 19, 1862, Cadwallader Jones Papers, SHC.

23. Wilson Oberry to Paul Cameron, July 27, 1862, March 22, 1863, CFP.

24. Wilson Oberry to Paul Cameron, December 8, 1862, CFP.

25. Paul Cameron to George Mordecai, September 18, 1863, George W. Mordecai Papers, SHC.

26. Ibid.

27. Ibid.

28. The forces of William Tecumseh Sherman had made a raid near Meridian, Mississippi, and it seemed likely they would move east into Alabama. Cameron got a later report from his cotton factor in New Orleans that Sherman was compelled to move back toward Vicksburg. Battle & Noble to Paul Cameron, March 5, 1864, CFP. Sherman and his troops occupied Meridian on February 16. Meridian was a major center of Confederate railroad stock. Union troops destroyed 120 miles of rails, sixty bridges, and twenty locomotives. Sherman left Meridian and moved back toward Vicksburg on February 20. Hannings, ed., *Every Day of the Civil War*, 396–399.

29. Paul Cameron to General S. F. Patterson, February 18, 1864; S. F. Patterson to Mrs. Paul Cameron, February 24, 1864, CFP.

30. Paul Cameron to George Mordecai, March 2, 1864; George Collins to George Mordecai, March 11, 1864, in George W. Mordecai Papers, SHC.

31. Paul Cameron to [General S. F. Patterson], August 16, 1864, Jones and Patterson Family Papers, SHC; Richard C. White Jr., *A. Lincoln, a Biography* (New York: Random House, 2009), 631–638. In a private memorandum of August 24, 1864, Lincoln wrote: "'This morning, as for some days past, it seems exceedingly probable that this administration will not be re-elected.'" If defeated, Lincoln recognized, he would lose to an opponent who would have won election "on such ground that he cannot possibly save" the Union. White, *A. Lincoln*, 638–639.

32. White, *A. Lincoln*, 640, 651–652; Paul Cameron to George Mordecai, September 27, 1864, CFP.

33. Paul Cameron to Duncan Cameron III, November 20, 1864, CFP.

34. Paul Cameron to Thomas Ruffin, March 21, 1865, in *Ruffin Papers*, III:448.

35. Paul Cameron to Thomas Ruffin, August 11, 1865, in *Ruffin Papers*, III:464.

6. Exile's Return

1. Paul Cameron to George Mordecai, September 18, 1863, George W. Mordecai Papers, SHC. Cameron's brother-in-law had asked whether Cameron could absorb some of his workers. Cameron replied that he couldn't, "having the care of at least 800 slaves."

2. Paul Cameron to Thomas Ruffin, September 28, 1860, in Ruffin, Roulhac, and Hamilton Family Papers, SHC, quoted in Jean Bradley Anderson, *Piedmont Plantation: The Bennehan-Cameron Family and Lands in North Carolina* (Durham, NC: Historic Preservation Society of Durham, 1985), 57–58. Jean Anderson's classic book details the dimensions and uses of what is today called the "Great Barn," a structure still standing and part of the Stagville Center for Historic Preservation, a historic site owned and staffed by the state of North Carolina.

3. Anderson, *Piedmont Plantation*, 57. Thanks to the state and to generations of Stagville site managers, supporters, and volunteers, the Horton Grove slave houses still stand, and are preserved, maintained, and interpreted as integral parts of Stagville.

4. Benson J. Lossing, *Pictorial Field-Book of the Revolution*, quoted in Anderson, *Piedmont Plantation*, 63.

5. Anderson, *Piedmont Plantation*, 60–61, 115.

6. John Webster to Paul Cameron, June 24, 1853, and February [n.d.] 1856, CFP; Anderson, *Piedmont Plantation*, 115.

7. Disruptive behavior among freed people on the plantation in December 1865 led Paul Cameron to request that military authorities place a protective guard at Fairntosh. Cameron anticipated that the army commander might question whether the conduct of his former slaves was justified—whether it was retaliation for poor treatment. Consequently, along with his request, Cameron presented a detailed portrait of himself as a fair and generous master. Cameron's undated December 1865 letter is found in the Cameron Papers, and is quoted in Anderson, *Piedmont Plantation*, 96.

8. Anderson, *Piedmont Plantation*, 111.

9. For Sherman's "hard war" strategy, the March to the Sea, and the burning of Columbia and other South Carolina towns, see the excellent synthesis of recent Sherman scholarship in the biography by Robert L. O'Connell, *Fierce Patriot: The Tangled Lives of William Tecumseh Sherman* (New York: Random House,

2014). In fact, when Sherman moved into North Carolina, he instructed his marchers to "deal as moderately and fairly by the North Carolinians as possible," and to pull back from the havoc and punishment inflicted on South Carolina, the state that initiated secession and war. See O'Connell, *Fierce Patriot*, 176. For Paul Cameron's fears and insomnia, see Paul Cameron to Thomas Ruffin, March 21, [1865], in *Ruffin Papers*, III:448.

10. Rebecca Cameron Anderson to Mrs. George Mordecai, April [15?], 1865, CFP; 1930s WPA interview with Cyrus Hart, a former Cameron enslaved worker, quoted in Anderson, *Piedmont Plantation*, 117.

11. Paul Cameron to Thomas Ruffin, May 11, 1865, in *Ruffin Papers*, III:451.

12. George Mordecai to Paul Cameron, August 30, 1865, CFP.

13. Willie Lee Rose, "Masters without Slaves," reprinted in Willie Lee Rose, *Slavery and Freedom*, ed. William W. Freehling (New York: Oxford University Press, 1982). Confirming and expanding on Rose's insight is James Roark, *Masters without Slaves: Southern Planters in the Civil War and Reconstruction* (New York: Norton, 1977).

14. Paul Cameron to Thomas Ruffin, May 11, 1865, in *Ruffin Papers*, III:451–452; Cameron to Thomas Ruffin, May 27, 1865, Thomas Ruffin Papers, SHC.

15. Samuel Piper to Paul Cameron, n.d. [July 5, 1865, and summer 1865], CFP. Overseer Samuel Piper sent a series of reports to Cameron in 1865 and 1866, all undated. All of Samuel Piper's undated reports are found in Cameron Papers, in the folder designated "Undated Files N-Q." From the context of Piper's letters, and from the content of dated Cameron letters elsewhere in the collection, I have made a best guess about the season or month of each report, and placed my conjecture in brackets. For the report of mutiny against the overseer and refusal to send milk or butter to Hillsborough, see Paul Cameron's "Appeal for Military Police to Come to Fairntosh" [n.d., May 1865], CFP. Cameron's appeal was composed in the handwriting of either Anne Ruffin Cameron or daughter Anne Cameron Collins. Cameron stated that freed people "in several instances have threatened the life of the overseer without the slightest provocation."

16. Paul Cameron to sisters Mildred Cameron and Margaret Cameron Mordecai, May 27, 1865, CFP.

17. Paul Cameron reported his wife's outrage to Thomas Ruffin, her father. Paul Cameron to Thomas Ruffin, November 20, 1865, Thomas Ruffin Papers, SHC.

18. Paul Cameron to Duncan Cameron, November 2, 1848, CFP.

19. See Chapter 5. Anderson asserts that Cameron was still shopping for additional Mississippi land in early 1861. Anderson, *Piedmont Plantation*, 115, 208 n. 2.

20. "My old slaves seem resolved to hold on to *me* or to my *land*." Paul Cameron to Thomas Ruffin, August 11, 1865, in *Ruffin Papers*, III:464.

21. Copy of work contract with Cameron freedmen, August 6, 1865, CFP; Samuel Piper to Paul Cameron, n.d. [August 1865], CFP. The contract approved by the Freedmen's Bureau agent differed significantly from the one devised in April 1865 by Cameron. Enumerated "violations" of the contract were fewer; they focused on work rather than deportment, and penalized violators for "lost time" rather than expelling them and their families with a total forfeit of compensation. See the proposed "Contract for Labor" [April 1865], in *Ruffin Papers*, III:449.

22. Samuel Piper to Paul Cameron, n.d. [September 1865], CFP. There was no reliance on any contract, Cameron reported; "nothing but want will bring them to their senses." Paul Cameron to Thomas Ruffin, October 4, 1865, in *Ruffin Papers*, IV:35.

23. Three letters from Samuel Piper describe this episode. See letters from Samuel Piper to Paul Cameron, n.d. [November 1865], CFP. Cameron reported the strike and its suppression by soldiers to his brother-in-law, who wrote back that he was "glad the Yankee brought the Stagville men to terms." Paul Cameron to Thomas Ruffin, November 20, 1865, in *Ruffin Papers*, IV:40; George Mordecai to Paul Cameron, November 21, 1865, CFP.

24. Undated notes of Samuel Piper to Paul Cameron, n.d. [summer 1865; September 1865; December 1865], CFP. Paul Cameron to Thomas Ruffin, October 4, 1865, in *Ruffin Papers*, IV:35.

25. Samuel Piper to Paul Cameron, n.d. [December 1865], CFP.

26. Paul Cameron to Thomas Ruffin, November 27, 1865, in *Ruffin Papers*, IV:42.

27. Samuel Piper to Paul Cameron, n.d. [December 1865], CFP.

28. If Cameron stuck with black workers, Piper urged, the owner should "rid yourself of a large lot of troublesome ones as there can be no living in a neighborhood with such a set of people." Samuel Piper to Paul Cameron, n.d. [November 1865], CFP. Later in November, George Collins reported that he'd advised Cameron's Alabama overseer to make a contract in Alabama "in accordance with your action in North Carolina": to wit, to "select such as deserve support from former good conduct," and discharge the rest that are objectionable. George Collins to Paul Cameron, November 22, 1865, CFP.

29. Paul Cameron to Archibald C. Wright, February 12, 1866, CFP.

30. Contract for Fairntosh and Eno quarters, November 1865, in CFP.

31. Paul Cameron to George Mordecai, March 10, 1865, CFP. Cameron urged Mordecai to confide nothing to his credulous brother Thomas Cameron, as he "gives his confidence without reserve to the slaves that he is partial to."

32. Paul Cameron to Duncan Cameron III, April 27, 1865; Thomas Ruffin to Paul Cameron, November 16, November 24, 1865; George Mordecai to Paul Cameron, November 21, 1865; Paul Cameron to Thomas Ruffin, November 27, 1865, CFP.

33. Herbert Gutman, *The Black Family in Slavery and Freedom, 1750–1925* (New York: Pantheon Books, 1976), 415, 619.

34. The entry for "Paul Cameron" and his wife, Dicey, can be found in the Negro Cohabitation Certificates for Orange County, North Carolina. The originals are on file at the North Carolina Department of Archives and History, Raleigh. See page 202 and the insert between pages 240 and 241. An examination of the original entry reveals that the name "Paul Cameron" was *written over* the original entry, "Paul Hargis." In the early 1970s, with the aid of North Carolina state archivist C. F. W. Coker, Herbert Gutman located and brilliantly used the North Carolina Cohabitation Certificates to confirm antebellum marriages among once-enslaved couples. Gutman, *Black Family*, 619 n. 34.

35. For the postwar turn to patronage and the exchange of personal loyalty for protection and benefits, see Gregory P. Downs, *Declarations of Dependence: The Long Reconstruction of Popular Politics in the South, 1861–1908* (Chapel Hill: University of North Carolina Press, 2011), 2–7, 77.

36. From his overseer and a neighbor, Cameron obtained affidavits about the alleged thefts, illicit sale of stolen goods, and resulting "exhibitions of the Negroes in dress." Affidavits of Phillip Southerland and William Vestal, September 29, 1866, CFP. In his own handwriting, Cameron made copies of the affidavits.

37. Paul Cameron to George Mordecai, July 24, September 29, October 28, 1866, George W. Mordecai Papers, SHC; Paul Cameron to George Collins, October 4, 1866, CFP.

38. Anderson, *Piedmont Plantation*, 121–122; Dorothy Spruill Redford, *Somerset Homecoming: Recovering a Lost Heritage* (New York: Doubleday, 1988), 109, 121. It took "some four propositions" from Cameron to get his reluctant son-in-law to take over plantation management in Mississippi. Paul Cameron to Thomas Ruffin, October 4, 1865, Ruffin, Roulhac, and Hamilton Family Papers, SHC.

39. George Collins to Paul Cameron, August 30, 1866, CFP.

40. Paul Cameron to George Collins, October 4, 1866, CFP.

41. Collins's request to the Freedmen's Bureau was rejected without comment on November 20, 1866. A comparable request to send freed people from North Carolina to Mississippi was made by a white resident of Concord, North Carolina, to the North Carolina commissioner of the Freedmen's Bureau, General O. O. Howard. Victor Barringer reported that during the war, his "safe" Piedmont county had "become the resort of a large number of refugees with their negroes," most brought from war-threatened plantations in Mississippi. Now, Victor Barringer stated, he was "applied to almost every day by some of the Freedmen from Miss to know if there be any means in the world for them to get Government transportation back to Miss." The "negroes all desire to return to their old homes, &,

in Miss., they do better & get more for their labor than they can possibly do here, where we do not raise much cotton." Victor Barringer to Maj. General O. O. Howard, August 16, 1866, published in Rene Hayden et al., eds., *Freedom: A Documentary History of Emancipation, 1861–1867*, series 3, volume 2, *Land and Labor, 1866–1867* (Chapel Hill: University of North Carolina Press, 2013), 827–829. No reply was found to Barringer's request.

42. Paul Cameron to George Mordecai, November 7, November 10, 1866, George W. Mordecai Papers, SHC.

43. *Alabama Beacon*, March 17, 1870.

44. The sale to four Edgecombe planters was noted in George Mordecai to Margaret Cameron Mordecai, November 24, 1859, CFP, and confirmed in a statement of debts by one of the purchasers. See the Statement of Debts by Dr. J. W. Powell, March 9, 1868, CFP. The main purchaser was R. R. Bridgers. Paul Cameron to George Mordecai, May 29, 1865, George W. Mordecai Papers, SHC. Cameron reported to his brother-in-law that Bridgers "is very full of a *large attempt* at planting with negroes under the new order of things."

45. George Collins to Paul Cameron, December 16, 1866, January 7, 14, 1867, CFP. In December 1865, George Collins, his wife, and a first contingent of North Carolina freed people traveled to Mississippi by train. The trip of five nights and four days took them from Raleigh to Lynchburg, Virginia, then through the length of Tennessee, with stops at Knoxville and Chattanooga, and finally to Memphis. I surmise that George Collins and his December 1866 group of Carolina freed people followed the same route, and conjecture that Paul and Dicey Hargis exited the train at Chattanooga. For the report on the route of the December 1865 trip, see Anne Collins to Anne Ruffin Cameron, December 26, 1865, CFP.

7. "Against All Comers"

1. Wilson Oberry to Paul Cameron, January 7 and January 20, 1867, CFP.

2. Interview with Louie Rainey, Cassimore, Alabama, July 29, 1979. Collins wrote that he had had tried to pick up a blacksmith in Atlanta on the way out in December 1866. Collins to Cameron, December 23, 1866, CFP.

3. Cameron's original draft of the labor contract, intended to start on May 1, 1865, contained stringent requirements and penalties. "All shall promise to be perfectly respectful in language and deportment . . . and the persons so offending shall be required to leave" without recompense. Any refusal "to perform any manner of work, shall be regarded as a violation of contract, and the party shall be required to leave with his family, without claim for compensation." Labor was to be ten hours a day "the year round—on each and every day—Sunday excepted."

See the "Contract for Labor" proposed by Paul Cameron to Negroes on his plantation, April 1865, published in *Ruffin Papers*, III:449–450.

4. Wilson Oberry to Paul Cameron, July 1, 1865, CFP.

5. Henry Crydenwise to his parents, Mr. and Mrs. Oliver Crydenwise, August 22, September 4, 1864, March 22, April 10, June 25, 1865, all in Henry M. Crydenwise Letters, 1861–1866, Stuart A. Rose Manuscript, Archives, and Rare Book Library, Emory University.

6. *Alabama Beacon*, June 23, 1865.

7. Interview with Louie Rainey, July 3, 1986. Rainey said that his grandmother told him that "Cryden White" waved "his hand up on that platform just like somebody up there preaching, and [told] them what they couldn't do—and what they could do. They was free. 'You're free, everybody.' [He] said, *'You're free, go where you want, do whatever you want to do.'* Wasn't much they could do, 'cause they didn't have a thing. They just threw up their hands and screamed and some of them fell out—just so glad."

8. Henry Crydenwise to Mr. and Mrs. Oliver Crydenwise, June 25, 1865, Crydenwise Letters, Emory. Emphasis in the original.

9. The competing views of what freedom meant—and of what labor contracts would mean—put freedmen, planters, and Freedmen's Bureau agents at odds from the first, and intensified in 1866. Freedmen's Bureau head Oliver O. Howard initially directed that his agents act to "bring together the southern planters and workers for the benefit of both." William McFeely, *Yankee Stepfather: General O. O. Howard and the Freedmen* (New Haven, CT: Yale University Press, 1968), 148–151. Bureau agents such as Crydenwise were to "'stand between the two classes' and make both aware of common interests they shared, if only they would recognize it." Conflict arose and persisted, in the view of historian Eric Foner, "not from misunderstanding, but from the irreconcilable interests of former masters and former slaves as each sought to define the meaning of emancipation." Caught in the middle, Bureau agents sought to get freedmen back to work on plantations; at the same time they strove to prohibit punishment and promote black advancement. The dilemma worsened a year later when agents were obliged to threaten arrest of those who refused to sign contracts or left plantations, and simultaneously to protect the freedmen's right to bargain freely. Eric Foner, *Reconstruction: America's Unfinished Revolution, 1864–1877* (New York: Harper & Row, 1988), 143–144, 156, 169–170.

10. Wilson Oberry to Paul Cameron, November 7, 1865, January 7, 1867, CFP.

11. *Alabama Beacon*, September 15, 1866.

12. Allen C. Jones to Cadwallader Jones Jr., July 29, 1866, Jones-Roulhac Papers, SHC.

13. Wilson Oberry to Paul Cameron, January 7 and January 20, 1867, CFP.

14. George Collins to Paul Cameron, January 14, 1867, CFP; Mary Ellen Curtin, *Black Prisoners and Their World: Alabama, 1865–1900* (Charlottesville: University of Virginia Press, 2000), 26.

15. Wilson Oberry to Paul Cameron, June 19, 1867, CFP.

16. Wilson Oberry to Paul Cameron, July 27, 1867, CFP.

17. For the enslaved foreman's role on the antebellum cotton plantation, see Walter Johnson, *River of Dark Dreams: Slavery and Empire in the Cotton Kingdom* (Cambridge, MA: Harvard University Press, 2013), 166. Johnson quotes once-enslaved Charles Ball, who reported in his narrative of enslavement that the "overseer had nothing to do but to keep" the foreman "hard at work, and he was certain that the others must work equally hard."

18. Wilson Oberry to Paul Cameron, July 27, 1867, CFP.

19. Michael W. Fitzgerald, "Extralegal Violence and the Planter Class: The Ku Klux Klan in the Alabama Black Belt during Reconstruction," in Christopher Waldrep and Donald G. Nieman, eds., *Local Matters: Race, Crime, and Justice in the Nineteenth-Century South* (Athens: University of Georgia Press, 2001), 157–158.

20. Wilson Oberry to Paul Cameron, January 20, April 12, May 1, 1867, CFP.

21. Freedmen's Bureau agent S. G. Spann to C. W. Pierce, April 12, 1867, Bureau of Refugees, Freedmen, and Abandoned Lands (hereafter BRFAL), Alabama, Letters Received, Book 80, Vol. 27, National Archives.

22. *Alabama Beacon*, August 31, 1867.

23. Wilson Oberry to Paul Cameron, May 1, 1867, CFP.

24. Wilson Oberry to Paul Cameron, April 12, 1867, CFP.

25. Wilson Oberry to Paul Cameron, July 27, 1867, CFP.

26. Wilson Oberry to Paul Cameron, August 11, 1867, CFP.

27. *Alabama Beacon*, May 25, 1867. For the pledge of moderation by the two black leaders, see James Green and Alex Webb to C. W. Pierce, May 15, 1867, BRFAL, Alabama, Demopolis, Book 80, Vol. 1, page 27, National Archives.

28. Peter Kolchin, *First Freedom: The Response of Alabama's Blacks to Emancipation and Reconstruction* (Westport, CT: Greenwood Press, 1972), 162. Michael W. Fitzgerald, *The Union League Movement in the Deep South: Politics and Agricultural Change during Reconstruction* (Baton Rouge: Louisiana State University Press, 1989), 142–143. The *Alabama Beacon* editor labeled James Green's response to Alex Webb's murder as "incendiary." *Alabama Beacon*, June 22, 1867.

29. Fitzgerald, *Union League*, 68. Charles Hays to C. W. Pierce, September 18, 1867; Henry Claus to C. W. Pierce, September 20, 1867, BRFAL, Alabama, Letters Received, Book 80, Volume 27, National Archives.

30. Wilson Oberry to Paul Cameron, August 11, 1867, CFP.

31. For Brister Reese's place and date of birth, see his entry in the 1870 Census for Cedarville, Hale County, Alabama, Roll M593_18, page 1608, Image 328, accessed via Ancestry.com. Reese became a landowner in 1870. See the deed from V. Gayle Snedecor to Brister Reese et al., October 22, 1870, in Record of Deeds, Book C, Page 143, Probate Office, Hale County, Greensboro, Alabama. In 1872, white Republican R. L. Bennett was elected to the Alabama House of Representatives as a legislator from Hale County. When Bennett unexpectedly died in Montgomery in December 1872, a special election was held to replace him. Brister Reese won that election on January 21, 1873. *Alabama Beacon*, January 23, 1873. *Beacon* editor John G. Harvey disdained all black officeholders, and contemptuously declared Reese unfit for the position. It was "humiliating" that "the intelligent of Hale should be represented" by "negroes who are as unfit to make laws as an elephant to teach music." *Alabama Beacon*, March 1, 1873.

32. Wilson Oberry to Paul Cameron, September 2, 1867, CFP.

33. A combination of circumstances fed the crop disaster, which would recur over the next three years. The winter labor holdout—to make the best bargain for the year—delayed the start of plowing for the crop. The sandy and red clay soils prevalent on the Cameron plantation produced cotton plants that grew slowly. The slow-growing plants proved most exposed to the army worm when it came. Summer drought further arrested the plants' growth and increased the crop's vulnerability to the worm.

34. Wilson Oberry to Paul Cameron, September 27, 1867, CFP.

35. Wilson Oberry to Paul Cameron, October 22, 1867, CFP.

36. Wilson Oberry to Paul Cameron, September 27, 1867, CFP.

37. Wilson Oberry to Paul Cameron, October 22, 1867, CFP.

38. Wilson Oberry to Paul Cameron, October 20 and October 22, 1867, CFP.

39. Paul Cameron to [Anne Ruffin Cameron], December 8 and December 13, 1867; contract between Paul Cameron and Wilson Oberry, December 15, 1867; Cameron to George Collins, December 22, 1867, CFP.

40. Paul Cameron to wife, September 20, 1873, CFP.

41. Wilson Oberry to Paul Cameron, January 30, 1868, CFP.

42. Wilson Oberry to Paul Cameron, July 1, 1867; Circuit Court Records, Hale County, Alabama, October 6, 1867; *Alabama Beacon*, April 4, 1868.

43. Wilson Oberry to Paul Cameron, January 30, April 6, 1868, CFP.

44. Wilson Oberry to Paul Cameron, April 6, May 10, June 17, 1868, CFP.

45. Wilson Oberry to Paul Cameron, June 17, 1868.

46. Wilson Oberry to Paul Cameron, August 13, 1868, CFP.

47. *Alabama Beacon*, October 29, 1870, reported that whites who left for California in 1868 were returning in 1870.

48. John Parrish to Henry Watson, September 30, 1868, Henry Watson Papers, David M. Rubenstein Rare Book and Manuscript Library, Duke University; *Alabama Beacon*, September 12, 1868.

49. S. Hillyer to C. W. Pierce, January 5, 1868, BRFAL, Alabama, National Archives; Wilson Oberry to Paul Cameron, November 26, 1868, CFP.

50. Allen C. Jones to Paul Cameron, January 23, 1869, CFP.

51. Wilson Oberry to Paul Cameron, January 16, 1869, CFP.

52. Wilson Oberry to Paul Cameron, January 16, 1869, enclosure, CFP.

53. Emphasis added.

54. Wilson Oberry to Paul Cameron, July 15, 1870, CFP.

55. George Collins to Paul Cameron, November 22, 1865, CFP.

56. Wilson Oberry to Paul Cameron, January 16, March [15], June 11, 1869, CFP.

57. Wilson Oberry to Paul Cameron, March [15], 1869, CFP.

58. George Collins to Paul Cameron, December 7, 1869, February 6, 1870, CFP.

59. George Collins to Paul Cameron, December 7, 1869, February 6, 1870; Duncan Cameron III to Paul Cameron, January 9, 1870, all in CFP.

60. George Collins to Paul Cameron, December 7, 1869, CFP.

61. Wilson Oberry to Paul Cameron, July 15, 1870, CFP.

8. "If They Can Get the Land"

1. Paul Cameron to George P. Collins, December 22, 1867, Anne Cameron Collins Papers, SHC.

2. Allen C. Jones to Paul Cameron, December 6, December 11, 1869, CFP.

3. George P. Collins to Paul Cameron, December 7, 1869, CFP.

4. Wilson Oberry to Paul Cameron, July 15, 1870, CFP.

5. Ibid.

6. Ibid.

7. Duncan Cameron III to Paul Cameron, January 9, 1870; George Collins to Paul Cameron, February 6, 1870, CFP.

8. John Parrish to Henry Watson, September 17, 1870, January 1, 1871, Watson Papers, Duke University.

9. Wilson Oberry to Paul Cameron, January 16, 1869, enclosure, CFP.

10. *Alabama Beacon*, October 10, 1868, April 24, 1869.

11. *Alabama Beacon*, June 26, July 17, 1869.

12. Allen C. Jones to Paul Cameron, June 27, 1870, CFP.

13. *Alabama Beacon*, September 4, 1870, April 20, 1872.

14. James Webb to Zemma Webb, August 14, 1870, James Webb Papers, Alabama Department of Archives and History; Allen C. Jones to Henry Watson,

September 4, 1870, Watson Papers, Duke University. *Alabama Beacon*, October 12, 1872.

15. *Alabama Beacon*, February 10, 1872. Forrest made this appeal in Jackson, Mississippi, and the *Beacon* reported it. He brought the same appeal to Greensboro that November. *Alabama Beacon*, November 16, 1872.

16. Allen C. Jones to Henry Watson, September 4, 1870, Watson Papers, Duke University; *Alabama Beacon*, October 4, 1873.

17. The exception was Kansas, the destination of a notable black exodus from the South during the 1870s. See Nell Irvin Painter, *Exodusters: Black Migration to Kansas after Reconstruction* (New York: Alfred A. Knopf, 1976).

18. Loren Schweninger, *James T. Rapier and Reconstruction* (Chicago: University of Chicago Press, 1978), 84–90.

19. Eric Foner, *Nothing but Freedom: Emancipation and Its Legacy* (Baton Rouge: Louisiana State University Press, 1983).

20. Interview with James Lyles, August 9, 1979.

21. Paul Cameron, memorandum summarizing Alabama land sales, February 15, 1875, CFP.

22. Wilson Oberry to Paul Cameron, May 15, 1872, CFP.

23. Ibid.

24. Jean Bradley Anderson, *Piedmont Plantation: The Bennehan-Cameron Family and Lands in North Carolina* (Durham, NC: Historic Preservation Society of Durham, 1985), 127; Paul Cameron to James Hunter Horner, August 9, 1872, CFP.

25. Paul Cameron to [Bennehan Cameron], January 20, 1873, CFP.

26. Paul Cameron to Anne Cameron Collins, May 20, 1867, Anne Cameron Collins Papers, SHC.

27. In 1868, Thomas Roulhac ventured to San Francisco and sought to practice law there. Thomas Roulhac to Thomas Ruffin, September 18, 1868, in *Ruffin Papers*, IV:209. In 1870, a Hale County emigrant to California reported that "it is anything but Paradise, and that he does not see what people want to go there for." James Webb to Zemma Webb, September 4, 1870, James Webb Papers, Alabama Department of Archives and History.

28. Henry Watson notes on a visit to Greensboro, November 28, 1870, Henry Watson Papers, Duke University.

29. Paul C. Cameron and Anne Cameron, power of attorney conveyed to Thomas R. Roulhac, November 8, 1872, Record of Deeds, Book G, page 196, Probate Office, Hale County Courthouse, Greensboro, Alabama.

30. Paul Cameron to Bennehan Cameron, January 20, 1873, CFP.

31. Wilson Oberry to Paul Cameron, January 16, 1869; Allen C. Jones to Cameron, October 6, 1869, CFP.

32. John Parrish to Henry Watson, July 23, 1873, Watson Papers, Duke University; Sven Beckert, *Empire of Cotton: A Global History* (Cambridge, MA: Harvard University Press, 2015), 263–266, 286–287, 289–293.

33. Thomas Roulhac to Paul Cameron, October 18, 1873, CFP.

34. Duncan Cameron III to Pauline Cameron, June 6, 1874, CFP.

35. Paul Cameron to George Collins, December 22, 1867, CFP.

36. George Collins to Paul Cameron, November 19, 1872, CFP; Archibald Wright to Paul Cameron, July 13, December 29, 1873, CFP. George Collins to Paul Cameron, December 1, 1873, CFP.

37. Roulhac's welcome and incorporation by Greensboro's elite is detailed in the journal of one of the region's leading planters. See Glenn M. Linden and Virginia Linden, eds., *Disunion, War, Defeat, and Recovery in Alabama: The Journal of Augustus Benners, 1850–1885* (Macon, GA: Mercer University Press, 2007), 21, 174–175, 209, 230. My thanks to Greensboro attorney and local historian Nicholas H. Cobbs Jr. for making the original Benners diary available to editors Linden and for providing a copy of their book to me.

38. C. W. Pierce, Superintendent, District of Demopolis, to O. D. Kinsman, Superintendent, Montgomery, February 13, 1867, BFRAL, Alabama, in the unregistered letters, Freedmen's History Papers Archives, College Park, Maryland. Pierce gave a list of murders, assaults, and outrages from January 1866 through February 1867. In May 1866, in Marengo County, assailants attempted to drive away several families of freedmen who had rented a plantation and were working it themselves.

39. William Miller to R. A. Wilson, Freedmen's Bureau sub-agent, September 22, 1868, enclosed in letter from Wilson to Governor W. H. Smith, September 26, 1868; Maggie Davis to W. H. Smith, April 1, 1870; Samuel Brown to W. H. Smith, April 5, 1870; A. A. Smith to W. H. Smith, April 7, 1870; all W. H. Smith Papers, Alabama Archives and History. Allen W. Trelease, *White Terror: The Ku Klux Klan Conspiracy and Southern Reconstruction* (New York: Harper & Row, 1971), 83–84, 252–253, 302–303.

40. Trelease, *White Terror*, 83–94, 304–305, 308; Michael W. Fitzgerald, *The Union League Movement in the Deep South: Politics and Agricultural Change during Reconstruction* (Baton Rouge: Louisiana State University Press, 1989), 83, 143, 213, 221, 223–224.

41. *Alabama Beacon*, June 11, 1870, August 15, 1873.

42. *Alabama Beacon*, September 28, 1872.

43. *Alabama Beacon*, March 7, 1874.

44. Paul Cameron wrote a memorandum summarizing the sales reported "in Mr. Roulhac's letter"; the memo was dated February 15, 1875, CFP. Roulhac

reported selling most of the Alabama plantation's 1,600 acres. One small parcel sold for $20 per acre; almost all the rest of the land brought from $9 to $12 per acre.

45. Paul Cameron memo on the sale of Alabama land, February 15, 1875, CFP. Thomas Roulhac to Paul Cameron, February 15, June 22, 1875, CFP.

46. Paul Cameron and Anne Cameron to Paul and James Hargess, Deed Book K, page 480, Probate Office, Hale County. Thomas Roulhac was the Camerons' agent for all the sales. In this case and others, there was a gap between the date of purchase and the date the deed was officially recorded. Roulhac's summary of purchases stated that all agreements to buy Cameron's land came by February 1875. The Hargis brothers' deed was recorded in 1884. Paul and Jim Hargess made their initial purchase of twenty acres in 1872. See Deed Book G, page 196. The second purchase of 80 acres for $640 was made on March 27, 1876. See Deed Book X, pages 614–615. The family name began its migration—from Hargis to Hargess and ultimately to Hargress—in the mid-1870s.

47. On October 18, 1873, acting as designated agent, Thomas Roulhac gave a mortgage of $1,600 to Sandy Cameron for 160 acres of the plantation. The acreage conveyed was known as Edwards Field. The mortgage loan was for the entire amount due. Cameron committed to pay for the land in five installments of $320 each, staring on January 1, 1874, and concluding on January 1, 1878. Cameron was able to pay for only thirty acres. In a 1960 affidavit, Sandy Cameron's son-in-law Forrest Hargress stated that an unrecorded deed was dated July 1, 1876. Hale Mortgage and Deed Book, Vol. 52, pages 276–277, Probate Office, Hale County. A 1917 mortgage on Edwards Field, signed by Sandy Cameron's daughter, states that the thirty acres was conveyed by Thomas Roulhac on January 1, 1875. Mortgage agreement of Bettie [Cameron] Hargress and For[r]est Hargress with L. K. Jackson, January 2, 1917, Deed and Mortgage Book R, page 309.

48. For example, purchaser Wilson Rainey worked on the Locke plantation, about seven miles up the road; purchaser Robert Cabbil worked even closer, on the Stollenwerk plantation. With his wagon, purchaser Champ Hall hauled for the city of Greensboro, where Thomas Roulhac was mayor. See the Hale County Commissioners Minutes for 1874–1877, Book 2, pages 67, 77, 103, 104, 241. As an attorney, Roulhac was a knowledgeable and "excellent collector" of payments. Entry for Thomas Roulhac, Alabama, Volume 1, page 111, R. G. Dun & Co. Credit Report Volumes, Baker Library, Harvard Business School.

49. Paul Cameron to Milly Coles Cameron, February 26, 1875, CFP. "Tom Roulhac writes me he has sold all my land in Ala. but 160 acres. I hope he may *get* the pay." The money didn't come. George Collins to Paul Cameron, February 27, 1876; Paul Cameron to Anne Ruffin Cameron, June 14, June 17, June 19, 1879,

CFP. "I have never had business with such a man. How unlike his father. . . . Do tell me what to do with such a man." When Cameron found out that Roulhac was visiting Hillsborough in 1880, Cameron declared he would "seek him out" and presumably confront him. Paul Cameron to Anne Ruffin Cameron, February 28 and 29, 1880, CFP. Cameron was not the only creditor to wait for payment from Thomas Roulhac. In the credit reports of R. G. Dun & Company, which contain confidential credit appraisals from reliable local sources, Roulhac was consistently characterized as "not prompt," "slow pay," and "constitutionally slow abt paying." Entry for Thomas Roulhac, Alabama, Volume 11, page 249, R. G. Dun & Co. Credit Report Volumes, Baker Library, Harvard Business School.

50. For 1875 buyers James Mosley, Robert Cabell, and James McCoy, deeds were recorded and sales confirmed in 1884; for Ned Smith, 1885; for David Jackson and Henry Wilson, 1886.

51. *Alabama Beacon*, September 13, September 27, 1873.

52. *Alabama Beacon*, January 13, 1872, September 21, December 20, 1872.

53. *Alabama Beacon*, October 3, 1874.

54. Mary Ellen Curtin, *Black Prisoners and Their World: Alabama, 1865–1900* (Charlottesville: University of Virginia Press, 2000), 8, 44, 53–54.

55. Thomas Roulhac to Mrs. D. H. Hamilton, November 14, 1880, Ruffin, Roulhac, and Hamilton Family Papers, SHC.

56. Thomas Roulhac to Catherine Ruffin Roulhac, May 20, 1871, Ruffin, Roulhac, and Hamilton Family Papers, SHC.

57. Thomas Roulhac to Mrs. D. H. Hamilton, November 14, 1880, Ruffin, Roulhac, and Hamilton Family Papers, SHC.

9. "Hallelujah Times"

1. Interview with Carrie Hargress Davis, July 2, 1980. Unless otherwise specified, all interviews were conducted by the author.

2. Interview with Carrie Hargress Davis, August 6, 1979.

3. Interview with Angeline Hargress Banks, August 18, 1978; interview with Louie Rainey, July 29, 1979.

4. Paul Hargress made the conditional bequests on November 13, 1912, with attorney W. M. Spencer as the notary public and witness. Hale County deed books record the arrangement separately for each of the eleven beneficiaries. Each recipient was also to pay one-eleventh of the cost of Paul Hargress's funeral. The agreements were recorded in Deed Book Y, pages 2, 27, 83, 151, 213, 275, Probate Office, Hale County.

5. Mortgage of Paul Hargis et al. to Stith Evans for $300, February 16, 1881, Mortgage Book 10, page 93, Probate Office, Hale County. Paul Hargress's lender of 1881, Stith Evans, was known locally as an accommodating creditor to black borrowers, an earthy man who built a "large trade and made money rapidly" despite intermittent "drunken sprees." Entry for Stith Evans, Alabama, vol. 11, page 234, R. G. Dun & Co. Credit Report Volumes, Baker Library, Harvard Business School.

6. In 1887 and 1889, Paul Hargress had a different creditor who required a mortgage on the land in return for an advance each year of $500. By 1890, however, creditor J. W. McCrary and Paul Hargress agreed that the coming crop, farm animals, and tools would be sufficient collateral to obtain the $500 advance. See Mortgage Book 19, page 85 (1887); Mortgage Book 22, page 195 (1889); and Mortgage Book 24, page 379 (1890), Probate Office, Hale County.

7. Interview with Louie Rainey, July 29, 1979, June 22, 1983.

8. Interview with Louie Rainey, August 19, 1978, July 29, 1979, July 3, 1986.

9. Interview with Louie Rainey, July 3, 1986.

10. Interview with Louie Rainey, June 20, June 26, 1983. Neighboring landowner Joseph Phillips also recalled seeing the "lady census taker." Interview with Joseph Phillips, July 1, 1983.

11. Both Champ Hall and Jonas McCoy also earned payments from Hale County for building or repairing bridges. Hale County Commissioners Minutes for 1874–1877, Book 2, pages 103–104, 241–242. Interview with Louie Rainey, June 20, 1983. Champ Hall's large wagon reputedly "was like a Cadillac in its time!"

12. Landowners Eli Williams and James Mosley were among those who sub-rented their land. Interview with Louie Rainey, June 20, 1983. The lead-hoe role taken by Eli Williams's wife was described by Williams' grandson Joseph Phillips. Interview with Joseph Phillips, July 1, 1983.

13. Interview with Louie Rainey, June 20, 1983.

14. Interview with Louie Rainey and Joel Wallace, June 22, June 26, 1983; interview with Joseph Phillips, July 1, 1983.

15. Interview with Louie Rainey, June 22, 1983.

16. Interview with Louie Rainey, June 30, 1983. Champ Hall died of a shotgun wound in November 1879. In the credit appraisal provided by a confidential source for the R. G. Dun credit agency, the entries about John O'Donnell obliquely intimated that O'Donnell had a liaison with a black woman. The informant reported that O'Donnell was "a single man of moderate capacity, bad character & habits. . . . This young man . . . has fallen into very bad habits & unless he changes his mode of life, cannot be considered a reliable or desirable customer." See the entry for John O'Donnell, Alabama, Vol. 11, page 253, R. G. Dun & Co. Credit Report Vol-

umes, Baker Library, Harvard Business School. John O'Donnell was tried and acquitted of Champ Hall's murder in 1881.

17. For the land division between Robert Cabbil and Jonas McCoy, see Deed Book L, pages 36–39, Probate Office, Hale County. McCoy was unable to pay off his debts. His land was sold in 1884 to white purchaser James M. Simpson. McCoy was the first black landowner in the community to lose his land. Interview with Louie Rainey, July 29, 1979.

18. Interview with Alice Hargress, August 19 and August 20, 1978.

19. The Hale County Tax Book for 1900–1910 listed Ruffin as owning 1,845 acres in 1900, valued at $10,000 for tax assessment. Hale County, Book of Assessment of Taxes, Cedarville, Beat Seven, page 75. Ruffin continued to buy property after 1900, so his total acreage continued to grow in the twentieth century.

20. Interview with Louie Rainey, August 19, 1978; interview with Lem Cabbil, June 29, 1983.

21. See the record of Tom Ruffin's birth and listing with his mother, Harriet, and brothers Wesley and Washington in the James Ruffin Plantation Record, 1841–1847, Marengo County, Alabama, found in the Ruffin, Roulhac, and Hamilton Family Papers, SHC.

22. Interview with Mary Ellen Ruffin Hayes, Bessemer, Alabama, December 6, 1980.

23. Interview with Louie Rainey, August 19, 1978; interview with Joseph Pratcher, June 29, 1983.

24. One who sold land to Tom Ruffin was the Greensboro town druggist; the other was the town's leading physician. Two other sellers were Cedarville merchants (John O'Donnell and Patrick Kelly) winding down their businesses.

25. When whites in the Cedarville area decided to sell property, Tom Ruffin's success in timber, as a merchant, and as an employer of tenants earned him early knowledge of impending land sales by whites and a first option to buy. His incremental early purchases (1880–1891) were recorded in the Hale County Deed Books: Book J, page 466, Book K, pages 209, 434, 466, 485, and Book M, pages 434 and 577. The $11,200 purchase, on December 17, 1895, was recorded in Book O, page 252. Tom Ruffin's land purchases continued through 1913.

26. Interview with Joseph Pratcher, June 29, 1983.

27. Interviews with Louie Rainey, August 19, 1978; James Lyles, August 9, 1979; and Lem Cabbil, June 29, 1983.

28. Interview with Louie Rainey, August 19, 1978; Interview with Robert Cabbil, July 28, 1979.

29. Even though Tom Ruffin died in 1921, a one-page account of his life and achievements was included posthumously in the Federal Writers' Project of the

1930s, which otherwise consisted of interviews done with living survivors of bondage. African American interviewer Louise Porter spoke with Tom Ruffin's physician son, Dr. Washington Ruffin, and others who knew "one of the largest landowners" in Hale County. See George P. Rawick, ed., *The American Slave: A Composite Autobiography*, supplement, series 1, vol. 1, *Alabama Narratives* (Westport, CT: Greenwood Press, 1977), 355–356.

30. Interviews with Louie Rainey, August 19, 1978, and James Lyles, August 9, 1979. Ruffin's plain garb was recalled by Lem Cabbil in an interview conducted on June 29, 1983. Mary Ellen Ruffin Hayes had also heard the story of her grandfather's pocketknife as Tom Ruffin's way to vouch for a borrower seeking a small loan from Ruffin's account with Greensboro businessman J. B. Stickney. Interview with Mary Ellen Ruffin Hayes, December 6, 1980.

31. Interview with Louie Rainey, June 22, 1983.

32. Interview with Louie Rainey, June 20, 1983.

33. Mary Ellen Curtin, *Black Prisoners and Their World: Alabama, 1865–1900* (Charlottesville: University of Virginia Press, 2000), 54–57; Eutaw (Alabama) *Whig & Observer*, November 26, 1874; Richard Bailey, *Neither Carpetbaggers nor Scalawag: Black Office Holders during the Reconstruction of Alabama*, 2nd ed. (Montgomery, AL: Richard Bailey, 1993), 207, 213, 230.

34. For the vote on the proposed new Alabama Constitution in 1875, polls were not opened in the heavily black Cedarville, Macon, and Laneville precincts (called "beats" in Alabama) on the grounds that black voters had previously cast their ballots at multiple sites.

35. "Testimony of James K. Green," Birmingham, Alabama, November 17, 1883, in *Report of the Committee of the Senate upon the Relations between Labor and Capital* (Washington, DC: Government Printing Office, 1885), IV:450–455.

36. Ibid., 451–453.

37. Douglas A. Blackmon, *Slavery by Another Name: The Re-Enslavement of Black Americans from the Civil War to World War II* (New York: Doubleday, 2008), 55, 328. With Thomas Roulhac as mayor, the newly installed white government of Hale County began leasing prisoners to private parties in August 1875. In July 1910, convict Archy Hargrove of Hale County died while leased and working in a coal mine.

38. Blackmon, *Slavery by Another Name*, 122; R. Volney Riser, *Defying Disfranchisement: Black Voting Rights Activism in the Jim Crow South, 1890–1903* (Baton Rouge: Louisiana State University Press, 2010), 112–144. By 1902, black voter registration in Alabama had fallen by 98 percent. Riser, *Disfranchisement*, 148. For the ongoing and crippling consequences of the 1901 state constitution, see Allen Tullos, *Alabama Getaway: The Political Imaginary and the Heart of Dixie* (Athens: University of Georgia Press, 2011), 3–5, 244.

39. *Greensboro Watchman*, April 13, 1916.

40. Interview with Louie Rainey, June 22, 1983, July 8, 1986.

41. Interview with Louie Rainey, July 8, 1986.

42. Interview with Louie Rainey, June 22, 1983.

43. Interview with Louie Rainey, July 29, 1979.

44. Paul Hargress to L. K. Jackson, February 12, 1915, Deed Book Y, pages 638–639, Probate Office, Hale County.

45. Interview with Louie Rainey, November 25, 1980, June 22, 1983.

46. For Paul Hargress's date of death, see Probate File Number 19, Probate Record Book M214, Probate Office, Hale County.

10. "A Game Rooster"

1. Interview with Carrie Hargress Davis, August 6, 1979.

2. See the list of enslaved persons on the Tunica plantation, January 1861.

3. It is entirely my conjecture that Dorsey (who was later called Dorothy by descendants) named her son to honor the Ned who was sold away in 1861. As noted earlier, it was a frequent practice, on the Cameron and other plantations, for children to be named after friends or family members who were lost, whether by sale or death. Dorsey's enslaved uncle, Washington—who witnessed Ned's attempt to defuse the confrontation—had supplied crucial details to a white lawyer. The details saved Ned from hanging, but not from sale. For full details of the episode, see Chapter 5

4. By early April 1865, Confederate communications were in disarray, and no dispatches or telegrams can definitively establish Forrest's location between April 4 and April 8. On April 4, he was at Marion, Alabama—about twenty miles east of the Cameron plantation. On April 8, he met Union commander General James H. Wilson, the victor at Selma, to discuss a prisoner exchange. In between, according to two recent biographers, he was "in the Cahaba area." Brian Steel Wills, *A Battle from the Start: The Life of Nathan Bedford Forrest* (New York: Harper-Collins, 1992), 310–311; Jack Hurst, *Nathan Bedford Forrest: A Biography* (New York: Alfred A. Knopf, 1993), 252–253. After the meeting with Wilson on April 8, Forrest gathered remnants of his troops and headed toward Gainesville, Alabama. That trajectory would have taken him toward Newbern and within a few miles of the Cameron plantation. Hurst, *Forrest*, 253. Wounded by a saber in hand-to-hand combat on April 1, Forrest had his arm in a sling during early April.

5. Interview with Alice Hargress, August 19, 1978; interview with Carrie Davis, August 18, August 20, 1978; interview with Angeline Hargress Banks, August 20, 1978; interview with Louie Rainey, November 25, 1980. The Hargress family Bible lists January 1, 1866, as the date of birth for Ned Forrest Hargress. Interview with

Louie Rainey, August 19, 1978, November 25, 1980; interview with Betty Hargress Washington, August 18, August 20, 1978.

6. Interview with James Lyles, August 9, 1979; interview with Angeline Hargress Banks, August 6, 1979. Forrest Hargress's three surviving daughters were interviewed by reporter Jim McKay for a story published in the *Demopolis Times*, March 9, 1972. In that interview, the sisters claimed "that Dorothy told her son when he was old enough that he was the son of the famous General." "Their father's nickname, as legend has it, was 'General.'" The McKay story placed Nathan Bedford Forrest in the area around 1870, when building the Selma-to-Memphis railroad, rather than in April 1865, while a commander in retreat from Union forces at Selma. In both accounts, Dorothy was summoned to be a cook at the Confederate general's encampment. Journalist McKay summarized local lore: "It was common knowledge back then that he was the bastard son of Forrest."

7. Cintha Hargress was born in Mississippi in 1862, and named her first daughter after her mother, Susan. See the 1880 Census for Cedarville, Hale County, Alabama, Roll 15, Microfilm #1254015, page 406A, Enumeration District 061, Image 0294, found in Ancestry.com.

8. Interview with Louie Rainey, August 19, 1978, November 25, 1980; interview with Betty Hargress Washington, August 18, 1978.

9. Interview with Betty Hargress Washington, August 19, 1978; interview with Alice Hargress, August 20, 1978; Forrest Hargress Affidavit, 1960, Hale County Mortgage & Deed Book, Volume 52, pages 276–277.

10. Interview with Betty Hargress Washington, August 18, 1978; interview with Elijah Banks, August 19, 1978; interview with Louie Rainey, July 29, 1979.

11. Interview with Louie Rainey, July 29, 1979, November 25, 1980.

12. Steven Deyle, *Carry Me Back: The Domestic Slave Trade in American Life* (New York: Oxford University Press, 2005), 280.

13. A black physician also scoffed. Greensboro's Dr. Wiley pointedly addressed Forrest Hargress as "Colonel" rather than "General." Interview with Angeline Hargress Banks, August 6, 1979.

14. Paul Hargress's bequest to his personal caretaker Dicey McCullough was explicitly "in consideration of the kindness and services [she] rendered" to him. Hale County Deed Book X, pages 616–617.

15. Dylan Penningroth, *The Claims of Kinfolk: African-American Property and Community in the Nineteenth-Century South* (Chapel Hill: University of North Carolina Press, 2003), 89, 137–138, 158–161, 192. Carrie Hargress Davis put it this way: her father and Forrest Hargress "got the same momma," but for Forrest Hargress, "a white man was his daddy," so as her family saw it, Forrest "went by Hargress but he wasn't really no Hargress." Interview with Carrie Hargress Davis, July 1, 1980.

16. Interview with Angeline Hargress Banks, December 9, 1980.

17. Interview with Louie Rainey, July 29, 1979.

18. Interview with James and Lillie Mae Cannon, August 5, 1979.

19. Interview with Alice Hargress, December 1, 1980.

20. Interview with Alice Hargress, July 6, 1988.

11. Sanctuaries

1. *Greensboro Watchman*, October 5, October 12, 1916, January 3, 1918.

2. *Greensboro Watchman*, October 7, 1920.

3. Isabel Wilkerson, *The Warmth of Other Suns: The Epic Story of America's Great Migration* (New York: Random House, 2010).

4. Family tradition put the total number of Cameron Cabbil's children at twenty-three. Interview with Carrie Hargress Davis, July 1, 1980; interview with Louie Rainey, December 7, 1980; interview with Alice Hargress, June 20, 1983; interview with Laura Cabbil Glover, July 5, 1988. The United States Census for 1880 and 1900 affirms the large number of children in the household of Cameron Cabbil and his wife, Laura Cabbil, and in the adjoining household of the unmarried woman, Cintha Hargress. The adjacent listing of the two households in the census confirms their proximity. The match of Cameron Cabbil's first name and Paul Cameron's last name was almost certainly a coincidence. Different census entries recorded Cameron Cabbil's date of birth variously as 1864 or 1861. His parents were on a different antebellum plantation and would not have known of Paul Cameron before the 1870s.

5. Interview with Alice Hargress, November 24, 1980, July 6, 1988; interview with Amanda Cabbil and Laura Cabbil Glover, July 5, 1988, Bessemer, Alabama.

6. Interview with Robert Cabbil, July 28, 1979; interview with Carrie Hargress Davis, July 1, 1980; interview with Alice Hargress, June 20, 1983.

7. Interview with York Banks, December 3, 1980.

8. Interview with Louie Rainey, August 19, 1979; interview with Alice Hargress, July 6, 1988.

9. The United States Census listed Pinkie and Toney Sledge with two sons and one daughter in 1910; the 1920 census listed Pinkie Sledge with six children.

10. Interview with York Banks, July 1, 1983.

11. *Greensboro Watchman*, March 25, June 10, October 25, 1915. The *Watchman* was the successor to the *Alabama Beacon*. Looking back on the previous decade, the newspaper's editor stated that the boll weevil first came to Hale County in 1913. *Greensboro Watchman*, April 1, 1920. A recent overview of the path of the boll weevil in Alabama asserted that it "advanced into twelve southwest Alabama counties"

in 1911. But the study goes on to note that it was in 1913 that "the entire cotton crop of southwest Alabama was devoured." *History of the Boll Weevil in Alabama, 1910–2000*, Alabama Agricultural Experiment Station, Auburn University, Bulletin 670 (December 2007), 4–5. On the basis of the editor's local information, I have accepted 1913 as the weevil's arrival date in Hale County.

12. *Greensboro Watchman*, May 27, September 30, 1915; October 5, October 12, 1916.

13. *Greensboro Watchman*, May 27, 1915.

14. Interview with Louie Rainey, July 8, 1986.

15. *Greensboro Watchman*, July 13, August 3, 1916.

16. *Greensboro Watchman*, July 13, July 20, 1916. Interview with Louie Rainey, June 26, 1983.

17. In the 1880 Census, Nancy Mosley's birthplace was given as North Carolina.

18. The 1880 United States Census listed Andrew and Rachel Lyles living next to James and Nancy Mosley, on Mosley land. In the 1910 Census, James Lyles was listed with one younger sibling, a brother named Eugene. In the 1930s, James Lyles would name a son Eugene, after the younger brother. Interview with James Lyles, November 25, 1980.

19. Lawrence Goodwyn, *Democratic Promise: The Populist Moment in America* (New York: Oxford University Press, 1976), 143–144, 294–295, 323–324, 402–407.

20. Andrew Lyles was the treasurer of the club. The charter for the Farmers Club in Co-partnership was recorded on February 22, 1890, in the Hale County Book of Corporations and Societies, Book 1, pages 18–19. The members agreed "to do business together" in "the line of cormerse."

21. Goodwyn, *Democratic Promise*, 323–324.

22. Interview with James Lyles, November 25, 1980.

23. Andrew Lyles to Thomas Ruffin, February 23, 1916, Hale County Deed Book Z, page 209. Lyles family tradition held that Ruffin transferred or sold part of the Lyles land to Cedarville merchant Patrick Kelly. Neither family members nor I have found a clear record of the transfer.

24. Interview with James Lyles, August 11, 1979.

25. Ibid.

26. Interview with James Lyles, August 9, 1979.

27. Interview with Louie Rainey, June 30, 1980.

28. Interview with Alice Hargress, July 6, 1988.

29. Interview with Lem Cabbil, June 29, 1983. The old cabins had "big planks" for flooring. Fitted snugly together when laid, they shrank in time, and strips were laid down to cover the cracks. "You could take the planks up," as happened to provide the Sledge casket. Interview with James Lyles, June 21, 1983.

30. Interview with Alice Hargress, June 20, 1983.

31. Interview with James Lyles, November 23, 1981.

32. Interview with James Lyles, August 9, 1979. The United States Census for 1920 listed a James Lyles as a boarder in a dwelling in Detroit, living with other boarders, one of whom was a Mosley. I've not been able to establish whether either the Lyles or the Mosley listed were related to each other.

33. Interview with James Lyles, August 9, August 11, 1979.

34. Interview with James Lyles, August 9, 1979.

35. Interview with James Lyles, May 21, November 23, 1981. Dispute over title to eighty acres of the property was never resolved. Interview with James Lyles, November 25, 1980.

36. Interview with James Lyles, August 11, 1979. See the death notice for Rev. James Eaton, April 1925, in *Alabama Deaths, 1908–59*, for Hale County, volume 17, roll 2, page 8315, accessed through Ancestry.com.

37. Interview with Alice Hargress, June 23, 1980.

38. Interview with Louie Rainey, December 7, 1980. Cameron Cabbil was charged with larceny in 1909. The charge was not prosecuted and was dismissed on April 12, 1909. Minutes of the Hale County Circuit Court, Book H, page 48. I've been unable to determine whether a behind-the-scenes land transfer smoothed the dismissal. In the U.S. Census of 1910, Cabbil was enumerated and listed as at home rather than in a prison camp. A different account of the land loss came from Lem Cabbil, who asserted that the destructive July flood led to the departure of Cameron Cabbil's family of workers. Without workers, and too aged and infirm to work the land himself, he sold all but seventeen acres of his land to adjacent white landowner Earl Compton. Interview with Lem Cabbil, June 29, 1983.

39. Interview with Alice Hargress, December 1, 1980; interview with Mathilda Biggs and Arie Sears, December 3, 1980.

40. Interview with Alice Hargress, June 20, 1983.

41. Interview with York Banks, July 1, 1983.

42. Interview with York Banks, November 28, 1980; interview with Mathilda Biggs and Arie Sears, December 3, 1980; interview with Gates Rainer Jr. and Elijah Banks, June 24, 1983.

43. Interview with Gates Rainer Jr., May 20, 1981, June 24, 1983.

44. Interview with Eugene Long, November 25, 1980.

45. By the mid-1920s, some Model T Fords sold for as little as $300. The price for those sold in Demopolis on Thanksgiving Day 1926 was $400.

46. Interview with York Banks, November 28, 1980; interview with Lem Cabbil, June 29, 1983.

47. Before he got an automobile, Tom Ruffin consulted with white contacts to be sure they approved his acquisition of a car. Interview with Mary Ellen Ruffin Hayes, December 6, 1980.

48. See the deed from Jonas McCoy to James M. Simpson, December 24, 1884, in Hale County Deed Book L, pages 37–39; and the sale from J. M. Simpson to G. E. Compton on October 23, 1919, in Hale County Deed Book 10, page 270, recorded on November 19, 1931. The Deed Books are in the Hale County Probate Office.

49. Interview with Alice Hargress, December 1, 1980.

50. Interview with Alice Hargress, July 2, 1980.

12. "That Thirties Wreck"

1. Interview with Alice Hargress, December 1, 1980.

2. Interview with York Banks, November 28, 1980.

3. Interview with Betty Hargress Washington, August 20, 1978.

4. Interview with James Lyles, August 9, 1979.

5. Will of Thomas Ruffin, Hale County, Will Record A, pages 809–814, and Probate Minute Book, Volume H, page 303. The Ruffin will was probated on September 2, 1921. Tom Ruffin's oldest child, Hattie Ruffin, married several times. In 1921, at the time of the probated will, her married name was Hudson. After remarriage, her surname became Harris. Both Tom Ruffin's granddaughter and one of his tenants recalled settlements with workers that "went on for days." Interview with Mary Ellen Ruffin Hayes, December 6, 1980; interview with Joseph Pratcher, June 29, 1983.

6. Interview with Eliza Lyles, August 9, 1979; interview with Joseph Pratcher, June 29, 1983.

7. Interview with Joseph Pratcher, June 29, 1983.

8. Interview with Louie Rainey, June 23, 1983.

9. Interview with York Banks, November 28, 1980.

10. Interview with Joseph Phillips, July 1, 1983.

11. Interview with Robert Cabbil, July 28, 1979, November 24, 1980; interview with Louie Rainey, June 22, 1983.

12. Interview with York Banks, November 28, 1980.

13. Ibid.

14. Interview with Louie Rainey, June 23, 1983.

15. Interview with James Lyles, August 9, 1979.

16. Interview with James Lyles, November 23, 1981.

17. Interview with James Lyles, August 9, 1979, November 23, 1981. He worked in the Edgewater Mine, between Bessemer and Birmingham. Interview with James Lyles, August 11, 1979.

18. Interview with Alice Hargress, August 20, 1978.

19. Interview with Alice Hargress, December 1, 1980.

20. Interview with Ambrose Hargress, July 5, 1988.

21. Interview with Betty Hargress Washington, August 17, 1978.

22. Interview with James Lyles, June 21, 1983.

23. Pete Daniel, *Breaking the Land: The Transformation of Cotton, Tobacco, and Rice Cultures since 1880* (Urbana: University of Illinois Press, 1985), 168–183; Pete Daniel, *Dispossession: Discrimination against African-American Farmers in the Age of Civil Rights* (Chapel Hill: University of North Carolina Press, 2014), 9–14.

24. Paul Conkin, *Tomorrow a New World: The New Deal Community Projects* (Ithaca, NY: Cornell University Press, 1959).

25. Interview with James Lyles, August 11, 1979, November 25, 1980, June 21, 1983.

26. Interview with James Lyles, June 21, 1983.

27. Interview with James Lyles, August 11, 1979, June 21, 1983; interview with Eugene Lyles, December 2, 1980.

28. Interview with James Lyles, November 25, 1980, June 21, 1983.

29. Interview with Eliza Pratcher Lyles, August 9, 1979.

30. Interview with Louie Rainey, July 29, 1979.

31. Interview with Louie Rainey, July 29, 1979, May 18, 1981.

32. Interview with Alice Hargress, December 19, 1986.

33. Interview with Louie Rainey, June 20, 1983.

34. Ibid.

35. Interview with Louie Rainey, June 30, 1980, November 25, 1980.

36. By 1940, Louie Rainey had become a resident member of Pinkie Sledge's household. United States Census, 1940, for Cedarville, Hale County, Alabama, Roll T 627_36, page 2A, Enumeration District 33-15, accessed through Ancestry.com.

37. Interview with Louie Rainey, November 20, 1980; interview with Joel Wallace, December 1, 1980.

38. Interview with York Banks, July 1, 1983.

39. Interview with Arie Banks Sears, December 3, 1980; interview with Alice Hargress and Joel Wallace, December 1, 1980; interview with Lem Cabbil, June 29, 1983.

40. Interview with James Lyles, June 21, 1983.

41. For the backgrounds of Claude and Alton Stillman, see the United States Census, 1940, Little River, Pemiscot, Missouri, Roll T627_2137, page 15A, Enumeration District 78-27, and the obituary for Claud Stillman, September 9, 1955, both accessed through Ancestry.com. For the obituary, the family spelled Stillman's first name as "Claud"; the federal censuses of 1930 and 1940 spelled his first name as "Claude." Alton Stillman died in August 1952.

42. *Greensboro Watchman*, August 27, 1916, June 24, 1920, August 4, 1921.

43. Interview with Elijah Banks and Alice Hargress, August 17, 1978.

44. Interview with Robert Cabbil, November 24, 1980.

45. Interview with Robert Cabbil, August 11, 1979; interview with Alice Hargress, December 1, 1980, June 23, 1983, June 30, 1983; interview with Eugene Lyles, December 2, 1980.

46. Interview with James Lyles, August 11, 1979.

47. Interview with Robert Cabbil, July 28, 1979; interview with Alice Hargress, December 1, 1980.

13. New Foundations

1. Interview with Louie Rainey, July 29, 1979.

2. The Cassimore Burial Society built a separate building as its Society Hall in the 1920s. The school moved from the church to the hall. The original Society Hall stood until the 1980s, when it was torn down and replaced by a newer building.

3. Interview with Alice Hargress, December 1, 1980; interview with Lem Cabbil, June 29, 1983.

4. Pete Daniel, *Breaking the Land: The Transformation of Cotton, Tobacco, and Rice Cultures since 1880* (Urbana: University of Illinois Press, 1985), chapters 4, 5, 8, and 11.

5. Interview with James Lyles, August 11, 1979, November 23, 1981; interview with Alice Hargress, December 1, 1980.

6. Interview with Alice Hargress, December 1, 1980, June 26, 1983.

7. Interview with Ned Forrest Hargress, July 1, 1980. Named after his father and great-grandfather, Ned Forrest Hargress was born in 1946 and grew up in Cassimore. His great-grandfather died in 1965 and his father in 1975.

8. Interview with Mary Cabbil, November 20, 1980; interview with Eugene Lyles, December 2, 1980.

9. Interview with James Lyles, August 11, 1979; interview with Eugene Lyles, December 2, 1980; interview with Alice Hargress, June 20, 1983.

10. Interview with Lem Cabbil, June 29, 1983.

11. Interview with Robert Cabbil, July 28, 1979; interview with Mary Cabbil, November 20, 1980.

12. Interview with York Banks, November 28, 1980.

13. Thomas J. Sugrue, *Sweet Land of Liberty: The Forgotten Struggle for Civil Rights in the North* (New York: Random House, 2008), 6–12, 60–82.

14. S. McEachin Otts, *Better than Them: The Unmaking of an Alabama Racist* (Montgomery, AL: New South Books, 2014), 46.

15. Interview with Louie Rainey, July 29, 1979; interview with Robert Cabbil, August 11, 1979.

16. Interview with Ned Forrest Hargress, July 1, 1980.

17. Interview with Ted Hargress, July 6, 1988.

18. Interview with Ned Forrest Hargress, July 5, 1988.

19. Interview with Betty Hargress Washington and Minnie Hargress Williams, August 17, 1978.

20. Interview with Alice Hargress, August 20, 1978.

21. Ibid.

22. Interview with Louie Rainey, July 29, 1979.

23. Douglas A. Blackmon, *Slavery by Another Name: The Re-Enslavement of Black Americans from the Civil War to World War II* (New York: Doubleday, 2008), 367–382.

24. Interview with Louie Rainey, August 9, 1979.

25. Interview with Alice Hargress, December 1, 1980; interview with York Banks, November 28, 1980.

26. Interview with Alice Hargress, August 18, 1978.

27. Interview with Alice Hargress, June 20, 1983.

28. C. Scott Graber, "A Blight Hits Black Farmers," *Civil Rights Digest* 10, no. 3 (1978): 21–22; Dylan C. Penningroth, *The Claims of Kinfolk: African-American Property and Community in the Nineteenth Century South* (Chapel Hill: University of North Carolina Press, 2003), 158–161, 188–192.

29. Interview with Alice Hargress, June 30, 1983. For Alice Hargress, respecting and retaining "heir land" was a moral duty that each family owed its members and their descendants. She abided by that obligation, and through her model urged others to do the same. At law, however, the practice of tenancy-in-common—shared ownership of landed property—has proved extremely vulnerable. A single owner, or an outsider who bought an owner's share, could force a court-ordered partition sale of the whole, compelling all to sell off land held in common. Thousands of rural African Americans have lost family land as a result. Efforts to reform partition law have been spearheaded by University of Wisconsin Law School professor Thomas Mitchell. Starting with a law review article in 2001, Mitchell and his collaborators have for a decade and a half highlighted the exposure of "heirs property" and sought to prevent further black land loss. See Thomas Mitchell, "From Reconstruction to Deconstruction: Undermining Black Land-ownership . . . through Partition Sales," *Northwestern University Law Review* 95 (2001). In 2011, the American Bar Association approved a new model law called the Uniform Partition of Heirs Property Act, designed to produce fairer outcomes if and when land is divided among heirs. With contributions from University of Alabama Law School faculty members, the Alabama legislature enacted a Uniform Partition of Heirs Property Act in 2014. For a comprehensive review of the vulnerability of heirs property and of ongoing effort to reform partition laws, see Thomas W. Mitchell, "Reforming Property Law to Address Devastating Land

Loss," *Alabama Law Review* 66 (October 2014): 1–58, also published as University of Wisconsin Legal Studies Research Paper No. 1329, October 29, 2014. See also the assessment of reform efforts and ongoing challenges by Sally Breitenbach, "Heirs' Property Challenges Families, States," July 15, 2015, *Stateline* (Pew Charitable Trusts, Research & Analysis), 1–9.

30. Interview with James Lyles, August 9, 1979.

31. Hardy Frye interview with Lewis Black, May 1972, Hardy T. Frye Oral History Collection, Auburn University Libraries, Special Collections and Archives Department.

32. Entry for Napoleon Black, 1930 United States Census, Pineville, Monroe, Alabama, Roll 42, page 9B, Enumeration District 16, Image 1070,0, Microfilm #2339777, accessed through Ancestry.com.

33. Interview with Lewis Black, May 21, 1981.

34. Stanley H. Smith interview with Lewis Black, October 1967, in the Civil Rights Documentation Project, Moorland-Spingarn Research Center, Howard University, Washington, D.C. The reputation of the Monroe County sheriff of the 1930s and 1940s persists to this day. "He'd slap you upside the head, cuss you out, beat you," recalled one black resident in 2015. See Paul Theroux's article on Monroeville, the home of Harper Lee, and the nearby hamlet of Beatrice, where Lewis Black grew up: "Return of the Mockingbird," *Smithsonian* 46, no. 4 (July–August 2015): 48.

35. Interview with Lewis Black, May 21, 1981.

36. Ibid.

37. Ibid.

38. Interview with James Lyles, August 9, 1979.

39. Report of Frank Prial, "Area 11, Alabama—Shelby, Bibb, Chilton, Perry and Hale Counties," October 11, 1965, Inspection Report Evaluation Community Action Programs, Box 1, Record Group 381, Office of Economic Opportunity Papers, National Archives, College Park, MD. For Prial's evaluation of the leadership of Lewis Black, see 8–9, 15. "Every Negro in Hale County knows who he is and that he fights for them. . . . The fact remains, he is sticking his neck far out. Few others are doing the same." See Susan Youngblood Ashmore, *Carry It On: The War on Poverty and the Civil Rights Movement in Alabama, 1964–1972* (Athens: University of Georgia Press, 2008), 130. Interview with Francis X. Walter, June 27, 2011, Sewanee, Tennessee. Said Lewis Black in 1981: "I'm not a religious fanatic. . . . Our savior ain't got here yet. . . . If I look in the mirror, I see *my* savior. That's the only somebody who's gonna save me." Interview with Lewis Black, May 21, 1981. On Lewis Black as a negotiator, see the interview with Rev. Arthur T. Days, July 4, 2011.

40. Interview with James Lyles, November 25, 1980, May 21, 1981.

41. Interview with Alice Hargress, December 1, 1980.

14. "Unless It's a Must"

1. Interview with Alice Hargress, June 29, 2011.

2. Interview with Arthur T. Days, July 4, 2011, Mobile, Alabama.

3. Interview with James Lyles, August 9, 1979.

4. Interview with Lewis Black, May 21, 1981.

5. Telephone interview with William Brault, June 25, 2011. Coming from Hartwick College in New York, William Brault was one of the four SCOPE volunteers who registered voters in Hale County in 1965.

6. Interview with Arthur T. Days, July 4, 2011, Mobile, Alabama. For a compendium of information about the preparations for the SCLC voter registration project—acronym SCOPE—see Willy Siegal Leventhal, *The Scope of Freedom: The Leadership of Hosea Williams with Dr. King's '65 Student Volunteers* (Montgomery, AL: Challenge, 2005).

7. Undated report on Hale County Voter Registration Drive [May 1965], Southern Christian Leadership Conference, Hale County File, Martin Luther King Jr. Center Archives, Atlanta, Georgia.

8. Interview with Alice Hargress, December 1, 1980, June 29, 2011. Interview with York Banks, November 28, 1980.

9. Interview with Alice Hargress, June 29, 2011.

10. Interview with Alice Hargress, December 1, 1980, June 29, 2011.

11. Interview with Alice Hargress, December 1, 1980; interview with York Banks, November 28, 1980.

12. Interview with Alice Hargress, December 1, 1980, June 20, 1983.

13. Interview with Alice Hargress, December 1, 1980, June 29, 2011.

14. Interview with James Lyles, November 25, 1980.

15. Interview with Alice Hargress, June 29, 2011. The description of Rev. Lyles's manner as "fiery" comes in an interview with Theresa Burroughs, June 30, 2011. Theresa Burroughs was a leader in the Hale County demonstrations of July 1965. In the 1980s, she founded the Safe House Museum of Greensboro, which houses photos and accounts of participants in the Hale County movement, and sponsors programs about the civil rights struggle in the Black Belt. In the 1960s, Rev. Martin Luther King came to the area to speak several times. On the last occasion, in late March 1968, local black leaders felt it was too late and too dangerous for him to leave. He spent the night safely at the Burroughs family home, protected by armed neighbors, and returned to Montgomery the next day. The Safe House Museum honors that moment as well as the movement in Hale.

16. Interview with Alice Hargress, August 19, 1978, June 29, 2011. Alice Hargress and James Lyles were among those blacks listed as registered to vote in 1964 by

the *Greensboro Watchman*, April 2, 1964. For a superb treatment of the civil rights and voting rights movement in Hale County and the Black Belt, and the economic struggle that accompanied and succeeded it after 1965, see Susan Youngblood Ashmore, *Carry It On: The War on Poverty and the Civil Rights Movement in Alabama, 1964–1972* (Athens: University of Georgia Press, 2008). The Hale County black registration number is on 127.

17. Interview with Alice Hargress, August 19, 1978.

18. Interview with Alice Hargress, August 19, August 20, 1978.

19. Stanley H. Smith interview with Lewis Black, October 1967, Tuskegee, Alabama, for the Civil Rights Documentation Project, on deposit at the Moorland-Spingarn Research Center, Howard University, Washington, D.C.

20. Ashmore, *Carry It On*, 127–128, 324 nn. 7, 8. Different sources give different dates for the major protest events in Greensboro in July 1965. I rely on the chronology—though *not* on the interpretation of events—given in the *Greensboro Watchman* of July 22 and July 29, 1965.

21. Interview with Alice Hargress, June 29, 2011.

22. Interview with Alice Hargress, December 1, 1980, June 29, 2011; interview with Arthur T. Days, July 4, 2011.

23. Interview with Alice Hargress, August 19, 1978, June 29, 2011.

24. Interview with Alice Hargress, December 1, 1980, June 29, 2011.

25. Interview with Alice Hargress, June 29, 2011.

26. Ibid.; interview with Arthur T. Days, July 4, 2011.

27. Interview with Alice Hargress, June 29, 2011.

28. Interview with Alice Hargress, August 19, 1979; Ashmore, *Carry It On*, 128; Stanley H. Smith interview with Lewis Black, October 1967, Tuskegee Institute, for the Civil Rights Documentation Project, transcript at Howard University.

29. Ashmore, *Carry It On*, 128.

30. Interview with Alice Hargress, August 19, 1978, June 29, 2011.

31. Interview with James Lyles, August 9, August 11, 1979, May 21, 1981.

32. Pete Daniel, "African-American Farmers and Civil Rights," *Journal of Southern History* 73 (February 2007): 3–38.

33. Interview with Lem Cabbil, June 29, 1983; interview with York Banks, July 1, 1983.

34. Report of Frank Prial, "Area 11, Alabama . . . ," October 11, 1965, OEO Papers, National Archives. The relentless role of the U.S. Department of Agriculture in accelerating black land loss in the civil rights era is meticulously and convincingly detailed in Pete Daniel, *Dispossession: Discrimination against African-American Farmers in the Age of Civil Rights* (Chapel Hill: University of North Carolina Press, 2013).

35. Ashmore, *Carry It On*, 129–130.

36. Stanley Smith interview with Lewis Black, October 1967; interview with James Lyles, August 11, 1979; Fortieth Annual Report of the Federation of Southern Cooperatives Land Assistance Fund, May 2007.

37. Interview with Lewis Black, May 21, 1981; interview with Arthur T. Days, July 4, 2011.

38. Julian E. Zelizer, *The Fierce Urgency of Now: Lyndon Johnson, Congress, and the Battle for the Great Society* (New York: Penguin Press, 2015), 132–145.

39. Ashmore, *Carry It On*, 224–236; Stanley Smith interview with Lewis Black, October 1967.

40. Interview with James Lyles, August 11, 1979.

41. Ibid. "Carry It On" is a stirring civil rights anthem composed in 1964 by Gil Turner, and is the title of Susan Youngblood Ashmore's indispensable 2008 book, which I have relied on deeply. Meticulously researched and lucidly written, *Carry It On* brilliantly chronicles the strivings of Lewis Black and others, against immense odds, to make the War on Poverty of benefit to rural blacks of Alabama.

Acknowledgments

I began research on this project in 1978. As years and then decades went by, I often jested that I didn't know which would make it first to a finish line—the book or the author. That the book is done at last is a testimony to the faith, forbearance, and generosity of family, friends, and colleagues. I wish that all who helped me had lived to see the day.

When I floated the idea of going out to Alabama to see if I could find descendants of those sent out in 1844—and to learn if they had an oral tradition about their enslaved forebears' migration—I got unstinting encouragement from colleagues, despite the outlandishness of my plan. Bill Chafe, who with Larry Goodwyn was starting the Duke Oral History Program, urged me to pursue the story. Bill Price, Larry Misenheimer, and Larry Tise, historians and leaders at the North Carolina Department of Archives and History, found funds to pay for my search for the fate of transplanted black North Carolinians. Alex Harris gave me a crash course in documentary photography. My former student Bill Wilkerson lent me his Nikon camera. With their support, westward I went.

Fortune smiled on my mission and my life when I met Alice Hargress in July 1978. A leader in her Alabama community, she became my guide and guardian, shared her past and urged others to share theirs, welcomed me to her home and church, and soon included me in family reunions. Her eight children, and her extended kin, likewise made me part of their lives. Her faith and her example were gifts beyond measure. In Alabama, the community's oral historian Louie Rainey and I spent years talking about people of the past, who came vividly to life as he told their tales.

Betty Hargress Washington and Angeline Hargress Banks helpfully shared accounts of their parents. The knowledge, vision, and determination of Reverend James and Eliza Lyles, who found me "in a wondering condition" and endured my endless questions, deepened my understanding at every point. The friendship, savvy, and wry humor of their son Gene and his wife Rose Lyles revitalized me with every visit to the Lyles Diner in Greensboro. The Lyles, father and son, introduced me to Lewis and Mildred Black, tenacious fighters for voter rights, black farmers, and economic cooperatives in rural Alabama.

When I breathlessly plunged ahead with this project in African American social history, generous scholars who were leaders in the field welcomed me to the fold and marshaled their support. John Blassingame, Herbert Gutman, Nell Painter, and Peter Wood all gave my quest their blessing, and with their help I received fellowships from the Guggenheim and Rockefeller Foundations. As the years passed, three Duke colleagues especially kept a watchful vigil on me and the project. Peter Wood, Raymond Gavins, and Bill Chafe buoyed me always with their conviction that what I was doing was worthwhile, and that however long it took, I must stay the course. No matter whether I was euphoric or despondent, dear friends Lorna and Bill Chafe always lent an ear and sustained me with their insight, devotion, and unflagging good cheer.

The archival foundation of the story started with the Cameron Family Papers, thousands of letters and documents housed at the Southern Historical Collection at the Wilson Library of the University of North Carolina. For almost forty years, I have turned and returned to the collection and have benefited from the assistance of generations of archivists at The Southern, as the archive is known to all. Carolyn Wallace, John White, Richard Shrader, Tim West, Matthew Turi, and myriad younger associates proved to be stalwarts of patience and alacrity. As my requests kept coming, none ever questioned—aloud—why I hadn't found what I wanted the time before. Happily, I had as my supplementary guide to both the Cameron story and the Cameron papers the research of and indispensable book done by Jean Bradley Anderson. Focused on the North Carolina part of the Cameron story, her superb 1985 book, *Piedmont Plantation*, is a model of meticulous research, empathy, and astute interpretation, and I and all who work on the Camerons, their enslaved workers, and their overseers, are deeply in her debt. Terry and Laurie Sanford graciously allowed me to visit Fairntosh on numerous occasions; the visual landscape complemented written accounts and photographs and enriched my understanding of a centerpiece of the story.

On the road, I made repeated trips to the Hale County courthouse in Greensboro, Alabama, where I spent days poring over land and mortgage records. There I was grateful for the aid of three Greensboro attorneys, who always took time to help a historian who began without the slightest idea of how to use such records. Charles Thigpen, though incredulous, patiently explained the deed-indexing system; "Spot" Williams showed me the original "patent" on land that Paul Cameron purchased. Over the years, in conversations in the small, musty room that held the deeds, or across the street in his office, always piled with documents, I learned the most from attorney Nicholas Cobbs. It was no secret to either of us that we had differing views of the past. But that never stopped Nick from welcoming me back, sharing his incomparable knowledge of the county, and conveying his viewpoint with a forthrightness, fairness, and humor that I treasured. My other road trips took me to Tunica County, Mississippi. There, I had hoped to find descendants of people sent to Tunica in the late 1850s, who might have a comparable oral tradition about that displacement. I came to know Katie Mae and Nathaniel Richardson, two wonderful people who labored on land once owned by Paul Cameron. They introduced me to others, all of whom conveyed the same message. The Mississippi Delta was "a land of émigrés," where sustained multigenerational rooting was a rarity.

In organizing and interpreting information on Cameron's enslaved workers, I built on the labors of many. The pioneer was Herbert Gutman, who used the Cameron and other slave lists to discern naming patterns and family commitment on the part of the enslaved. In the mid-1970s, the state of North Carolina acquired "Stagville," the first outpost of the Cameron plantation, and the nearby slave quarter of Horton Grove and designated both as state historic sites. By design, the Stagville Center became a magnet for research on its African American inhabitants. Young historian George McDaniel led the way. He found and interviewed dozens of descendants of Horton Grove forebears and constructed genealogies from their oral testimony and from slave registers. Alice Eley Jones's subsequent interviews with other black descendants captured crucial insights. A monumental synthesis of information from slave lists and Cameron letters by researcher Chris Hughes, and far-sighted leadership by Stagville site manager Jennifer Farley, produced a comprehensive printed 2003 "Database of Slaves." I turned to it time and again to supplement my own compilation of persons sent to Alabama and Mississippi, systematically coded by student assistants. George Waldrep attentively entered hundreds of coded names into a program designed to reveal distant family relationships.

When I undertook this project, I did not have or ever imagine I would have a "church family." But in time I came to have two. George McDaniel introduced me to descendants of those who had formed the Cameron Grove Missionary Baptist Church of Durham, and its members soon embraced me as one of their own. Janie Cameron Riley, Addie Cameron Whitted, Dorothy Peaks Johnson and her sisters, Lonnie and Annie Lloyd, and Rev. and Mrs. Jesse Alston were among those who welcomed me to their stirring Sunday services. With songs, sermons, and fellowship, Cameron Grove lifted my spirits. In Alabama, members and ministers of the Cassimore A.M.E. Zion Church likewise came to receive me as an honorary church member. Always—with Alice Hargress and Nancy Lawson leading Sunday School, Elijah Banks and Gates Rainer starting morning prayer, Clereatha Ryans conducting special services, and Rev. William Scott in the pulpit—I was "at home" with friends. My visits to both churches affirmed the faith and confirmed the resilience of the people I was writing about.

Early and often, I drew on friends for encouragement, and generously they obliged. David Paletz and Walter Dellinger never tired of hearing excerpts of the Alabama story, whether on the jogging trail or at the lunch table. The same was true for Steve Channing and Nancy Clapp-Channing, and for Peter Burian and Maura High, though the setting shifted to the sands of Sunset Beach. Jean McLendon and Martin Groder, brilliant therapists both, listened to more history than any other client brought them and gamely tried to disentangle my obsession from my self. Talking was one thing, writing another, and other friends focused on teasing prose out of me. Marianna Torgovnick bravely invited me to join her writing group, for which I will always be grateful. David Donald arranged for me to be a fellow at the Warren Center at Harvard, where center director Bernard Bailyn, incomparable administrator Susan Hunt, and creative colleagues set a tone that brought forth my first synthesis of Alabama material. Coincidentally, the year in Cambridge launched me for a time on a different project—the story of a woman named Mary Walker who escaped the Cameron plantation but left her children behind. I rationalized that telling the Mary Walker story would take just a short time and build momentum for the Alabama book. I was half right. *To Free a Family* took twenty-five years, but words flowed. Those who joined me on that journey—Mary and Ed Wolff, Linda Cowan, Clare Kenney, Donna Hryb, Dorothy O'Shaughnessy, and their many family members—helped advance me on this one.

My two therapists and a friend in my men's group, Bill Thorp, all at different times inquired whether I might benefit from an *editor*. I didn't just balk, I recoiled. "I guess you just like to do things the hard way," Bill Thorp concluded. Louis Galambos, my long-ago senior thesis advisor at Rice, broke that impasse when he suggested a "developmental editor" and recommended Madeleine Adams. Her counsel helped, and it set the stage for me to send the Mary Walker manuscript to Joyce Seltzer, whom I had met years before, and whose penetrating questions about the point of my work had set the bar high, just where it should be. When I turned back to Alabama, I knew I would want her judgment and suggestions at the end. This time I recognized that I needed help to finish, for the Alabama story covered 200 years and involved a vast and shifting cast of characters. I turned again to Madeleine Adams as well as to a gifted writing coach in Denver, Shari Caudron. From both, I received the same blunt challenge. What's the through-line? What holds the story together? Their insistent questions, and subsequently the astute suggestions of Joyce Seltzer and two readers for the Harvard Press, brought to fruition the final manuscript. In different ways, Denver friends escorted me and the manuscript to the finish line. Harold and Susan Skramstad urged me to hold fast to the entire story. Charles Dewey and Andrea Williams endorsed my title. And as always, Peter and Deedee Decker leavened my life with their generosity, warmth, and wit.

When I began to inhabit the universe of the people in this book, my daughter Heather was ten and my son Steve was almost nine. My disappearances—to the archives or to Alabama or into a tiny home study that could barely hold all of my notes—came to be part of their lives. I am thankful that whenever I resurfaced, they welcomed me back, and that even when young, they fathomed my fervor for finding and telling this story and my care for the people who were part of it. Great admirers as we all were of Alex Haley, it may have helped when they learned that on research trips, their dad came to be identified as "the Roots man." Over the decades, it's been a supreme joy to witness both Heather and Steve become extraordinary writers and fashion wonderful families, all without disappearances.

The appearance of Judith White in my life changed it forever. Her radiance has blessed me, our kin, our friends, our church families, and many people in this story who have met her. To all, Judith has brought sunshine, wisdom, and affection. On me, she has bestowed the gift of love and the windfall of infinite patience. She buoyed me when I was blocked, read endless drafts when I was productive, and made all observations in the most heartening way. For us and for this project, she has always had a mind to stay. I am profoundly indebted to all those who helped in the making of this book. More than ever, I am grateful to Judith for our journey together.

Index

Enslaved people known only by their first names are indicated by *italics*.